LIBRARY
UNIV OF MAINE

LIBRARY
UNIV OF MAINE

AMERICA AND THE
STRIFE OF EUROPE

THE UNIVERSITY OF CHICAGO PRESS ✶ CHICAGO
THE BAKER & TAYLOR COMPANY, NEW YORK; THE CAMBRIDGE UNIVERSITY
PRESS, LONDON; THE MARUZEN-KABUSHIKI-KAISHA, TOKYO, OSAKA
KYOTO, FUKUOKA, SENDAI; THE COMMERCIAL PRESS, LIMITED, SHANGHAI

AMERICA AND THE STRIFE OF EUROPE

By
J. FRED RIPPY
PROFESSOR OF AMERICAN HISTORY
THE UNIVERSITY OF CHICAGO

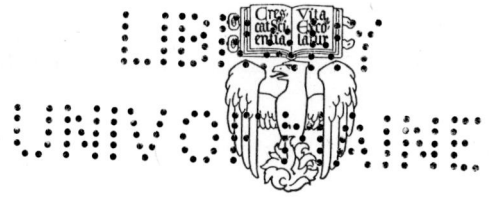

THE UNIVERSITY OF CHICAGO PRESS ∗ CHICAGO

COPYRIGHT 1938 BY THE UNIVERSITY OF CHICAGO. ALL RIGHTS RESERVED. PUBLISHED SEPTEMBER 1938. COMPOSED AND PRINTED BY THE UNIVERSITY OF CHICAGO PRESS, CHICAGO, ILLINOIS, U.S.A.

TO MY CALIFORNIA ALMA MATER

132092

PREFACE

WRITTEN history is to a considerable extent a series of illustrated or documented concepts. Each generation of historians has its own particular frames of reference which it fills in by a selective process from the vast multitude of past ideas and events. Each individual even is in many respects his own historian, seeking light and satisfactions from what he thinks has gone before.

In the present critical stage of international affairs it has seemed worth while to examine the history of the European relations of the United States with the concept of Europe's strife as a unifying theme. It is surprising how much of that history centers about such a concept. It has been present in almost every phase of the relations of the United States and Europe since the American nation was born and before it was born.

The nation has been largely isolated from Europe in politics, but not in its thought and feelings about politics. Like all men who use their minds and imaginations, Americans have viewed themselves in a universal environment. Their vision has not been limited by the boundaries of their nation, nor have their individual and national activities been conceived as having merely a local significance. Americans have always been vividly conscious of participating in a world-drama, and among the other actors of whom they have been most keenly aware the Europeans were politically of highest importance.

The strife of Europe has been influential alike in the genesis of basic ideology and in the formation of programs

PREFACE

of action. In so far as this strife originated in the struggle of the European masses for fuller opportunities and larger political rights, it aroused our deepest sympathies and strengthened our devotion to our own democratic experiment. In its more emphatically international aspects it was mainly responsible for the development of isolationism and the isolation maxim of our foreign policy. The desire was not merely to keep out of European politics but to keep clear of European turmoil as well and to exclude a contentious Europe from participation in American political affairs. European strife thus produced thought and action with reference to territorial expansion. Expansion was considered a means of enlarging the area of freedom and peace in opposition to the domain of oppression and conflict as likewise a means of reducing the chances of involvement in European wars. And not expansion alone but the ability to regulate European conduct in the New World has been possible in great measure because a divided and discordant Europe was helpless to prevent the one or resist the other.

European strife often has proved a distinct practical advantage to the United States. Yet the American people have never exulted because of Europe's international conflicts or displayed an inclination to foment its international discords, however prompt they may have been to take advantage of them. The American people have always deplored the calamitous situation. At times their devotion to democracy and peace has been so fervent as almost to smother their isolation sentiment. In their eagerness to aid those who were struggling for liberty and to release Europe as a whole from the bondage of war, they were ready to depart from the sacred maxim. The danger that Europe's strife might involve them increased with the growing complexity and integration of modern life and therefore became a factor of

PREFACE

increasing importance to them, but it is probable that their concern throughout was based primarily on altruism.

In the volume here presented much attention has been given to the motivation of our foreign policy. Fundamentally it has been determined by considerations of national interest as defined by those who were controlling or seeking to control the foreign relations of the nation. But the concept of national interest is broad enough to embrace both material and ideal values. Considerations of immediate self-interest, economic and otherwise, have, no doubt, had great weight. Yet it is extremely unlikely that they have invariably determined national action. It is a circumstance signifying much in respect to American character that the people of this country are reluctant to admit they are impelled by such motives. They are usually quick to conceal them beneath a cloud of rationalizations and idealizations. Is not this a high tribute to American ideals? Americans will cheerfully defend the vital interests of the nation when convinced that they are menaced, and they will strive to promote its economic welfare. It should be remembered, however, that the nation is not merely some material thing, not merely an organization for economic competition with other national units; it is also an assemblage of ideals and sentiments, illusory and unsound though some of them may be. Appeals to considerations of pure self-interest are rarely made to the people of the United States on weighty questions of foreign policy, presumably because American leaders know the people cannot be summoned to their side by such appeals. The people must be made to feel that they are serving a larger and grander cause. Americans like to envisage themselves as engaging in noble enterprise. They are most profoundly stirred when they are convinced that they are taking part in a contest between titanic world-forces.

PREFACE

The foreign relations of the United States have been shaped by idealisms as well as by material interests.

But the subject of the motivation of American foreign policy need not be pursued farther at the moment. The reader may observe its operation more fully in the pages that follow and reach his own conclusions. In its more fundamental ramifications it is a part of the general problem of the dynamics of history.

I have not ventured to give any advice with reference to the course which the nation ought to follow in the midst of the crisis that the world now confronts. I have merely tried to weigh the forces, material and sentimental, which tend or have tended to influence its conduct in its most important relationships with Europe. I confess I know not what to advise. Both isolation and co-operation have their discouraging obstacles and their grave risks. In dealing with the plight of the isolationists I have used the word "messiah" to describe some of our most active idealists. I hasten to declare that I have not intended any disparagement and to apologize for the word which I have used for lack of a better term.

If I were to offer any suggestions at all, they would be somewhat as follows: The history of our own enthusiasms, shortcomings, and aggressions recommends tolerance toward other nations. In weighing the irritating and seemingly irrational acts of foreign governments, we should ask ourselves what our own would do now or would have done in the past in similar circumstances. After all it must not be forgotten that we have annexed a vast territorial domain, much of it by violence, and have ordered other nations to remain politically aloof from the world that Columbus discovered. If we can continue to enforce that order and hold the possessions we have, such an achievement alone ought

PREFACE

to be sufficient to satisfy the most ardent patriot. I might also remark that the efforts of the United States to allay the strife of Europe have not been attended with signal success, but perhaps this would be a little beside the point. History seldom, if ever, exactly repeats itself. Statesmen therefore should not be too closely bound by their conceptions of the past. With respectful but not servile consideration for national experience and traditions, they should take a long and clear view of the national interest, material and psychological, and make that their goal. Above all, they should never be unduly swayed by the passions of the moment or allow alarmists to hurry them forward into precipitate action. The nation must defend its material domain and its political principles whenever such defense is clearly demanded. But the danger should be real and immediate, not remote and in some respects imaginary. Even aggressive defense might conceivably be necessary, but we should avoid the error of undeliberate haste.

This volume contains in its footnotes no citations to authorities. Indeed it contains few footnotes of any kind. I have omitted them for the sake of economy and in order to avoid distracting those who are sufficiently interested to follow the narrative. But I have appended a critical bibliography for the convenience of any who may wish to check my facts or examine my concepts more searchingly. For the maps illustrating the territorial and political expansion of the United States I am indebted to Professor Herbert E. Bolton. They are based upon maps in his illuminating syllabus on the *History of the Americas*.

J. FRED RIPPY

TABLE OF CONTENTS

IDEOLOGY

CHAPTER	PAGE
I. ISOLATIONISM	3
II. THE DEMOCRATIC EXPERIMENT IN PERIL	22
III. PACIFISM	41
IV. EXPANSIONIST IDEALISM AND RATIONALIZATIONS	55
V. ENTHUSIASMS OF 1898 AND AFTER	77

EUROPE'S DISCORDS AMERICA'S ADVANTAGE

VI. EXPANSION: FIRST PHASE	103
VII. THE REGULATION OF EUROPEAN CONDUCT IN AMERICA	122
VIII. EXPANSION: SECOND PHASE	138

THE UNITED STATES AND THE PEACE OF EUROPE

IX. THEODORE ROOSEVELT AND THE PEACE OF EUROPE	169
X. BRYAN AND THE PEACE OF EUROPE	186
XI. WILSON AND THE PEACE OF EUROPE	201
XII. THE PLIGHT OF THE ISOLATIONISTS	217
CRITICAL BIBLIOGRAPHY	235
INDEX	253

LIST OF MAPS

THE AMERICAS IN 1763	104
TERRITORIAL EXPANSION OF THE UNITED STATES (1776–1867)	105
THE ENTRY OF THE UNITED STATES INTO THE PACIFIC	154
THE UNITED STATES IN THE CARIBBEAN (1898–1933)	165

IDEOLOGY

CHAPTER I

ISOLATIONISM

I

IN A farewell address of 1796 George Washington gave this nation some advice. It was important, but not strange or even original. In urging the people and their leaders to avoid permanent European alliances, Washington merely expressed a conviction of long standing, a sentiment even then almost hallowed with age. Isolationism was a natural, almost a spontaneous, reaction to social and political conditions in Europe, and particularly against Europe's military strife.

No doubt many of the early settlers of North America as they thought of the turmoil, oppression, and misery that characterized much of the old country felt a comforting sense of security when they reflected that the Atlantic was broad, stormy, and difficult to cross. At any rate this theme runs through the writings of the Pennsylvania Germans. Pastorius wrote in the seventeenth century: "After I had sufficiently seen the European provinces and countries, and the threatening movements of war, and had taken to heart the dire changes and disturbances, ... I was impelled through a special guidance from the Almighty to go to Pennsylvania." William Penn talked of founding a model colony, a sort of "holy experiment" which might be observed with benefit by all nations. In a letter written to the colonists in 1710 he remarked: "Friends, the eyes of many are upon you; the people of many nations of Europe look on that country [America] as a land of ease and quiet, wishing for themselves in vain the blessings they conceive you enjoy."

The most convincing evidence of the fundamental nature of the American desire for isolation is the general expression of that desire at the outbreak of the war for independence. Even before independence was declared, statesmen were willing to formulate a policy of isolation for a nation as yet unborn.

From the fall of 1775 to the beginning of 1778 isolationism was rife among the colonial leaders. The feeling was so strong in 1775 that it took John Adams and the small group who supported him a year to convince the Continental Congress that commercial connections with Europe would not be dangerous. The plan for negotiation with European governments, adopted in September of 1776, was a definite victory for a conscious policy of isolation. A few leaders, in desperation, had urged the necessity of intimate political relationships, but after the issue had been hotly debated the isolation policy prevailed.

As the prospects of the insurgents grew more discouraging certain modifications were made. The first of these occurred within a fortnight or so when the Continental Congress drew up instructions for its diplomatic agents to France. These agents were authorized to sign a pledge that America would never submit to the mother-country or grant her any privileges denied to France, and if France would join in the war they might agree that neither associate should make peace without six months' notification to the other. This was the first breach in the isolationist policy.

At the very end of the year others were authorized. Commissioners sent to Spain, the Hapsburg Empire, Prussia, and Tuscany were instructed to guarantee that the United States would agree to no peace with England short of inde-

ISOLATIONISM

pendence. They were to urge these courts to prevent Great Britain from enlisting foreign troops against the rebellion and to endeavor to effect the recall of such of these troops as were already in America. France was to be incited to attack the Electorate of Hanover, then an English possession, as well as British possessions in the West Indies or elsewhere, except Canada, which the Americans intended to capture. Spain was also to be urged to participate in the war. The Continental Congress fully expected that France and Spain would acquire some of the British colonies across the Atlantic: France the English West Indies and Spain the Floridas. The fact is, the Continental Congress even authorized its diplomats to promise co-operation in these conquests.

For more than a year the diplomats negotiated without much success, and in many quarters relief was expressed that Europe did not respond favorably. The general impression seemed to be that after all it was better that America should fight its battles alone. Then in the early spring of 1778 came news of the signing of the treaty of alliance with France.

In agreeing to this treaty on February 6, the agents of the revolting colonies had transcended their instructions. The treaty provided that the allies should *wage war together and make peace together*. The insurgents might capture and annex the Bermudas or any English territory on the American continent (Canada); France was to keep any islands she might seize in the West Indies. The Americans guaranteed to France the colonies then possessed in the New World as well as those she might acquire by the peace treaty, while France guaranteed to the revolting colonists their unlimited independence with the territory then in their possession as well as that to be acquired as a result of the war.

AMERICA AND THE STRIFE OF EUROPE

The allies also invited other nations hostile to England to make common cause with them, and a separate, secret act offered Spain the opportunity to accede to the treaty under similar conditions.

Thus the infant nation in America was becoming involved in European politics. Yet there was wild rejoicing when news of the alliance reached America. The diplomatic agents were applauded and not censured. Full realization of the dire need for foreign assistance caused misgivings to vanish or rendered those who still felt them momentarily inarticulate. But the involvement had been accepted primarily with the view of forestalling England, for the colonial leaders feared that the British government might obtain outside aid at the price of a new distribution of territory in America that would include also a partitioning of the revolting thirteen.

During the next four years the new nation tended to become more fully enmeshed in the complex fabric of European politics. But this took place only under the insistent compulsion of a desperate emergency. The distrust of Europe and the dread of involvement persisted and was expressed even with reference to the most valuable ally of the colonists. Opinion during the period vacillated between gratitude to the "generous ally" and distrust of the "intrigues of the French court." Co-operation against a common enemy seemed at one time to be drawing the two allies closer together. The final instructions to the commissioners appointed to participate in the peace negotiations with England intrusted almost everything to France. But deep suspicion of the Spanish associate never abated, and distrust of France finally prevailed in the councils of the peace commissioners. The envoys eventually broke their instructions and proceeded alone, negotiating a separate treaty with

ISOLATIONISM

England before the French government was notified. And once more diplomats who had exceeded their authority were commended. The end of the Revolution brought a distinct feeling of relief that America was done with Europe and renewed determination to uphold a policy of isolation.

The years immediately following the termination of the war witnessed a definite revival of isolation sentiment. The desire to sever all possible connection with the rest of the world permeated all the rejoicing at the conclusion of peace in 1783. Even a movement to cut off diplomatic intercourse with Europe made some headway, and men of such opposite views as John Adams and Thomas Jefferson went so far as to lament the commercial impulses and genius of their countrymen that made it impossible to prevent them from venturing on the high seas in search of markets. Issues regarding public policy were supported and opposed by the same argument: their adoption or rejection would open the way for European intrigues in America. Statesmen most responsible for foreign policy held all but unanimously that isolation should be a settled principle of American diplomacy.

Isolationism was an important factor in the deliberations of the Philadelphia Convention of 1787 and was embodied in an express provision of the new constitution framed there: no person holding any office of profit or trust under the United States should, without the consent of Congress, accept any emolument, office, or title of any kind whatsoever from any king, prince, or foreign state (Art. I, sec. 9). And isolationism was also a factor in the final ratification of that document. During the campaign for ratification the supporters of the instrument pointed out repeatedly that a strong central government was necessary to enable the United States to maintain a neutral position in European affairs as well as a dominant position on the American continent.

When the new government came into power in 1789 the isolation policy was reaffirmed both by the attitude of Congress and by the acts of the Washington administration. The desire for detachment from European politics was not shaken by the Nootka Sound controversy between England and Spain—a controversy that threatened to lead to a violation of the territory of the United States and fighting in Louisiana and the Floridas adjacent to its boundaries. Nor was that desire smothered by the wild demonstrations of sympathy caused by the events of the French Revolution. Isolationist statesmen made their own interpretation of the alliance treaty of 1778 with France and kept out of the European war. Despite the ardent sympathies of perhaps the vast majority of the people for struggling French democracy, neutrality was proclaimed in 1793. And although sympathies for one belligerent or the other became an issue in party politics as the trend in France became uncertain, the policy of isolation was maintained. The independent nation encountered the first temptations with success.

II

Such in brief outline is the background of the American policy of isolation. In his farewell address Washington merely expressed sentiments which had long prevailed in the nation as well as in his own mind. Other statesmen of the year 1796 might have expressed them with greater emphasis. A comparison of his statement at that time with previous utterances of his countrymen will reveal at any rate that more emphatic assertions of isolationism had been made in the past. In Washington's well-known address of 1796 he said:

ISOLATIONISM

The rule of conduct for us in regard to foreign nations is in extending our commercial relations to have with them as little political connection as possible.... Europe has a set of primary interests which to us have none or a very remote relation. Hence she must be engaged in frequent controversies, the causes of which are essentially foreign to our concerns. Hence, therefore, it must be unwise in us to implicate ourselves by artificial ties in the *ordinary* vicissitudes of her politics or the *ordinary* combinations and collisions of her friendships or enmities.

The reader will observe that Washington here used the word "ordinary" twice (italics are my own). Did a cautious statesman mean to imply that with reference to some future emergency the nation should act differently or at least maintain an attitude of reserve? In the next paragraph he said: "It is our true policy to steer clear of *permanent* alliances with any portion of the foreign world, so far, I mean, as we are now at liberty to do it....." It will be noted that he used the word "permanent" (italics mine again) and seemed to suggest that the United States had already impaired its liberty of action to a certain degree. He doubtless referred to the French alliance of 1778 and desired to indicate that temporary alliances formed for specific national objectives might be necessary in the future as in the past. The Father of his Country had a keen sense of honor. Already, in another passage of his address, he had remarked: "So far as we have already formed engagements let them be fulfilled with perfect good faith." His view and that of his cabinet was, however, that the alliance bound the United States to support France only in a defensive war and, even then, only in America.

In the writings of Washington's contemporaries stronger statements of isolationism may be found as well as additional reasons for the existence of this sentiment. Washington rested his advice on the *prevalence of strife* in Europe and the *divergence* of American and European interests. He rarely condemned the political system of Europe or its morals; with the exception of the policies of England toward his compatriots, it was not often that he denounced the policies of European governments. He was not only cautious but dignified and reserved. This was less true of other leaders of the period. It is necessary at this point to review their opinions.

John Adams and Thomas Jefferson set forth the clearest and most complete statements of their views, but others left sufficient record to remove all doubt regarding their attitude. An examination of the writings of the Fathers will confirm all that has been said.

During the first months of the Revolution when the insurgents were thinking of looking to Europe and especially to France for some sort of aid, Adams declared:

> That we ought not to enter into any alliance with her, which would entangle us in any future wars in Europe; that we ought to lay it down, as a first principle and a maxim never to be forgotten, to maintain an entire neutrality in all future European wars. . . . . If we united with either nation [namely, either France or England], in any future war, we must become too subordinate and dependent on that nation, and should be involved in all European wars, as we had been hitherto; that foreign powers would find means to corrupt our people, to influence our councils, and, in fine, we should be little better than puppets, danced on the wires of the cabinets of Europe. We should be the sport of European intrigues and politics; that, therefore, in preparing treaties to be proposed to foreign powers, and in the instructions to be given our ministers, we ought to confine ourselves strictly to a treaty of commerce.

Adams' view prevailed and the Continental Congress finally decided to solicit foreign aid without entanglements. And when the states of Europe proved unresponsive as the desperate months of 1777 dragged on, Adams was consoled by the thought that their seeming reluctance might turn out to be a blessing. "If we could have a free trade with Eu-

ISOLATIONISM

rope," he wrote, "I should rather run the risk of fighting it out with George and his present allies, provided he should get no other." "I do not love to be entangled in the quarrels of Europe," he declared; "I do not wish to be under obligations to any of them, and I am very unwilling [that] they should rob us of the glory of vindicating our own liberties." And both George Washington and Samuel Adams agreed with him.

One of the main concerns of the year 1777 was to keep England from gaining assistance on terms detrimental to the success of the insurgent colonies and calculated to violate their territorial integrity. The principal diplomatic aim of the Continental Congress at that time was to prevent European intervention in behalf of England.

It was fears on this score, as already noted, that led to the acceptance of the French alliance. Americans were forced by their conception of expediency from a policy of strict isolation dictated by their most fundamental beliefs. Referring to the matter, Adams said in April, 1780, that Americans had "proceeded with reluctance and regret to the treaty." "That that is true," Adams remarked, "I know and feel to this very moment." And although he declared that he felt "no such reluctance" himself and strongly approved the step, he expressed his vexation early in 1781 that America had been forced to appeal to Europe in order to anticipate England. Writing to Franklin, he said:

America has fought Great Britain and Ireland six years, and not only Great Britain, but many states of Germany, many tribes of Indians, and many negroes, their allies. Great Britain has been moving earth and hell to obtain allies against us, yet it is improper in us to propose an alliance! Great Britain has borrowed all the superfluous wealth of Europe, in Italy, Germany, Holland, Switzerland, and some in France, to murder us, yet it is dishonorable in us to propose to borrow money! By heaven, I would make a bargain with all Europe, if it lay with me. Let all

AMERICA AND THE STRIFE OF EUROPE

Europe stand still, neither lend men nor money nor ships to England nor America, and let them fight it out alone. I would give my share of millions for such a bargain.

Although Adams staunchly defended the alliance of 1778 and disavowed on his part all reluctance to accept its terms, he nevertheless was among those who were not always free from distrust of the ally, along with the other states of Europe. In April, 1780, for instance, he said he was convinced that all Europe, possibly excepting Austria, desired American independence. But he added:

Yet I have many reasons to think that not one of them, not even Spain nor France, wishes to see America rise very fast to power. We ought, therefore, to be cautious how we magnify our ideas, and exaggerate our expressions of the generosity and magnanimity of any of these powers. Let us treat them with gratitude, but with dignity. Let us remember what is due to ourselves and to our posterity, as well as to them. Let us, above all things, avoid as much as possible entangling ourselves with their wars or politics. Our business with them and theirs with us is commerce, not politics, much less war. America has been the sport of European wars and politics long enough.

It was this distrust of Europe which embraced even France, that caused Adams along with John Jay to disregard instructions and negotiate independently with England. As Adams was on the point of entering upon these negotiations he wrote to Congress: "America has been long enough involved in the wars of Europe. She has been a football between contending nations from the beginning, and it is easy to foresee that France and England both will endeavor to involve us in their future wars." He was sure, he said, that Jay agreed with him; regarding Franklin, who was also associated in the peace enterprise, he was less certain. Adams expressed similar sentiments to his British diplomatic adversary, to whom he remarked that "all the powers of Europe" would be scheming continually "to work us into their real or imaginary balances of power." And while in the midst of the negotiations he pointed out to friends at home the need of strengthening the national government in order to prevent America from becoming "the sport of transatlantic politicians of all denominations, who hate liberty in every shape, and every man who loves it, and every country that enjoys it."

His conviction of the selfishness and general depravity of Europe deepened with his lengthening sojourn abroad. While Adams was in London the Swedish ambassador at St. James's had remarked to him that he took it for granted the people of the United States would "have sense enough to see us in Europe cut each other's throats with philosophical tranquility [sic]." By the beginning of 1784 Adams admitted that he was "quite in sentiment with" the Scandinavian diplomat. The next year he was lamenting the fact that his countrymen were "as aquatic as the tortoises and sea-fowl," and hence unwilling to cut themselves off from commerce with the rest of the world. He was convinced, he said, that, "if all intercourse between Europe and America could be cut off forever, if every ship we have were burnt, and the keel of another never to be laid, we might still be the happiest people on earth, and, in fifty years, the most powerful." And it was during the same period that he wrote to Rufus King: "Every day will furnish America with fresh proofs of the fallacious nature of all her hopes of prosperity, grandeur, and glory from the friendly disposition of foreign powers. Whatever assistance she may ever derive from any of them must be purchased at a greater price than it will be worth."

With such sentiments Adams came home to serve as vice-president under Washington and later as president. Surveying his public career in 1805, he declared:

AMERICA AND THE STRIFE OF EUROPE

The principle of foreign affairs which I then advocated [1776] has been the invariable guide of my conduct in all situations, as ambassador in France, Holland, and England, and as Vice-President and President of the United States, from that hour to this. . . . . This principle was, that we should make no treaties of alliance with any European power; that we should consent to none but treaties of commerce; that we should separate ourselves, as far as possible and as long as possible, from all European politics and wars.

Although Jefferson did not actively engage in diplomacy until the end of the Revolution, between 1785 and 1793 his views in most respects were in accord with those of Adams. Like Adams, he regretted that his countrymen must engage in foreign commerce. "Were I to indulge my own theory," he wrote in 1785, "I should wish them to practice neither commerce nor navigation, but to stand with respect to Europe precisely on the footing of China. We should thus avoid wars, and all our citizens would be husbandmen."

He expressed even greater disgust than did Adams with the European regime—the endless wars and intrigues, the heartless tyranny, and the bitterness toward the United States. In June, 1785, he urged young James Monroe to come to Paris as an exercise in patriotism. "It will make you adore your own country," said Jefferson, "its soil, its climate, its equality, liberty, laws, people, and manners. My God! How little do my countrymen know what precious blessings they are in possession of, ... which no other people on earth enjoy. . . . . Come then and see the proofs of this, and on your return add your testimony to that of every thinking American, in order to satisfy our countrymen how much it is to their interest to preserve uninfected by contagion those peculiarities in their government and manners to which they are indebted for these blessings."

The unhappy state of Europe was his constant theme during these early days. In 1786 he referred to the region as a place "where the dignity of man is lost in arbitrary distinctions, where the human species is classed into several stages of degradation, where the many are crushed under the weight of the few, and where the order established can present to the contemplation of a thinking being no other picture than that of God almighty and his angels tramping under foot the hosts of the damned." During the same year he wrote that a comparison of the American system of government and those of Europe was analogous to "a comparison of heaven and hell." "England, like the earth," he said, "may be allowed to take the intermediate station." Already he was rejoicing that we were "happily free" from European broils and praying that God might long keep us so. And at the end of 1787 he wrote: "I know .... that it is a maxim with us, and I think it a wise one, not to entangle ourselves with the affairs of Europe." Nearly fifteen years later, in his inaugural address as president, he was to restate the maxim thus: "Peace, commerce, and honest friendship with all nations, entangling alliances with none."

These views of the sad state of Europe held in common by Adams and Jefferson were likewise shared by others. One of the best expressions of them, aside from those of Jefferson, was that of Richard Henry Lee in March, 1785. "The selfishness and corruption of Europe I have no doubt about," said Lee, "and therefore wish most sincerely that our free Republic may not suffer themselves to be changed and wrongly wrought upon by the corrupt maxims of policy that pervade European councils—where artful and refined plausibility is forever called in to aid the most pernicious designs."

From all these expressions four motives for isolationism emerge: the memory of unpleasant experiences, especially during the period since 1689 when the colonial wars of modern Europe began in earnest; the conviction of the superiority of our political system and moral standards; the belief that European and American interests were not parallel; and the fear that our diplomats would be no match for the unscrupulous and subtle schemers of the Old World—in other words, the fear that the young nation would be drawn into Europe's strife.

Washington and Jefferson added two more: an intervening ocean and the prospect of profiting from Europe's inevitable discords. It was Washington himself who stressed the geographical aspect of the subject. In a letter written to a French friend in February, 1788, he remarked: "Separated as we are by a world of water from other nations, if we are wise, we shall surely avoid being drawn into the labyrinth of their politics, and involved in their destructive wars." And in another letter of the same year he observed: "We who live in these ends of the earth only hear the rumors of war like the roar of distant thunder. It is to be hoped that our local situation will prevent us from being swept into its vortex." It was also Washington who suggested the possibility of commercial profit to be derived from maintaining a neutral position. In 1788, for instance, he remarked that a general war was likely to be "kindled" among the European states at any time, and then added: "Whenever a contest happens among them, if we wisely and properly improve the advantages which nature has given us, we may be benefitted by their folly, provided we conduct ourselves with circumspection and under proper restrictions." A letter written to Lafayette in 1790 was still more definite: "It seems to be our policy to keep in the situation in which nature has placed us, to observe a strict neutrality, and to furnish others with those good things of subsistence which they want and which our fertile soil abundantly produces."

ISOLATIONISM

Jefferson shared Washington's views regarding the geographical basis of isolation as well as his desire to profit by increased commerce as a neutral power. And Jefferson saw, along with others, still further advantages to be derived from Europe's discords: America might be free to expand its boundaries and able in some measure to regulate the conduct of the European nations with reference to the New World.

But while Jefferson was the most influential of the early prophets of territorial expansion and perhaps the first to suggest that the United States should object to the transfer of territorial domain from one European power to another in America, the clearest expression of the general idea of limiting Europe's freedom of action on this side of the Atlantic came from another source. Alexander Hamilton, writing for the *Federalist* in 1788, enunciated the idea of two spheres of influence with the United States dominant in one of them. He said:

> By a steady adherence to the Union, we may hope, erelong, to become the arbiter of Europe in America, and may be able to incline the balance of European competitions in this part of the world as our interest may dictate. . . . . Under a vigorous national government the natural strength and resources of the country, directed to a common interest, would baffle all the combinations of European jealousy to restrain our growth. . . . .
>
> Our situation invites and our interests prompt us to aim at an ascendant in the system of American affairs. The world may politically, as well as geographically, be divided into four parts, each having a distinct set of interests. Unhappily for the other three, Europe, by her arms and by her negotiations, by force and by fraud, has, in different degrees, extended her dominion over them all. The superiority she has long maintained has tempted her to plume herself as the Mistress of the World, and to consider the rest of mankind as created for her benefit. . . . . It belongs to us to vindicate the honor of the human race and to teach that assuming brother moderation. . . . . Let the thirteen States . . . concur in erecting one great American system, superior to the con-

AMERICA AND THE STRIFE OF EUROPE

trol of all transatlantic force or influence, and *able to dictate the terms of the connection between the old and the new world* [italics mine].

These illustrations of isolationism taken from the writings of the outstanding leaders of the period would seem sufficient to prove the existence of that sentiment long before 1796 or even 1793. Yet one is loath to abandon the subject.

Early in 1776 Thomas Paine advanced isolationism as an argument for a declaration of independence. "Dependence on Great Britain," he said, "tends directly to involve this continent in European wars and quarrels." "It is the true interest of America," he declared, "to steer clear of European contentions, which she can never do while, by her dependence on Britain, she is made the make-weight in the scale of British politics."

Although he finally approved the French alliance, Samuel Adams was reluctant and apprehensive. He thought the honor and security of the United States would be better served if its liberty and independence were established "with as little foreign aid as possible." He said in 1777 that he dreaded the influence of foreign diplomats on the American people. "It is presumed," he said, "that they will always have too high a sense of their dignity to suffer themselves and their nation to be degraded. But when peace is happily settled and a number of foreign ministers are about our court, it will require men of great knowledge of the world and experience in affairs to penetrate their various intrigues." And in 1783 he wrote: "I deprecate the most favored nation predominating in the councils of America, for I do not believe there is a nation on earth that wishes we should be more free or more powerful than is consistent with their ideas of their own interest."

In April, 1781, George Mason of Virginia wrote of the "opinion prevailing" in his state "that our allies are spinning out the war in order to weaken America as well as Great Britain and thereby leave us at the end of it as dependent as possible on themselves." Shortly after the Revolution terminated (1783) he declared: "We reflect with gratitude on the important aids France has given us; but she must not, and I hope will not, attempt to lead us into a war of ambition or conquest, or trail us around the mysterious circle of European politics." He heartily approved the following sentiment expressed by his young son who was in Paris: "I wish America would put her trust only in God and herself, and have as little to do with the politics of Europe as possible."

Similar expressions were placed on record as early as 1785 or 1788 by James Madison and James Monroe, who were later to conduct the foreign policy of the United States during another critical period, as well as by almost every leader of the independence epoch. The sentiments of Washington's Farewell Address had filled the atmosphere for twenty years. That address set no precedent; it merely confirmed an established policy.

III

Nevertheless there was ample justification for such a final message. Temptations to depart from the isolation policy had been confronted in the past, and Washington knew that they would have to be faced in the future—even the immediate future. The European nations were neither willing to consider America a realm set apart from their political activities nor content to assume that the United States could not be induced to participate in European politics. Offers of material advantage, provocative attacks on commerce, apparent threats to national security, and moving appeals to American ideals would all have to be resisted if the United States were to keep clear of the European system. Moreover, the strife of Europe would continue, the economic interests of the United States abroad would increase, and technological progress would reduce the importance of the geographical factor.

At its most intense stages European strife would make it almost impossible for the United States to remain aloof, especially if certain American ideals and interests should converge or seem to converge. Such a stage was that which embraced the years from 1789 to 1823. During this period many influences tended to involve the nation in European politics: The French alliance, necessary in order to achieve independence but tending to entail subsequent obligations; political sympathies reaching out to France, Greece, other parts of Europe, and Hispanic America; repeated invitations to form alliances with one European antagonist or the other; threats of war which might result in hostilities in adjacent European colonies; likelihood that the territory of the United States might be violated by the belligerents; threats of European intervention in Spanish America; and danger that neighboring colonies might be transferred from a weaker to a stronger power with increased peril to national security. At the end of this period, however, isolationism was strengthened by the promulgation of the Monroe Doctrine.—Such a stage of intense strife was likewise that which embraced the period extending from 1896 into an indefinite future, when bitter rivalries in Europe led to one catastrophe and threatened to result in others. Once again diplomats from across the Atlantic appealed to the United States for alliances or for aid of one sort or another. Between 1898 and 1916 invitations came from both Germany and England, and after 1919 appeals came from Geneva as well as from Paris and London. Between these two epochs of intense strife separated by an era of seventy-five years, solicitations

ISOLATIONISM

were made of a more restricted nature for commitments with reference to Cuba, Central America, the Hawaiian Islands, China, and Samoa; and in an epoch of domestic crisis another phase of the isolation policy was menaced: European states tried to extend their possessions or controls in America.

Moreover, attempts to profit commercially by supplying Old World belligerents with Washington's "good things of subsistence" and Jefferson's "necessaries of war" would tend to involve the nation in military conflicts with Europe. Washington lived only three years after issuing his farewell advice, but he lived long enough to see his successor, who was none other than the isolationist John Adams, launch the country into a little "informal war" with France in an attempt to protect our maritime commerce. A similar endeavor was to be one of the factors that would involve us again in 1812 and in 1917; and by 1937 baffled statesmen would conclude that the United States could not reap a commercial harvest from Europe's discords without itself being drawn into Europe's wars.

The way of isolation was beset with temptations and obstacles of almost every sort, and the perils seemed to increase rather than diminish. Both interests and ideals formed parts of the problem; either of them when taken separately tended to weaken isolationism; and when both coalesced to form a common impulse to act, the United States would be in grave danger of departing from the maxim of the Fathers. It would not be easy for the Americans to preserve their tranquillity while the Europeans cut one another's throats. George Washington's forebodings were not unfounded.

CHAPTER II

THE DEMOCRATIC EXPERIMENT IN PERIL

I

THE people of the United States are capable of being deeply touched by ideals as well as by interests. And when these ideals are placed in a broad setting in which they are confronted by a world-antagonist, as ideals often are, the impulse to action is almost irresistible, even though such action should run counter to the sacred maxim of isolation.

The American experiment in democracy has been conducted in a universal environment. The movement for independence from England was based at the outset on an invocation of the rights of Englishmen, but its ideology was soon expanded so as to embrace the rights of man and an appeal to the laws of Nature and of Nature's God. Let him who doubts this assertion re-read the Declaration of Independence:

> When in the course of *human* events, it becomes necessary for one people to dissolve the political bands which have connected them with another, and to assume among the *powers of the earth* the separate and equal station to which the *Laws of Nature and of Nature's God* entitle them, a decent respect to the *opinions of mankind* requires that they should declare the causes which impel them to the separation.—We hold these truths to be self-evident, that *all men* are created equal, that they are endowed by their Creator with certain unalienable Rights, that among these are Life, Liberty, and the pursuit of Happiness.—That to secure these rights, Governments are instituted *among Men*, deriving their just powers from the consent of the governed.—That whenever any form of Government becomes destructive of these ends, it is the Right of the

THE DEMOCRATIC EXPERIMENT IN PERIL

People to alter or abolish it, and to institute a new Government, laying its foundation on such principles and organizing its powers in such form as to them shall seem most likely to effect their Safety and Happiness [italics my own].

Within this world-setting antagonists were confronted, sometimes real and sometimes imaginary. Always Americans felt there were enemies of the democratic system in Europe, and occasionally the enemy was thought to be within our gates. The Nullifiers and the Secessionists were the important domestic antagonists, although the Abolitionists were occasionally included. The antagonist was envisaged as ever present, to be berated, denounced, ridiculed, and feared. Awareness of his existence always aroused strong emotions of one kind or another. Confidence of early triumph mounted high at certain epochs; others were filled with dread, almost with despair.

The French Revolution inspired fervent hope among Americans, but ended in the discouragement of Napoleonic tyranny and was followed by the awesome spectacle of despotic reaction. The little Corsican cast an ominous shadow over America. The Holy Alliance seemed to threaten the suffocation of all popular aspirations for freedom and self-government, including perhaps those of the New World and especially those of Hispanic America.

With the frustration of European designs against America at the close of the first quarter of the nineteenth century, the champions of the American experiment breathed more freely. As republics were established from the Río Grande to Cape Horn, and as one popular movement after another swept over Europe, the strident phrases of democratic eloquence rose to dizzy heights. Perhaps the culmination was reached in the "Roaring Forties" when almost every orator on nearly every occasion imagined he was speaking from a world platform whence he was being heard by the teeming millions of the earth—where he was watched with approval by the Almighty Himself.

Ensuing years were scarcely less clamorous, but the flowing periods were intended for friends and for the enemy within as well as for the antagonist without, and the eloquence was inspired by fear of defeat more than by confidence of victory. All were reminded, nonetheless, that they were acting upon a universal stage. The day of general triumph might be more distant than at one time assumed and proclaimed, but "government of the people, by the people, and for the people," as Lincoln was finally to assert in 1863, must not "perish from the earth." Nor should European monarchies be permitted to take advantage of internecine strife in order to expand their hostile power in America.

Recovery from the ravages of civil war and the exploitation of a magnificent physical environment largely occupied the next thirty years. But the overseas antagonist was never wholly forgotten. Liberal uprisings in France and Spain as well as in Brazil were observed with jubilation, and efforts were made both to reduce the area of European possessions in the New World and to safeguard national security by dominating the Isthmian routes. Ulysses S. Grant and William H. Seward wished to annex almost every European colony in America, while Rutherford B. Hayes and James G. Blaine intimated their impatience regarding European presumptions with reference to the control of the canals.

The last years of the nineteenth century gave birth to American enthusiasms not altogether in harmony with some of the idealism of previous epochs. While the new emotions swept the nation far out beyond its continental moorings, opposition sentiment was not inarticulate. The old and the new ideology were sufficiently related, however, to insure the temporary triumph of imperialism. In the main, the path of empire was followed with glee, and in its Caribbean ramifications it was followed the more freely because the European antagonist was actually confronted or supposed to be. Rapidly the notion of the German menace developed, conceived first as a threat to national progress or national security, then as a menace to the great experiment, and finally as a threat to all of these and the peace of the world besides.

Soon after 1900 pacifism was so closely associated with the democratic ideal that many believed world-peace and the democratic system would stand or fall together. American leaders, therefore, actively concerned themselves with the peace of Europe as well as with the progress of popular government in distant lands beyond the Atlantic. Theodore Roosevelt and Bryan and Wilson and House all lent a hand; and a nation already profoundly irritated by drastic interference with its efforts to profit commercially from Europe's strife cheerfully entered a war to end war and make the world safe for democracy.

Since the World War the peace ideal and the democratic ideal have not been fully dissociated. Those who threaten peace imperil democracy, and those who menace democracy threaten peace. The enemies of both are the dictators of the totalitarian states, and especially the Fascist and Nazi dictators, some of them in league with militarist and autocratic Japan. The antagonist is still present, vividly etched in a vast terrestial background.

II

Evidence of the American conviction that this democratic experiment in North America was a matter which concerned all the world exists in overwhelming abundance. It

AMERICA AND THE STRIFE OF EUROPE

may be found in a thousand orations celebrating the Fourth of July, in the speeches of nearly every member of Congress for more than a century, in the records of numerous constitutional conventions, in the addresses of a multitude of political campaigns, in preachments from almost every pulpit, on the front pages of hundreds of journals, and in the addresses and declamations issuing from the auditoriums of every educational institution. The most exalted and dignified expressions of the conviction may be read in the presidential messages. For the purposes of this volume little more evidence can be required. George Washington may speak first, and most of the others may follow in their turn.

In his First Inaugural Washington said:

> No people can be bound to acknowledge and adore the Invisible Hand which conducts the affairs of men more than those of the United States. Every step by which they have advanced . . . . seems to have been distinguished by some token of providential agency; . . . . the preservation of the sacred fire of liberty and the destiny of the republican model of government are justly considered perhaps, as *deeply*, as *finally*, staked on the experiment intrusted to the hands of the American people.

And in his last presidential message to his fellow-citizens he told them that he would descend to his grave with the prayer "that Heaven may continue to you the choicest tokens of its beneficence; that your union and brotherly affection may be perpetual; that the free Constitution which is the work of your hands may be sacredly maintained; that its administration in every department may be stamped with wisdom and virtue; that, in fine, the happiness of the people of these States, under the auspices of liberty, may be made complete by so careful a preservation and so prudent a use of this blessing as will acquire to them the glory of recommending it to the applause, the affection, and adoption of every nation which is as yet a stranger to it."

THE DEMOCRATIC EXPERIMENT IN PERIL

Not so much can be anticipated from John Adams who "panted" for an aristocracy and was suspected of wavering faith. Yet, upon taking his oath, he ventured to remark:

> To a benevolent human mind there can be no spectacle presented by any nation more pleasing, more noble, majestic, or august, than an assembly like that which has so often been seen in this and the other Chamber of Congress, of a Government in which the Executive authority, as well as that of all the branches of the Legislature, are exercised by citizens selected at regular periods by their neighbors to make and execute laws for the general good. Can anything essential, anything more than mere ornament and decoration, be added to this by robes and diamonds? Can authority be more amiable and respectable when it descends from accidents or institutions established in remote antiquity than when it springs fresh from the hearts and judgments of an enlightened people? . . . . Such is the amiable and interesting system of government . . . . which the people of America have exhibited to the admiration and anxiety of the wise and virtuous of all nations for eight years . . . . .

With the arrival of the philosophic Jefferson to the presidency the vision of the cosmic drama is fully developed. Europe had been at war for ten years, and the struggle would continue for ten years more. It involved issues linked with American ideology, and its reverberations had reached the United States. Lengthy quotation from his Inaugural Address can hardly be resisted:

> During the throes and convulsions of the ancient world, during the agonizing spasms of infuriated man, seeking through blood and slaughter his long-lost liberty, it is not wonderful that the agitation of the billows should reach even this distant and peaceful shore; that this should be more felt and feared by some and less by others, and should divide opinions as to measures of safety. But every difference of opinion is not a difference of principle. We have called by different names brethren of the same principle. . . . . If there be any among us who would wish to dissolve this Union or to change its republican form, let them stand undisturbed as monuments of the safety with which error of opinion may be tolerated where reason is left free to combat it. I know, indeed, that some honest men fear that a republican government can not be strong. . . .;

AMERICA AND THE STRIFE OF EUROPE

but would the honest patriot, in full tide of successful experiment, abandon a government which has so far kept us free and firm, on the theoretic and visionary fear that this government, the world's best hope, may by possibility want energy to preserve itself? .... Sometimes it is said that man can not be trusted with the government of himself. Can he, then, be trusted with the government of others? Or have we found angels in the forms of kings to govern him? Let history answer this question.

Jefferson then proceeded to state the "essential principles" upon which the American experiment in government was based; and, although these have subsequently been modified in some particulars, no better statement of the American ideal has ever been formulated with such brevity. These principles were enumerated as follows:

Equal and exact justice to all men, of whatever state or persuasion, religious or political; .... the support of the State governments in all their rights, as the most competent administrations for our domestic concerns and the surest bulwarks against antirepublican tendencies; the preservation of the General Government in its whole constitutional vigor, as the sheet anchor of our peace at home and safety abroad; a jealous care of the right of election by the people—a mild and safe correction of abuses which are lopped by the sword of revolution where peaceable remedies are unprovided; absolute acquiescence in the decisions of the majority, the vital principle of republics, from which is no appeal but to force, the vital principle and immediate parent of despotism; .... the supremacy of the civil over the military authority; .... the diffusion of information and arraignment of all abuses at the bar of the public reason; freedom of religion, freedom of the press, and freedom of person under the protection of the habeas corpus and trial by juries impartially selected.

In thus attempting to describe the basic principles of the American political system at the beginning of his administration, Jefferson was setting an example to be followed for many years. If the people were to defend, perpetuate, and extend this noble experiment, it was necessary that men everywhere should understand it and appreciate its merits.

THE DEMOCRATIC EXPERIMENT IN PERIL

Like his predecessors, James Madison had serious difficulties in preventing his country from becoming involved in the wars which harassed Europe. Indeed, because of the determination of the nation to claim the full measure of what was conceived to be its commercial rights and to take advantage of Europe's strife in order to expand its territorial domain, it proved impossible to avoid military conflict. Madison, however, while thoroughly convinced of the superior merits of the great democratic experiment, was less disposed to view it in its universal setting. His messages, therefore, lacked the dramatic appeal of the earlier presidents.

It remained for James Monroe to recall the vision of the cosmic setting and the antagonist. This he did in his First Inaugural and with greater effectiveness in his Annual Message of 1823 which contained what later became famous as the Monroe Doctrine.

In taking his oath as president he remarked:

> From the commencement of our Revolution . . . . almost forty years have elapsed, and from the establishment of this Constitution twenty-eight. Through this whole term the Government has been what may emphatically be called self-government. And what has been the effect? To whatever object we turn our attention, whether it relate to our foreign or our domestic concerns, we find abundant cause to felicitate ourselves in the excellence of our institutions. During a period fraught with difficulties and marked by extraordinary events the United States have flourished beyond example. . . . . Dangers from abroad are . . . . deserving of attention. Experiencing the fortune of other nations, the United States may be again involved in war, and it may in that event be the object of the adverse party to overset our Government, to break our Union and demolish us as a nation.

His message of 1823, directed at both England and the members of the reactionary Neo-Holy Alliance of Continental Europe, evinced a resolution to act upon the Hamiltonian concept of 1788; namely, "to dictate the terms of the

AMERICA AND THE STRIFE OF EUROPE

connection between the old and the new world." In this message Monroe warned the European states that his nation would be disposed to resist the extension of their political system to America, whether in the form of colonies or of political controls of any other type. Monarchies should not expand their dominion at the expense of the area reserved for the operation of democratic governments. America was to be the land of freedom. The world was definitely divided into two vast spheres—the homes of two antagonistic forms of political organization and two opposing political ideologies—neither of which was to meddle in the political affairs of the other. Thus, like Washington's farewell admonition, Monroe's doctrine was less the establishment of a precedent than the confirmation of an old ideal. It merely repeated the maxim of isolationism with emphasis on its expanded American phase, recalled the universal setting, and once more directed attention to the old antagonist. America would not use military force or political intervention to extend its principles to Europe; as a recompense for this exercise of restraint the combination of European belligerent despotisms should refrain from coercion in America.

With the inauguration of John Quincy Adams the spirit of nationalism was fully developed. It was based upon the proud sense of achievement and the pride of vast possessions in land and resources. But it also rested upon a more unique emotion, which was none other than the certainty that the democratic experiment had been an immense success. For the moment the enemies of the system were almost forgotten:

> The year of jubilee since the first formation of our Union has just elapsed; that of the declaration of our independence is at hand. . . . . Since that period a population of four millions has multiplied to twelve. A territory bounded by the Mississippi has been extended from sea to sea.

THE DEMOCRATIC EXPERIMENT IN PERIL

[Louisiana, the Floridas, and an unperfected title to the Oregon country had been acquired.] New States have been admitted to the Union in numbers nearly equal to those of the first Confederation. . . . . The people of other nations, inhabitants of regions acquired not by conquest but by compact, have been united with us in the participation of our rights and duties, of our burdens and blessings. The forest has fallen by the ax of our woodsmen; the soil has been made to teem by the tillage of our farmers; our commerce has whitened every ocean. The dominion of man over physical nature has been extended by the invention of our artists. Liberty and law have marched hand in hand. All the purposes of human association have been accomplished as effectively as under any other government on the globe. . . . . Standing at this point of time, looking back to that generation which has gone by and forward to that which is advancing, we may at once indulge in grateful exultation and in cheering hope. . . . . Our political creed is, without a dissenting voice that can be heard, that the will of the people is the source, and the happiness of the people the end, of all legitimate government upon earth.

But rivals and antagonists were never long lost from view. An English visitor at a Boston public school was reminded of this in 1827 when one of the pupils recited a "furious philippic" against Great Britain and another began his oration by asserting that the world had slumbered for "eighteen hundred years . . . . in ignorance of liberty and the true rights of freemen" before America arose to teach its salutary lesson. Like sentiments might have been observed in almost any school in the nation.

Within five years, however, the enemy within the gates—the enemy of domestic discord viewed by Washington in 1796 not without apprehension, tolerantly alluded to by Jefferson in 1801, and seen with dismay by both Madison and Monroe—seriously disturbed the tranquillity of Andrew Jackson. The Nullification Movement was under way in South Carolina. The democratic experiment was still in peril, and the hero of New Orleans once more placed it in its universal setting. In his annual message of December 4,

1832, he declared that the domestic problems of the nation were a subject of "anxious concern to the friends of freedom throughout the world," and in his special message of January 18, 1833, he invoked the same vast conception, substituting "hopes" for "anxious concern" and "civil liberty" for "freedom." The nation must determine, he said, whether the Union possessed the means of self-preservation to continue the experiment. And in the role of another Washington delivering another farewell exhortation to the people of his country, he warned them against the menace arising from within. "You have the highest of human trusts committed to your care," he said. "Providence has showered on this favored land blessings without number, and has chosen you as the guardians of freedom, to preserve it for the benefit of the human race."

Already Joel Roberts Poinsett, the leader of the friends of the Union in South Carolina, had made a similar appeal. Envisaging a world-stage with South Carolinians acting thereon, he brought them a message from the venerable Lafayette. "Tell your countrymen," said the illustrious Frenchman who had once fought for their liberties, "that if they are so mad and so wicked as to quarrel among themselves about the mere matter of interest, about five or six per cent more or less for [import] duties, ... they will discredit republican government throughout the world. [Tell them] we are looking anxiously to them, for if they are so blind as to dissolve the Union, and cause the failure of the great experiment . . . . , we who are contending for freedom on this side of the Atlantic must lie down in despair and die in our chains."

This particular domestic crisis soon passed, but others arose in a rapid series and for three decades the country was not free from dread engendered by the presence of an in-

THE DEMOCRATIC EXPERIMENT IN PERIL

ternal foe. As the champions and beneficiaries of the democratic experiment contemplated the antagonists at home and abroad the spirit of nationalism was transformed into a delirium. Domestic enemies must be converted by an avalanche of oratory and purified in a glorious blaze of expansionist enthusiasm; foreign foes must be held at bay by an aggressive defense. The "Roaring Forties" had arrived. Viewing the situation from close range, another English traveler observed in 1848: "This country, as a field for increase of power, is in every respect so infinitely beyond ours that comparison would be absurd." He was amazed at the vigor and prosperity of Americans. All circumstances, he said, "combine to promise them, a few years hence, a degree of strength which may endanger the existing state of things in the world. They only wait for matured power, to apply the incendiary torch of Republicanism to the nations of Europe."

As James K. Polk took his oath in March, 1845, he had his heart set on Texas and Oregon and his eyes upon the enemies of the experiment wherever they might reside. His air was that of triumph, and he spoke to all the world:

> Who shall assign limits to the achievements of free minds and free hands under the protection of this glorious Union? No treason to mankind since the organization of society would be equal in atrocity to that of him who would lift his hand to destroy it. He would stop the progress of free government. . . . . He would extinguish the fire of liberty, which warms and animates the hearts of happy millions and invites all the nations of the earth to imitate our example. . . . . Foreign powers do not seem to appreciate the true character of our Government. . . . . To enlarge its limits is to extend the dominions of peace [and freedom] over additional territories and increasing millions.

The limits of the nation were enlarged, and the management of the new acquisitions aroused menacing protests among its citizens, but in 1853 Franklin Pierce was equally defiant and equally confident. Referring to the initiation of the democratic experiment and viewing it in the universal environment, he declared: "The oppressed throughout the world from that day to the present have turned their eyes hitherward, ... to be constantly cheered by . . . . steady and . . . . increasing radiance. . . . . The apprehension of dangers from extended territory . . . . and augmented population has proved to be unfounded." His administration would not be "controlled by any timid forebodings of evil from expansion."

But the reader must be hurried on. Domestic enemies of the system increased. A large section of the nation seceded in order to protect its investment in Negro slaves and follow its own peculiar way of life. The experiment faced catastrophe, but the catastrophe was not conceived as one confined to North America. The crisis was a crisis in human government; the success of the North was supposed to involve the world's best hope. The people's philosopher stands now, gaunt and sad, on the bloody field of Gettysburg (November 19, 1863). For two years his utterances have been replete with cosmic conceptions, and on this occasion he speaks these immortal words:

> Fourscore and seven years ago our fathers brought forth upon this continent a new nation, conceived in liberty, and dedicated to the proposition that all men are created equal.
>
> Now we are engaged in a great civil war, testing whether that nation, or any other so conceived and so dedicated, can long endure. We have met on a great battlefield of that war. We have come to dedicate a portion of that field as a final resting-place for those who here gave their lives that that nation might live. . . . .
>
> . . . . The brave men, living and dead, who struggled here, have consecrated it far above our powers to add or detract. The world will little note nor long remember what we say here, but it can never forget what they did here. . . . . It is rather for us . . . . to be here dedicated to the great task remaining before us: that from these honored dead we take

THE DEMOCRATIC EXPERIMENT IN PERIL

increased devotion to that cause for which they gave the last full measure of devotion; that we here highly resolve .... that government of the people, by the people, and for the people shall not perish from the earth.

Victory and a martyr's death soon made Lincoln a national hero, and his vivid utterances associated with the manner of his rise to power and service later converted him into a symbol of the democratic ideal. The years that followed the close of the Civil War were filled mainly with domestic problems, but the end of the old century and the beginning of the new was also characterized by a new outburst of aggressiveness and the appearance of the old antagonist in a new form: the military autocracy of Germany. And a few months before the United States launched itself upon its most aggressive defense of democracy and world-peace, Woodrow Wilson, whose mind never wandered far from the *kosmos*, went to Kentucky to dedicate Lincoln's birthplace as a national memorial. As he stood there before that national shrine Lincoln rose before him as the personification of almost all that was significant in American history:

.... How eloquent this little house within this shrine is of the vigor of democracy! There is nowhere in the land any home so remote, so humble, that it may not contain the power of mind and heart and conscience to which nations yield and history submits its processes. Genius is no snob. .... It affects humble company as well as great. .... No man can explain this, but every man can see how it demonstrates the vigor of democracy, where every door is open, in every hamlet and countryside, in city and wilderness alike, for the ruler to emerge when he will and claim his leadership in the free life. .... It is likely that in a society ordered otherwise than our own Lincoln could not have found himself or the path of fame and power upon which he walked serenely to his death.

Wilson would soon lead a society so ordered on a transoceanic crusade. Already, by this and similar stirring appeals, he had prepared the nation emotionally for such an enterprise. The vibrant phrases of his war message of April 2, 1917, scarcely need to be recalled. Germany was the dangerous enemy of freedom and peace everywhere. "The world must be made safe for democracy. Its peace must be placed upon the tested foundations of political liberty. . . . . We are but one of the champions of the rights of mankind. We shall be satisfied when those rights have been made as secure as the faith and freedom of nations can make them."

But the world was made safe neither for democracy nor for peace. The strife of Europe continued. And at the close of 1936 another spokesman, descrying other antagonists, went to Buenos Aires to advocate the merits of democracy before men who were losing faith. With dauntless good cheer he had been trying at home to demonstrate its efficiency, and he had now gone abroad to strengthen the faith of his American neighbors. Since he was attending a peace conference he had much to say about peace; but in his mind peace and democracy were inextricably linked, and in his utterances the great experiment received the major emphasis:

. . . . Your first concern, like ours, is peace—for we know that war destroys not only human lives and happiness, but destroys as well the ideals of individual liberty and of the democratic form of representative government which is the goal of all American republics. I think I can say that if in the generation to come we can live without war democratic government throughout the Americas will prove its complete ability to raise the standards of life for those millions who cry for opportunity today. . . . . In seeking peace, perhaps we can best begin by proudly affirming the faith of the Americas; the faith in freedom and its fulfilment which has proved a mighty fortress beyond reach of successful attack in half the world.

The democratic experiment was still in peril. Could it be safeguarded without another campaign across the seas? The ideal of isolation was endangered by another ideal.

THE DEMOCRATIC EXPERIMENT IN PERIL

III

This, however, was by no means a new dilemma in American history. At many critical periods the two ideals had been in conflict. Whenever the democratic experiment in the United States is confronted or supposed to be confronted by an immediate and real threat from abroad, there is always danger that isolationism will be smothered. And at periods when devotion to the democratic system rises to high fervor, the policy of isolation is exposed to violation, even though one of the undisputed principles of the system is noninterference in the affairs of other nations. The threat from without has been viewed as clearly impending only twice, namely, during the Civil War and in 1917 when the United States intervened in the World War, but it aroused considerable apprehension during the epoch of the Holy Alliance and again perhaps in the early years of the present century when Germany was supposed to be seeking a foothold in America. At other times the danger has been discussed, but the extent to which it has been genuinely feared is impossible to determine because of a disposition on the part of American leaders to employ the European menace as a cloak for expansionist designs. And, of course, hostilities with a militant European power in America would not necessarily violate the policy of isolation. It is only when the United States undertakes an aggressive campaign beyond the seas that the policy is violated. It may be observed, however, that an aggressive war engaged in by the United States under the impulse of democratic enthusiasm would most likely be proclaimed as a defensive war. Aggression is seldom admitted by any nation, and it would be easy for ardent Americans to convince themselves that they were undertaking a campaign of long-range defense.

The United States has never entered a war solely for the

AMERICA AND THE STRIFE OF EUROPE

purpose of facilitating the progress of the democratic ideal, but many of its citizens have often been tempted to do so. Moreover, the government or its agents have more than once hovered on the verge of intervention in violation of the isolationist maxim.

The first instance occurred during the infancy of the republic in connection with the French Revolution. John Adams, who was not in full sympathy with the movement, declared that in 1790 the whole nation was aglow "with sanguine hopes and confident expectation of a revolution in France that should produce a free, democratical republic, as sister to ours, in the first nation of Europe." "I saw a disposition everywhere," he said, "to enter into closer connections with our sister republic, and unite with her in a war against all her enemies." This was probably an exaggeration, but sympathy for France was undoubtedly strong and tended for many months to crowd out the sentiment of isolation. In the end, moreover, the government championed the right of revolution by proclaiming de facto recognition as one of the tenets of its foreign policy.

A whole series of impulses to go crusading developed with reference to the insurgent movements in Spanish America. Private individuals enlisted in the cause, diplomatic agents lent encouragement and support, the government expressed its kindly interest, and the principle of nonintervention might have been overridden if the enthusiasm had not been checked by fear of provoking European reprisals and the desire to obtain the Floridas from Spain without a war. And it may be added that early recognition of the independent governments of the region and the issuance of the Monroe Doctrine were official actions which tended to support self-government in America.

After Spain was expelled from its colonies, the Washington government gave encouragement to the establishment of democracies among its neighbors to the south. Diplomats sent out to the new nations were instructed to explain the practical operation and the great advantages of the democratic system, and the dispatch of a minister to Mexico was delayed in order to avoid contributing to the stability of a monarch who had seized control of the independent government there. Within five years two American diplomats—Joel Roberts Poinsett and William Henry Harrison—were given their passports because of their obtrusive zeal in promoting liberalism. Lincoln's agents in Spanish America during the period when monarchical intervention was threatened from Europe likewise were instructed to stimulate the devotion of the leaders to the democratic system. Years later (1889), the overthrow of America's last monarch, Dom Pedro II of Brazil, was observed with gratification in spite of the fact that he was considered the best of rulers, and war vessels were sent to the Brazilian coast to guard against his return with the backing of any European government. And finally Woodrow Wilson, with honorable but mistaken enthusiasm, sought to promote democracy among the Latin Americans by denying them the right of revolution; that is to say, by refusal to recognize any executive who secured power by revolt or a coup d'état.

Meantime a long series of popular movements in Europe had been observed with undisguised sympathy, the first of them the Greek revolt of 1821–28 and the last the demise of the monarchies at the termination of the World War. The Americans regarded with deep interest "the noble and patriotic struggle of the Modern Greeks to rescue from the foot of the infidel and the barbarian the hallowed land of Leonidas and Socrates," and many of them urged the government to offer recognition at once. A resolution authorizing the sending of a diplomatic agent was introduced in Congress, but only a resolution of sympathy was passed and isolationism emerged triumphant. The wide-spread European revolts of 1830 aroused further enthusiasm, and those of 1848 forced the government to the brink of intervention in the case of the ill-fated Hungarian Republic. A secret agent was sent with the view of granting speedy recognition in case circumstances seemed to warrant it; an influential element in the Democratic party clamored for active support of Europe's oppressed; and when the revolutionists were subdued, its leader, Louis Kossuth, was accorded a vociferous welcome and offered asylum in America. All of these demonstrations naturally displeased the Hapsburg monarch, and rupture of diplomatic relations was barely avoided. The downfall of Louis Napoleon in 1870 and the establishment of the Third French Republic were accorded similar acclaim, and admiration for Emilio Castelar and the Spanish democrats was so great that sympathies for insurgent Cubans, which might have led to intervention in 1874 when American citizens were executed by the government at Havana, were almost suffocated.

It will be observed, therefore, that devotion to democracy and devotion to the maxim of isolation have frequently tended to become conflicting sentiments. Action under the powerful impulse of democratic enthusiasm alone has usually been prevented by the restraint of isolationism supported by the general democratic principle of nonintervention in the domestic affairs of other nations. But when democratic fervor becomes exceedingly strong and is reinforced by the profit motive or by considerations of national defense, immediate or even somewhat remote, or by some other national interest or ideal, the policy of isolation is likely to be abandoned.

CHAPTER III

PACIFISM

I

IN AUGUST, 1848, an earnest and grim New Englander silently made his way past the liberty trees in the squares of Paris and through its recently barricaded boulevards to the quarters of A. Dudley Mann, an attaché of the American legation. His large, stout hands were those of one who had swung the hammer on the anvil; otherwise the visitor bore the appearance of a scholar. He had spent years poring over languages, contemplating the will of God and the ways of Nature, and devising remedies for the worst affliction of men and nations. His tired blue eyes gleamed with the zeal of an apostle. He had come to make final arrangements for an international peace conference in the very storm center of revolutions, and he wished to persuade Colonel Mann to preside over the assembly. The American pacifist was Elihu Burritt, the "learned Blacksmith" of Worcester.

Burritt's ardent appeal to Mann was rejected. The diplomat could not be convinced that it was America's mission at that moment to lead the world to peace. Mann thought his country had a more immediate and urgent mission. He was on the point of embarking on his official visit to Hungary, where he hoped to find conditions that would warrant recognition by the United States of Kossuth's insurgent government, and he believed it was the first duty of America to help Europe's struggling people to achieve their

AMERICA AND THE STRIFE OF EUROPE

democratic and nationalist aspirations. Presumably Mann and hundreds of others back home desired to grant such aid even at the risk of war. Peace must await the attainment of democracy and national self-definition by armed force. Amid the flare of revolutions two American ideals clashed.

Seventy years later another American apostle, a scholarly statesman who had harmonized and merged the two ideals, would appear in Paris on a more official mission. He had led his nation on a distant crusade for democracy *and* peace, and he had come to Europe in order to organize the world on that basis. Both Elihu Burritt and Woodrow Wilson, although differing in the scope of their pacifism, were the products of the American peace movement.

The organized peace movement in the United States dates back to August, 1815, when the New York Peace Society was formed by a Connecticut merchant. Between that date and 1828 more than fifty of such societies were established. They were in part a reaction against the Napoleonic Wars and the War of 1812 between the United States and England. In part also they were the result of humanitarian sentiment arising from the conception that it was the duty of America to uplift common men everywhere. And in part they sprang from the teachings of the New Testament as interpreted by the Quakers in particular. The Quakers, although in some sense the pioneers, were seldom, however, the prominent leaders in the movement. The outstanding leaders of this early period were David Low Dodge, the Connecticut merchant; Noah Worcester, a Massachusetts divine; Reverend Henry Holcombe, a Baptist pastor of Pennsylvania; and William Ladd, a merchant of Maine.

On May 8, 1828, the American Peace Society was organized in New York by Ladd, and during the next few

PACIFISM

years nearly all the local peace societies either perished or became affiliated with that national organization. Meantime the American pacifists were preaching their gospel in England and on the Continent of Europe. In France, and especially in England, they found sympathetic and able coadjutors. A peace society was organized in London in 1816 and in Paris in 1821. Perhaps the first international conference of pacifists in history met in London in June, 1843. The one which Burritt attended in Paris in 1848 was the second, and the fifth convened in 1851.

By this time Ladd had passed from the scene and George C. Beckwith, another Massachusetts minister, had taken his place as secretary of the American Peace Society. Moreover, Beckwith, Burritt, and their associates as well as the earlier leaders had already attempted to make their influence felt by the politicians and governments of the period.

At the very outset, in fact, circumstances seemed propitious to men somewhat blinded by their enthusiasm. On September 26, 1815, Tsar Alexander of Russia succeeded in inducing the Emperor of Austria and the King of Prussia to sign with him the so-called Holy Alliance. By its terms these monarchs pledged themselves "to manifest before the whole universe their unshakable determination to take as their sole guide, both in the administration of their respective states and in their political relations with other governments, the precepts of religion, namely, the rules of Justice, Christian Charity, and Peace, which, far from being applicable only to private life, should on the contrary govern the decisions of Princes. . . . ." To this pious pact all the sovereigns of Europe, save the Pope and the Sultan, were invited to subscribe; and all hastened to comply, with the exception of the ruler of England, who pointed out the constitutional limitations upon his authority. Officials of the

AMERICA AND THE STRIFE OF EUROPE

Massachusetts Peace Society were deeply impressed. In April, 1817, Noah Worcester wrote the Tsar a jubilant letter alluding to the fact that the "Holy League" and the Boston society had been organized at the same time and declaring that the object of the American organization was to "disseminate the very principles avowed in the wonderful alliance." Alexander replied immediately, giving his blessing to his co-workers in America, and a few months later Thomas Dawes eulogized the Russian monarch in an anniversary address:

> The Holy League of august sovereigns, in which the Emperor of all the Russias has taken so conspicuous a part, is a strong indication of the future prevalence of the cause of Peace. Jealous politicians may have doubted the motive. But they had not then read the undisguised answer of that illustrious man to the corresponding secretary of this Society. Some of our friends in New York have been favored with similar expressions of the Emperor's regard for that peace and good will towards men which were celebrated by the angels at the Redeemer's birth. We should be blind indeed not to perceive in such signs of the times the operations of an overruling Providence.

The *Friend of Peace*, official journal of the Massachusetts Peace Society, scolded the English Prince Regent for not becoming a member of the alliance, and Noah Worcester repeatedly expressed the hope that the United States would join, while William Ellery Channing even went so far as to memorialize Congress on the subject. American statesmen, however, were suspicious of the alliance almost from the beginning.

John Adams, who refused to have anything to do with the early peace movement, remarked in 1816 that if the principles of the Massachusetts organization were acted upon by the people "the human flock would soon be fleeced or butchered by one or a few." Writing to Worcester, he said: "Our beloved country, sir, is surrounded by enemies, ...

most dangerous, ... most powerful, and most unprincipled. .... Collisions of national interest, of commercial and manufacturing rivalries, are multiplying around us. Instead of discouraging a martial spirit, in my opinion it ought to be excited. We have not enough of it to defend us by land or sea." Adams probably had the European powers in general and England in particular in mind.

His distinguished son John Quincy, in a letter to Alexander H. Everett written near the end of 1817, was more pointed. Enraged because the peacemakers were corresponding with the Tsar, he declared:

> If our Peace Societies should fall into the fashion of corresponding upon the objects of their institutions with foreign Emperors and Kings, they may at some future day find themselves under the necessity of corresponding with attorney generals [sic] and petit juries. Philip of Macedon was in very active correspondence with a Peace Society at Athens, and with their coöperation baffled and overpowered all the eloquence of Demosthenes. Alexander of the Neva is not so near nor so dangerous a neighbor to us as Philip was to the Athenians, but I am afraid his love of peace is of the same character. . . . . .

The Tsar was admired in America, and his original intentions may have been wholly benign; but he allowed himself to be dominated by Metternich. The repressive activities of the alliance during the next few years transformed its pacific nature, and on May 12, 1821, a circular dispatch issued from Laibach boldly announced: "Useful and necessary changes in the governments of states must emanate only from the free will and the thoughtful and enlightened consent of those whom God has made responsible for power."

Despite repeated invitations from the Russian government, the United States, with John Quincy Adams in charge of the execution of its foreign policy, revealed not the slightest disposition to join the quasi-peace concert of the monarchies. As early as July, 1820, in the polite—even

AMERICA AND THE STRIFE OF EUROPE

false—language of diplomacy, he instructed his minister to Russia as follows: "The President, approving its general principles, and thoroughly convinced of the benevolent and virtuous motives which led to the conception and presided at the formation of this system by the Emperor Alexander, believes that the United States will more effectually contribute to the great and sublime objects for which it was concluded by abstaining from a formal participation in it. . . . ." To the Russian suggestion that the Tsar might interpose his influence on the side of America in its disputes with England or some other European nation, Adams replied that Russia would doubtless expect the favors to be reciprocal and would soon be asking the aid of the United States against the Tsar's opponents. The New Englander was so filled with distrust and isolation sentiment that the offer of an alliance from one of Europe's strongest powers was not even a temptation.

By this time the American peace leaders were suffering bitter disappointment. All the world seemed to be on the point of adopting the "delusive pretext of fighting for peace." In 1823, after the French invasion of Spain, the *Friend of Peace* observed: "It must be a miserable policy to revive military ambition to check the spirit of revolution. This is indeed like attempting to cast out demons by Beelzebub."

The important facts to notice, however, are two: Americans were interesting themselves in the peace of Europe, and they were discovering that their peace sentiments were conflicting with those of isolationism and of sympathy for the oppressed. What were the proper limits of pacifism? Were there just wars, and should pacifism ever become militant? These issues led to many arguments which lasted for years. Few of the peace advocates seemed to admit that pacifists should ever employ force in the attempt to promote their ideal, but there were more who believed that a defensive war against a foreign foe was just. With reference to the European masses who were struggling for their "long-lost freedom," they appear to have been less sympathetic than one might have expected, or at any rate to have allowed their attachment to peace to outweigh their devotion to democracy. If they likened the military operations of the reactionary monarchies to Beelzebub, they called the popular revolutions demons—at least in their more radical manifestations. In the main, the pacifists opposed any sort of war, whether reactionary, international, or revolutionary, save a war of national defense. Yet, as the popular movements in Europe continued, many of the peace advocates reached the conclusion that reasonable freedom was an indispensable condition for world-peace.

Their experience with the Holy Alliance was but the beginning of their disappointments. They lived in a century of both civil and international wars. Their efforts to co-operate with the English pacifists in preventing the war of 1850 between Denmark and Austria over Schleswig-Holstein proved futile. Their attempts to convince statesmen at Washington that the United States should assume official leadership of the world's peace forces were equally vain. In 1846–48 their own country even fought a war with Mexico. It was not possible to persuade their government to mediate in the Crimean War; and in 1861 civil strife began in their very midst. In spite of all their propaganda, despite all their conferences, memorials, and remonstrances, the world blandly ignored the peace advocates and continued its strife. Only the Anglo-American convention of 1817 limiting the armed forces of the two countries on the Great Lakes and the arbitration clause in the treaty of 1848 between the United States and Mexico lightened their despair—and for neither could they justly claim much credit.

Yet in some respects they had made positive achievements. They had not only kept the peace movement alive but had laid the foundations for future efforts. They had solved the problem of organization and finance so that by 1860 there were both in the United States and in England peace organizations with assured permanence no matter what the opposition or how serious a war was raging. They had established efficient machinery for publicity: periodicals, lectures, sermons, memorials, field agents, conferences—all these devices made the peace agitation well known and kept the peacemakers informed of developments at home and abroad. By 1860 governments were aware that the various peace societies numbered among their membership not merely clergymen but those of other professions, including lawyers, businessmen, and politicians. They had also worked out more or less definite plans for world-peace and secured international co-operation in their activities. British peace advocates worked hand in hand with Americans from the first, and they were later joined by those of France and the Germanies. Among the peace devices of the pioneers were arbitration clauses in international treaties, a court and a congress of nations, disarmament by international agreement, and plans for the development of international harmony and peace through education, propaganda, and the codification of international law.

Still more important perhaps was the development of a body of arguments against war. By 1860 practically every argument now familiar had been elaborated or suggested as well as almost every current plan for securing peace. Chiefly religious, moral, and philanthropic at the beginning, these arguments tended more and more to emphasize economic and political considerations: the wastefulness of war, the burdens it imposed on the working classes, its threat to democracy, and the relation between economic imperialism and war. Bankers were urged to refuse war loans; workers were told to organize internationally against war. Elihu Burritt even asserted that if a court and a congress of nations were not established for the purpose of preventing war, a general strike of the world's laborers might be the only alternative in a crisis; and in 1850, anticipating the idea of another mechanic of a more recent day, he actually asked the government of the United States for a peace ship to carry the American crusaders to Europe!

II

After the close of the Civil War in their own country these pioneers and their successors—too numerous to mention in this brief sketch—renewed their peace efforts. They demanded that the United States offer mediation in the Franco-Prussian War. They set up new organizations—there were more than sixty of them by 1914. They carried on campaigns at home and abroad for arbitration and the codification and reform of international law. They opened peace colleges and institutes. They established headquarters in Washington and used persuasion and pressure on public men. Observing the connection between war and the race for colonies, they urged the United States to participate in the Berlin Conference of 1884–85 relating to Africa and the Congo Basin in particular. They furnished suggestions regarding the policies which should be advocated at this international assembly. They wrote to friends in Europe and interviewed its monarchs and men of power. They helped to inject the peace issue into the Pan-American conferences. They attacked militarism, navalism, and imperialism. They were instrumental, along with their collaborators in Europe, in promoting two official peace conferences at The Hague. In fact, the peace movement became so influential on both sides of the Atlantic that even statesmen seemed hopefully devoted to the cause. By 1913 permanent peace seemed to many to be almost within reach.

The first Hague assembly was perhaps the most important step in the history of the peace crusade prior to 1900. It was not a conference of private individuals. It was an official peace conference consisting of diplomats called together by another Tsar of Russia, and the peace advocates felt that the Tsar's initiative was largely the result of their efforts. It is likely that they exaggerated their influence over Nicholas II. It is also probable that, as in the case of his predecessor Alexander, they were too confident of the purity of Nicholas' motives. He too would one day disappoint them. There is little doubt, however, that the peacemakers were mainly responsible for the participation of the United States in the conference. Neither the Washington authorities nor the press showed much interest until the friends of peace "moved heaven and earth to whip up enthusiasm." They interviewed statesmen, including President McKinley, founded a special propaganda journal, enlisted the aid of numerous civic and religious organizations, and held meetings in city after city until favorable sentiment was fully developed.

History must be recalled again in order to appreciate the full significance of their achievement. Dread of European entanglements came into general existence with the birth of the nation. The maxim of isolation was associated with the nation's founders and heroes. Isolationism had become a tradition, a sentiment almost as sacred as that of religion. No government since the year 1783 had completely succumbed to the temptation to depart from that policy.

PACIFISM

Moved by the desire for commercial expansion and by intimate relationships with Liberia, and possibly influenced to a very small degree by the pacifists, the United States had sent delegates to the Berlin conference on the Congo. But the government was severely criticized for the step by many of the newspapers and the majority of Congress. Actuated by the commercial motive in the main, the United States had also become somewhat involved with other powers in Samoa and China. Actuated by similar motives, as well as by various idealisms and rationalizations soon to be described, the nation, moreover, had just seized the Philippines despite the danger that such action might lead to larger participation in world-affairs. But the country as a whole was still strongly attached to isolationism. Efforts of the peace advocates to persuade the government to mediate in the war between France and Prussia had been only a little more successful than their previous efforts with reference to the Crimean War. The pressure of 1870 had resulted merely in a single cautious proffer of mediation. The final act of the Berlin conference of 1884–85 had never been ratified. The triple agreement with England and Germany regarding Samoa was on the point of being dissolved by a partition of the islands. The first Hague conference must be viewed with this record in mind. It was definite indication of the growing influence of the peace movement as well as of the sentimental desire of the United States to act a larger part on the world-stage. The sending of official representatives to the peace assembly of 1899 and ratification of the agreements reached marked a distinct departure from traditional policy, even though the ratification was qualified by a reservation definitely alluding to that policy.

The work of the conference was viewed by the peace champions with a mixture of delight and disappointment.

AMERICA AND THE STRIFE OF EUROPE

The Permanent Court of Arbitration finally agreed upon fell short of the hopes of the pacifists, but in many respects it conformed with their ideas. American pacifists were also grateful for the Draft Convention for the Pacific Settlement of International Disputes as well as for the agreement to set up commissions of inquiry to deal with controversies in times of acute crises between states. The friends of peace were disappointed, however, at the failure of the conference in the matter of disarmament, and they felt no pride when they learned that the American delegation had voted against a ban on poisonous gases. Weighing the conference's achievements against its failures, Benjamin Trueblood, then secretary of the American Peace Society, hailed the assembly as the "beginning of the Parliament of Man," nor was Alfred Love of the Universal Peace Union less enthusiastic.

Such were the achievements of the American peace advocates during the first eighty-four years of their organized effort in behalf of peace. At the close of last century the people of the United States, while strongly isolationist still, were by no means indifferent to the strife of Europe. Their devotion to peace was becoming intense, and, strengthened by the dynamic belief that the United States should play a leading role in world-affairs, it would soon become active. Further intensified by anger against Germany and by emotional attachment to democracy, it would finally become militant. Within two years after the opening of the new century the White House would be occupied by a man ready to display active concern with reference to Europe's peace. Within fourteen years a pacifist would become secretary of state. And in less than two decades another chief executive would summon the nation to "fight for the things which we have always carried nearest to our hearts."

The World War was followed by a period of emotional

calm and material prosperity. The nation was less interested for a time in the peace of Europe, although not uninterested in its markets. It refused to join the League of Nations, refused for months even to communicate with it. Yet the peace advocates were not extinct. America had seen war and America hated war. The people of the United States were still vividly aware of Europe; they observed the crosscurrents of European politics with utmost diligence. Pacifism grew and finally waxed strong as new phrases were coined, phrases not without power to convince and electrify: collective security, the renouncement of war as an instrument of national policy, the outlawry of war, sanctions, the punishment of the aggressor, the sanctity of treaties, the consultation of enlightened statesmen, and other appealing concepts. In 1928 Secretary Frank B. Kellogg and Aristide Briand offered to the world their anti-war pact; Henry L. Stimson soon promulgated his doctrine against the recognition of territorial acquisitions secured by military force; and the Franklin Roosevelt administration moved to accept a policy of consultation in world-affairs. In 1935–37 the battle of the sanctions took place in Congress, largely between the internationalists and the isolationists, with victory, although by no means complete victory, going to the isolationists. In the meantime democracy was becoming more emotionalized in face of economic catastrophe and in face of critics at home as well as new antagonists abroad.

Democracy was becoming militant, liberalism of all types was growing militant, and pacifism was already of an active species akin to militancy. A nation emotionally attached to democracy and peace fused in a common ideology and at the same time fully aware of the existence of dangerous antagonists is a nation stripped for action. The explosives were all present at the beginning of 1938. A touch of anger caused by some insult, some injury to national interest, or some threat to national security even broadly defined might be all that was required to supply the igniting flame. For both material and sentimental reasons the country was finding it increasingly difficult to retain its philosophical tranquillity while Europeans prepared to slaughter one another on the bloody altars of Mars.

Before describing the official efforts of the United States to preserve the peace of Europe, however, it seems advisable to examine still other sentiments which have influenced its foreign policy and to note briefly the manner in which Europe's strife permitted the United States for one hundred and fifty years largely to have its way in America. The other sentiments demanding consideration are those which produced a policy of expansion, a policy which was also a possible peril to the maxim of isolation. Isolationism was not merely threatened by democratic zeal and pacificism. It was besieged by expansionism which tended to provoke European concerts and European interventions in America against the United States, and in its later stages tended also to launch the nation out into far-flung fields of international competition as well as of national endeavor based upon notions of world-service and world-leadership.

CHAPTER IV

EXPANSIONIST IDEALISM AND RATIONALIZATIONS

I

History has no more difficult problem than that of motivation. Yet motivation is a problem which the historian is not permitted to neglect. His readers constantly are asking why individuals and groups, large or small, acted as the records indicate. If the actors were always motivated by the reasons they allege the problem would be simplified, for men and groups usually announce their motives. But the problem hinges mainly on this point. The actors frequently do not announce all their motives or their real motives. They often seek to deceive others and not infrequently they deceive themselves. Thus there are alleged motives and actual motives, and often it is impossible to distinguish between them.

In the United States, as in all modern states, the most fundamental motives influencing foreign policy are rooted in the idea of national interest, which embraces two large concepts: security and prosperity or progress. This idea of national interest, an idea broad enough to include both tangible material interests and less tangible ideal interests, is defined and redefined continually by leaders and groups who control or seek to control the policies of government. Sometimes both those at the helm and those determined to replace them are in pursuit merely of their own security and prosperity. But they usually pretend, often convince others,

AMERICA AND THE STRIFE OF EUROPE

and perhaps rarely fail to convince themselves that their own interests harmoniously blend with the national interest—as sometimes they may.

The problem of motivation is difficult even in the case of such a familiar movement as American expansion, especially in its territorial phase. One may assert that the expansionist movement in the United States, like all movements in history, was largely the result of prevailing material interests and ideals. But to ascertain what these were and which of the two groups was the more powerful at a given moment of action is not an easy task. With reference to the actual motivation of American territorial expansion from the outset until the acquisition of Alaska, the following generalizations are offered:

1. The pride of empire, a motive which began to emerge as early as 1755 and reached its full development during the two decades following 1840.
2. The exclusion of Europe—a Europe rent with strife—from certain areas in accordance with the American phase of the isolation policy and the Monroe Doctrine.
3. The desire to secure the use of certain rivers for the transportation of the commodities of the frontier inhabitants.
4. The strategic motive (closely related to No. 2), which was a factor in developing the desire for regions conceived to have an important relation to national defense.
5. The abatement of a nuisance; the inhabitants of some areas competed with citizens of the United States in the fur trade, instigated Indian attacks on its frontiers, or furnished an asylum for runaway slaves and a rendezvous for escaping criminals.
6. Land speculation on the part of capitalists and land hunger on the part of the masses, influences which often combined to create a national impulse to expand.
7. The acquired habit of migration, especially westward migration, originating perhaps in a sort of wanderlust, on the part of many inhabitants who finally helped to induce the government to act.
8. Rivalry between the sections, which led to demands for territory

EXPANSIONIST IDEALISM AND RATIONALIZATIONS

north or south, but this rivalry tended to check as well as to promote expansion.
9. The desire to extinguish domestic discord by creating enthusiasm for grand enterprise abroad.

As the territorial phase of expansionism approached its culmination, it became an intense emotion and acquired a significant name: Manifest Destiny. It then became one of the potent sentiments of nationalism. It was rooted in the vivid feeling of mission, the principal characteristic of nationalism, for nation *is* mission. Americans felt that they were a chosen people, the providential agents for the spread of their system of politics and their general culture. They submitted with reluctance to the provisions of international law or any other restraints established by man. They lived, as it were, under the regime of higher law, although they invoked the principles of international law when these served their purposes.

Such were probably the important actual motives for territorial expansion, but there were also alleged motives—some of them perhaps genuine—which have not been included in the list. It is advisable to turn now to the literature of expansion. This literature, which is immense, will be examined with most profit if one reads it with the view of discovering not merely the genuine reasons for territorial expansion but the apologies or arguments for expansionist objectives as well. Apologies may set forth real motives or pretended motives, and the pretended motives of the propagandist may become the actual motives of those convinced by his arguments. The primary concern here is with the idealization and rationalization of territorial expansion, for it is believed that idealizations and rationalizations are important instruments in the creation of national purpose and the national will to act.

AMERICA AND THE STRIFE OF EUROPE

II

The desire for expansion like the sentiment of isolationism developed very early. Its first manifestations were based upon pride of empire as well as the optimism of land speculators and the anxiety to exclude dangerous contentious neighbors from adjacent territory. As early as 1755 John Adams wrote:

> Soon after the Reformation a few people came over into this new world for conscience sake. Perhaps this apparently trivial incident may transfer the great seat of empire into America. It looks likely to me: for if we can remove the turbulent Gallicks, our people, according to the exactest computations, will in another century become more numerous than England itself. Should this be the case, since we have, I may say, all the naval stores of the nation in our hands, it will be easy to obtain the mastery of the seas; and then the united force of all Europe will not be able to subdue us. The only way to keep us from setting up for ourselves is to disunite us.

Benjamin Franklin made in the same year a similar prediction with reference to the growth of population in the colonies, but expressed no anticipation with regard to their independence. And, curiously enough, it was during this same year that Thomas Pownall, who later became governor of Massachusetts and was then planning to establish a colony south of Lake Erie, predicted that his projected settlement would in time become the manufacturing center of the continent.

Moreover, Benjamin Franklin at that moment or shortly thereafter was also becoming interested in western lands, and his vision of the future of America expanded as he contemplated the profits to be obtained from his projected settlement in the Illinois country. In 1767 he wrote to Lord Kames that "America, an immense territory, favoured by nature with all advantages of climate, soil, great navigable

EXPANSIONIST IDEALISM AND RATIONALIZATIONS

rivers, and lakes, ... must become a great country, populous and mighty; and will in less time than is generally conceived, be able to shake off any shackles that may be imposed on her, and perhaps place them on the imposers." And it was in this very year that he urged his plan for the Illinois settlement upon Lord Shelburne and Lord Conway.

Land speculators must have optimism and impose it upon others! They also develop soaring imaginations and a lust for empire. But poets and philosophers likewise have imaginations: In 1771 Philip Freneau envisaged an America peopled from the Atlantic to the Pacific by Anglo-Saxons, and between 1781 and 1783 Jefferson was looking with covetous eyes upon fair lands between the Mississippi and distant Oregon. That the American Revolution was characterized by attempts to conquer the trans-Appalachian region and Canada, the one successful and the other a failure, hardly needs to be mentioned. It was Jefferson also who made this startling statement in 1786: "Our confederacy must be viewed as the nest from which all America, North and South, is to be peopled."

Some of the geographers, too, possessed the long-range vision. As Washington took charge of the government in 1789, Jedidiah Morse of New England published his *American Geography*. It was a well-known fact, he said in this work, that "empire" had been "travelling from east to west":

> Probably her last and broadest seat will be America. Here the sciences and arts of civilized life are to receive their highest improvement. Here civil and religious liberty are to flourish, unchecked by the cruel hand of civil or ecclesiastical tyranny. Here Genius, aided by all the improvements of former ages, is to be exerted in humanizing mankind—in expanding and enriching their minds with religious and philosophical knowledge, and in planning and executing a form of government, which shall involve all the excellencies of former governments, with as few of

AMERICA AND THE STRIFE OF EUROPE

their defects as is consistent with the imperfection of human affairs, and which shall be calculated to protect and unite, in a manner consistent with the natural rights of mankind, the largest empire that ever existed.

Such an empire would "comprehend millions of souls west of the Mississippi," for that great river "was never designed as the western boundary of the American empire." "The God of nature," declared Morse, "never intended that some of the best part of his earth should be inhabited by the subjects of a monarch 4,000 miles from them." He ventured to predict that when the "rights of mankind" should be "more fully known, ... the power of European potentates" would be "confined to Europe." Three years later Gilbert Imlay, a Kentucky geographer, displayed equal optimism. He predicted that posterity would not "deem it extraordinary should they find the country settled quite across to the Pacific Ocean in less than another century." (Exactly a century later the continental area was occupied and the frontier disappeared!) To establish the capital city on the Potomac would be shortsighted folly, Imlay declared; it should be located at Lake Pepin or St. Anthony Falls. From the heart of the continent Americans would migrate in all directions. "Thus in the center of the earth," he said, "governing by the laws of reason and humanity, we seem calculated to become at once the emporium and the protectors of the world."

For the moment, however, the ambitious young nation was surrounded by the territorial possessions of the European powers. This circumstance tended to impede its expansion, to interfere with the free use of adjacent rivers, and even to involve America in European politics. It was an embarrassing situation, and as early as March, 1785, Richard Henry Lee wrote Samuel Adams: "A word more upon the point of our just wishes to be detached from European

EXPANSIONIST IDEALISM AND RATIONALIZATIONS

politics and European vices; of course I wish it most sincerely. But unfortunately Great Britain is upon our northern quarter and Spain upon the southern. We are therefore compelled to mix with their councils in order to be guarded against their ill designs."

But this situation did not extinguish the optimism of Jefferson. He observed that Spain's weakness and Europe's strife would make it possible to obtain the far-flung Spanish borderlands in one way or another. "Those countries," he said in 1786, "cannot be in better hands. My fear is that they are too feeble to hold them till our population can be sufficiently advanced to gain it [*sic*] from them piece by piece." He hoped that these lands might not pass into the hands of a stronger European power, but even in that event there was no reason for despair. They might be purchased, seized, or obtained as the price of neutrality when Europe's discords should result in a general war. In an emergency, even an alliance with one group of belligerents or the other might not be too dear a price to pay for the removal of European territorial domain from our borders.

Thus the expansionist impulse was rapidly developing, and the Europeans themselves did not fail to observe it. As early as December, 1782, the *Morning Post* of London remarked: "The pride of empire will awaken, and conquests will be multiplied on neighboring borders . . . . ; and as they increase in power, that power will reach the limits of the Southern Ocean [namely, the South Sea or the Pacific], and dispossess the Europeans of every hold upon the great continent of America." At the same time a Frenchman declared that the Americans would sooner or later expand to the Pacific, and a Spaniard, then or shortly after, predicted that the "pygmy" would become a "giant," a "colossus" which would soon menace all Spain's possessions in North

America. And in 1794 the Spanish governor of Louisiana repeated the warning.

III

It should cause no surprise to discover that natural rights and self-defense became the first justifications of territorial expansion. A prevalent slogan of the period was natural rights, and national security is one of the most urgent aspects of national interest. In fact, in the minds of the Fathers national security was itself a natural right.

It was soon urged that the United States could claim a natural right to navigate the Mississippi and other rivers flowing into the Gulf of Mexico as well as a natural right to possess a deposit near its banks. These two rights were asserted by Jefferson and Madison, by Rufus King and certain members of Congress, and by the western settlers alike. And to these two claims were soon added two others: the natural right to annex any territory essential to national security and the natural right to control in the interest of that security the transactions of other powers in North America. On January 28, 1803, when commenting upon the unpleasant news that weak Spain had transferred Louisiana to a stronger power, the *New York Evening Post* boldly affirmed:

> It belongs *of right* to the United States to regulate the future destiny of *North America*. The country is *ours;* ours is the right to its rivers, and to all the sources of future opulence, power, and happiness which lay scattered at our feet; and we shall be the scorn and derision of the world if we suffer them to be wrested from us by the intrigues of France.

After Louisiana had been purchased from France, however, Jefferson blandly ignored the natural right of its inhabitants to liberty of choice in their national allegiance. But others did not ignore the inconsistency; they rationalized their way around it. A circular sent out apparently by

EXPANSIONIST IDEALISM AND RATIONALIZATIONS

the officials of Mississippi Territory made this ingenious appeal:

Nature designed the inhabitants of Mississippi and those of New Orleans to be one single people. It is your peculiar happiness that nature's decrees are fulfilled under the auspices of a philosopher who prefers justice to conquest, whose glory it is to make man free and not a slave, and who delights in benevolence instead of splendor. Yet, although he is careful with your happiness, he will not permit you to destroy it by obstructing our rights. . . . . Would you . . . . try vainly to prevent New Orleans from fulfilling its destiny?

A member of Congress, however, discovered a more rational justification. "I am," he said, "one of those who believe that the principle of liberty can not suddenly be ingrafted on a people accustomed to a regimen of a directly opposite hue. The approach of such a people to liberty must be gradual. I believe them at present totally unqualified to exercise it."

From this time forward the right of self-defense, strengthened by isolation sentiment, which was in turn reinforced by the Monroe Doctrine, continued to be a weighty argument of the expansionists. And as the years went by this right was enlarged from the modest conception of immediate self-preservation in face of an actual menace to the extravagant notion of permanent security against all future contingencies. Self-defense, therefore, assumed an aggressive aspect.

Congratulating Americans on the Louisiana Purchase, Edward Livingston and James Monroe wrote: "We separate ourselves in great measure from the European world and its concerns, especially its wars and intrigues. We make, in fine, a great stride to real and substantial independence." The attempts to seize the Floridas and Canada in 1811 and subsequently were justified by the argument that in no other way could the menace of European neighbors—contentious and warring neighbors—be removed or "the torch that

AMERICA AND THE STRIFE OF EUROPE

lights up savage warfare" be extinguished. Thereafter an aggressive self-defense often closely associated with isolationism was offered as a justification for almost every territorial acquisition that was urged.

Senator Lewis Cass, for instance, declared in 1853: "We do not intend .... to have this hemisphere ruled by maxims suited neither to its position nor to its interests, and divided into political communities, dependencies of European monarchies, or under their influence, and, therefore, liable to be involved in every war breaking out in the Old World, and thus extending its dangers and difficulties to the New. . . . ." Five years later, November 23, 1858, the *New York Herald* was advocating the annexation of Mexico, Cuba, and Central America in the name of defensive isolation, pointing out with emphasis that, "if we look unconcernedly on while a few selfish European intriguers endeavor to establish a European protectorate and Spanish despotism, we shall only consent to their being immersed in more savage civil wars than they have yet witnessed, and become finally involved ourselves in a general war with the European alliance." Hostile gestures on Europe's part during the American Civil War served to give point to the argument and furnish justification for those who sought even during Reconstruction to revive the expansionist sentiment of an earlier day. But at that epoch and for the next thirty years expansionism was curbed by other considerations, among them the fear of destroying the moorings of isolationism and embarking the nation on the "trackless sea" of empire. Thus the sentiment of isolation, based mainly on the fear of being involved in European strife, stood at the beginning and at the end of territorial expansion and swept through its whole course.

Meantime the maxim of self-defense had expanded so as

EXPANSIONIST IDEALISM AND RATIONALIZATIONS

to embrace every contingency: possible future attack from an adjacent base by an enemy in an existing war; possible future conflict with a powerful neighbor which had replaced or was about to replace a weak one; the danger that a weak neighbor might be unable to resist conquest by a European power; possibility of attack by such a power along an indefensible boundary; the alleged likelihood that the United States might suffer economic injury because of the establishment of a European power in contiguous countries; injury to the institution of slavery through the abolition of slavery in Texas or Cuba at the instigation of England; danger that the spread of American democracy might be checked through the influence of European absolutism in adjacent countries; the possibility that an American state might seek and obtain European protection against marauding Indians or the threat of anarchy; and the possibility of future attack by European nations from a group of islands out in the Pacific Ocean more than two thousand miles away. All these contingencies at one time or another were presented as justifications for annexation of the areas involved. Self-defense was truly a colossal concept!

IV

These, however, were not the only arguments for expansion. Besides these three closely related justifications—natural law, isolation from a contentious Europe, and self-defense—there were at least a half-dozen others employed by 1872 when the first tremendous impulse flickered out: geographical predestination; divinely ordained use of the soil; the extension of the area of freedom; the mission of regeneration; political gravitation and the kindred concept of political affinity; and the law of natural growth—a veritable arsenal of defense and offense.

AMERICA AND THE STRIFE OF EUROPE

Americans who read natural law in the hearts of men soon began to discover it also, as Albert K. Weinberg has observed, in the configuration of the earth. The principle of natural boundaries which was mainly a doctrine of restraint in Europe became an apology for expansion in America. The leaders developed a passion for territorial unity and symmetry. Boundaries must be extended so as to include territorial appendages, territorial nexuses held together by a great river or two rivers with interlocking tributaries, and all lands lying between the national boundaries and more remote natural barriers. Topography was always inviting Americans to advance their frontiers.

Louisiana was scarcely acquired when it was discovered that other areas belonged to the United States by geographical predestination. Men began to declare at once that God and Nature, or reason and Nature, or Nature alone, or God alone, had decreed that the Floridas must become ours. This could be discovered by looking at the map. And before the Floridas were safely annexed Canada beckoned, because the St. Lawrence united it with the Mississippi. Later the Río Grande beckoned also, and the Rocky Mountains invited the nation to advance. Nor did even those natural boundaries satisfy all. Some declared that the mountains beyond the Río Grande constituted a better natural boundary to the south, or that the "symmetry of this republic" required the absorption of all Mexico and even of all beyond to the southern limits of the Isthmus of Panama. Others, and one of them—Francis Baylies, a member of Congress—as early as 1823, looked across the lofty western mountains to the great ocean. "If we reach the Rocky Mountains," he said, "we should be unwise did we not pass that narrow space which separates the mountains from the ocean. . . . . Gentlemen are talking of natural boundaries. Sir, our natural boundary is the Pacific Ocean. The swelling tide of our population must and will roll on until that mighty ocean interposes its waters, and limits our territorial empire." John Quincy Adams, who had been engaged in negotiations with Great Britain and Russia with reference to the Pacific Coast, agreed with Baylies. More than ten years before, Representative John A. Harper had declared: "To me, sir, it appears that the Author of Nature has marked our limits in the south by the Gulf of Mexico; and on the north, by the regions of eternal frost."

The American empire would be bounded by the oceans and its glory by the stars. But any who imagined that even the oceans would be accepted by all as a final barrier were mistaken. Harper and Baylies had overlooked the territorial appendages: Cuba, the Dominican Republic, and the Hawaiian Islands. The first two were soon discovered to be a "part of the American continent" that "naturally" belonged to the nation which possessed it, and Hawaii, it was said, was nearer to America than to any other great land mass. With reference to Cuba, William H. Seward pointed out in 1859 that "every rock and every grain of sand in that island were drifted and washed out from American soil by the floods of the Mississippi, and the other estuaries of the Gulf of Mexico."

It is not surprising that superior utilization of the soil should have been employed to justify the territorial expansion of the United States. The argument had been used against the Indians since the middle of the seventeenth century, when it was asserted that they had failed to obey the divine command to till the soil and might therefore be deprived of their lands by efficient agriculturalists. Property claims based upon a nomadic mode of life were invalid against those who were willing to sow and reap. "Is one of the fairest portions of the globe," asked William Henry Harrison in 1812 with regard to the Old Northwest, "to remain in a state of nature, the haunt of a few wretched savages, when it seems destined by the Creator to give support to a large population and to be the seat of civilization, of science, and of true religion?" "There can be no doubt," said Lewis Cass in 1830, "that the Creator intended the earth should be reclaimed from a state of nature and cultivated." He had the Indians of the same region in mind. And in that very year the Georgia representatives in Congress were making similar assertions regarding the natives of the Southwest. James M. Wayne declared that the "Almighty's command to his creatures to till the earth" invalidated the Indian's right to uncultivated domain. And Richard H. Wilde asserted: "Jacob will forever obtain the inheritance of Esau. We cannot alter the laws of Providence, as we read them in the experience of the ages."

Spanish-American neighbors, it is true, were tillers of the soil, but they tilled it indifferently and in spots. The earth was really created for those who would make better use of it. This was the implication contained in a report of the Democracy of New York in 1848, which urged the acquisition of Mexican domain and observed: "Labor was the consecrated means of man's subsistence when he was created. To replenish the earth and subdue it, was his ordained mission and destiny." Ten years later Caleb Cushing, with his eyes still on Mexico, asked: "Is not the occupation of any portion of the earth by those competent to hold and till it, a providential law of national life?" The question was merely rhetorical, yet it was soon answered by Representative Samuel E. Cox, who declared that "no nation" had "the right to hold soil, virgin and rich, yet unproducing." In 1858 the *United States Democratic Review* even asserted that

EXPANSIONIST IDEALISM AND RATIONALIZATIONS

"no race but our own can either cultivate or rule the western hemisphere"; but the argument was usually applied only to the neighbors on the south. And it applied to mining as well as to agriculture, for as early as 1853 another expansionist magazine had declared:

> Silver coin will never be abundant in the United States until the boundary of the South includes the mineral fields of Central Mexico, now occupied by a people who have no knowledge, or no appreciation of their value. .... The time is not far distant when the enterprise of the South will direct itself upon those regions, which belong to it .... by the well-founded and legitimate rights of industry and intelligence; .... the same that confirms the title of every free people to the soil upon which they stand.

Far more frequently employed was another argument discovered in the course of the war with Mexico: the regenerating mission. In the latter part of 1847 the mission of the United States to regenerate Mexico by extending its benevolent rule over the country was proclaimed in many quarters. John L. O'Sullivan, who popularized the phrase "manifest destiny," was rather cold-blooded about the matter. "The Mexican race," he said, "now see in the fate of the aborigines of the north their own inevitable destiny. They must amalgamate and be lost in the superior vigor of the Anglo-Saxon race, or they must utterly perish." Others were more kindly. A letter printed in the *New York Journal of Commerce*, for illustration, declared: "The supreme Ruler of the universe seems to interpose, and aid the energy of man towards benefitting mankind. His interposition .... seems to be identified with the success of our arms. .... That the redemption of 7,000,000 of souls from all the vices that infest the human race is the ostensible object of both, appears manifest." But the United States withdrew its armies and annexed only the sparsely populated areas and left the most ardent of the expansionists to lament the error.

AMERICA AND THE STRIFE OF EUROPE

"Poor Mexico needs to be brought under radically transforming influences," declared Gerritt Smith in 1854. "Indeed, she is perishing for the lack of them." She must be annexed to the United States; "our nation is the mightiest of all civilizing and renovating agencies." In fact, one of the expansionist magazines declared in 1858 that the nation was strong enough to do anything that required strength: "It is vital enough to inject life into the dead."

Nor did the regenerating mission confine itself to Mexico. Representative Milton S. Latham asserted in 1854 that it extended to all the "feeble and misgoverned people grown on the debris of Spanish power in America, and [to] the colonies still subjected to the withering influence of her rule." A year later he declared that our "proud mission" was to "cultivate, fertilize, regenerate" even "to the most remote part of this continent and to its neighboring islands." Many of the contemporary leaders agreed with him; and as late as 1871, when the impulse had almost faded away, Benjamin F. Butler eloquently announced: "I believe that within my day I shall see the stars and stripes floating as evidence of our control and beneficent power at the Isthmus of Darien, while the traveler at the north pole will mistake the radiance of its red and white for the glow of the Aurora."

Very closely associated with this concept of the divine mission of regeneration was the notion of the duty to extend the area of freedom. Regeneration was to be effected through superior energy, intelligence, and institutions. The concept of expanding the area of freedom emphasized the superior institutions. The word freedom was employed to stress what was considered most unique and valuable in the democratic system of government. The American political experiment was viewed in its world-setting with the an-

EXPANSIONIST IDEALISM AND RATIONALIZATIONS

tagonist absolutism in menacing opposition. The result was emotional exaltation which tended to express itself in an aggressive defense. Extension of the area of freedom was the defiant answer of America to the supposed determination of the European nations to set bounds to the democratic experiment by expanding their own system in the New World.

The idea first took form in 1837 in connection with a revolt in Canada, when the insurgent leaders proclaimed their admiration for American institutions and declared that they were fighting for self-government. The "slumbering genius of Freedom woke" and the champions of democracy rushed to the frontier. The British authorities in Canada accepted the challenge. The lieutenant-governor declared: "The enemy of the British Constitution is its low-bred Antagonist, Democracy in America." The fight was on, and the revolutionists were defeated. "The Republicans," reported the British official, "stood their ground until the monarchical troops arrived within about twenty yards of them, when, abandoning their position as well as their Principle that all men are born equal, they decamped in the greatest confusion."

Thereafter the slogan was invoked with reference to Oregon, Texas, California, Mexico, Central America, and the islands of the Caribbean; and Great Britain continued to be the main antagonist, but other European nations and supposed combinations of nations were involved as well. All were alleged to be aggressively hostile to the rights of man and the expansion of free principles. Referring to the dynamic convictions of the Americans of 1846, a member of Congress said:

> Their doctrine was, that this continent was intended by Providence as a vast theatre on which to work out the grand experiment of Republican government. . . . . If the worn-out and corrupt monarchies of the

AMERICA AND THE STRIFE OF EUROPE

Old World had colonies here, let them be kept within the narrowist limits consistent with justice and the faith of treaties. Let all which remains be preserved for the growth and spread of free principles of American democracy.

With reference to European possessions in America, this orator's definition of the doctrine was too restrained. During the same year Seward proclaimed: "Our population is destined to roll its resistless waves to the icy barriers of the North, and to encounter oriental civilization on the shores of the Pacific. The monarchs of Europe are to have no rest while they have a colony on this continent." Influenced in part by the desire to distract attention from domestic troubles, others were soon agreeing with him. Senator Hershel V. Johnson expressed the conviction in 1848 that Providence had designed "the whole of North America . . . . to become the theatre of the highest civilization and freedom." Samuel S. Cox declared in 1859 that if the nation gave proper regard to the great principle of local autonomy it could "Americanize this continent and make it what providence intends it shall become." Agreeing with Cox with reference to the sanctity of local institutions, Reuben Davis thought we might "expand so as to include the whole world." "Mexico, Central America, South America, Cuba, the West India Islands, and even England and France [we] might annex without inconvenience or prejudice, allowing them . . . . to regulate their local affairs in their own way," said Davis.

The nation must expand in order to eliminate the hostile exponents of absolutism. It must also expand in order to root out evils springing up within: not slavery alone, whose malevolent influence might be checked by multiplying the free states (freedom was conceived as applying mainly to white men), but the evil of plutocracy as well. As early as

EXPANSIONIST IDEALISM AND RATIONALIZATIONS

1846 Representative Alexander Duncan was pointing out that "personal liberty is incompatible with a crowded population." Developing the idea, he said further:

> By whatever means the lands and wealth of a country fall into the hands of a few individuals, it establishes a feudal system . . . . and . . . . enslaves the people. . . . . The inability of the weak, the humble, and the non-assuming to contend with the overbearing, the cunning, and the grasping monopolist makes it necesssry, to . . . . equality of circumstances and personal liberty, that the advantages of territory should constantly be kept open to all who wish to embrace it.

And before he was through the cosmic Duncan presented a third reason for the expansion of freedom's domain. "If ours is to be the home of the oppressed," he said, "we must extend our territory . . . . to the demand of the millions who are to follow us, as well of our own posterity as those who are invited to our peaceful shores to partake in our republican institutions." Remembering his Bible, Representative James E. Belser declared:

> Long may our country prove itself the asylum of the oppressed. Let its institutions and its people be extended far and wide, and when the waters of despotism shall have inundated other portions of the globe, and the votary of liberty be compelled to betake himself to his ark, let this government be the Ararat on which it shall rest.

William Cullen Bryant gave poetic wings to the sentiment:

> There's freedom at thy gates and rest
> For Earth's down-trodden and opprest,
> A shelter for the hunted head,
> For the starved laborer toil and bread.

V

But still other rationalizations were brought forth to justify territorial aggrandizement. There was the notion of political gravitation and its kindred concept of political affinity. It is not strange that this argument of political affinity should be applied to the Canadians, who were supposed after 1837 to be devoted to liberty. They were, as John Bell remarked in 1853, "bone of our bone, flesh of our flesh, deriving their origin from the same Anglo-Saxon source." Neither is it surprising that it should have been asserted in reference to the Texans, concerning whose annexation Thomas Hart Benton remarked: "Man and woman were not more formed for union, by the hand of God, than Texas and the United States are formed for union by the hand of nature." The attempt to apply the concept of political affinity to people of a different race and culture, however, is rather startling. Yet the argument was offered as an inducement to annex Mexico in 1847, and within the ensuing decade many felt that a number of the neighbors to the south were sufficiently related to the United States to permit their absorption without injury to the political system. In their minds the United States was endowed with remarkable power to assimilate foreign elements. To Representative Latham in 1855 it seemed that America was to "expand by assimilating" and that the process would result in "elevating those who have been misgoverned and oppressed to the rank of freemen."

More frequently employed, however, was the similar concept of political gravitation. Speaking of Canada in 1805, James Madison remarked that when the "pear is ripe it will fall of itself." Referring to Cuba in 1823, the second Adams declared: "There are laws of political as well as physical gravitation." An apple severed from the parent-tree could but fall to the ground. Cuba, disjoined from its "unnatural connection with Spain," could but gravitate toward the North American Union, "which by the same law of nature" could not "cast her off from its bosom." Generalizing the concept in 1846, the *New York Herald* asserted: "The law

EXPANSIONIST IDEALISM AND RATIONALIZATIONS

of nature which enforces the union and embodiment of small globules of water with a larger quantity of the element with which they come in contact, is not more sure in its operation than that [law] by which the small territories adjoining the United States will ultimately unite with the central power—and become part and parcel of this republic." The *United States Democratic Review* stated the principle more briefly in 1858, defining political gravitation as "a natural law of attraction which makes large bodies overcome smaller ones." For more than fifty years, and particularly between 1846 and 1870, the expansionists saw poised bodies all about them, and as far away as Hawaii, bodies ready to be attracted into the American political sphere as soon as interferences could be removed—ripening fruit almost ready to drop. Sir Isaac Newton was a helpful friend!

Having appropriated a law of physics, the expansionists next employed a principle of biology. Evolving an organismic theory of the state, they asserted that a state must grow like other organisms—must increase in population, in resources, and in the extent of its territorial domain. National growth was natural, necessary, inevitable. In 1845 Edwin de Leon portrayed America as a young giant which the Old World could not restrain. Thereafter it was Goliath who confronted the antagonist; the conception of powerful "Young America" was born. Said Stephen A. Douglas in 1853 alluding to the Clayton-Bulwer Treaty by which England sought to restrain a youthful nation: "You may make as many treaties as you please to fetter . . . . this giant Republic, and she will burst them all from her, and her course will be onward to a limit which I will not venture to prescribe." Edward Everett discovered in 1852 "the law of American growth and progress"; it was the overwhelming tendency to expand, a tendency "as organic and vital in the youth of states as [of] individual men." Shortly afterward Caleb Cushing confused these two conceptions borrowed from science. Could one say to the tide that it ought not to flow, or to the rain that it should not fall? Cushing declared that they must, but seemed unconscious that he was contemplating the law of gravity, for he added, evidently with Everett's law of growth in mind: "And so it is with well-constituted . . . . nations. They cannot help advancing; it is the condition of their existence." Others elaborated the concept and reached the conclusion that the law could not be violated with impunity. A Senate committee asserted in 1859 that when nations "cease to grow they will soon commence that period of decadence which is the fate of all nations as of individual man." Another writer had already observed: "The law of a republic is progress. Its nature is aggressive. It is founded on the conflagration of ancient and polluted things, and it must have play and action on surrounding nations, or, like Saturn, devour its own offspring."

In behalf of the national union and in the name of freedom some of the republic's own offspring were soon to be devoured. The course of empire was checked by internal conflict, ocean barriers, and clash with other idealisms. Expansionist sentiment diminished, almost vanished. But under the stimulus of conceptions both old and new it would revive. A new imperialism would develop in response to its dynamic impulses.

CHAPTER V

ENTHUSIASMS OF 1898 AND AFTER

I

EXPANSIONIST sentiment became so lifeless during the Civil War that it could not be fully revived at its close. Alaska and the Midway Islands were the sole achievements of its devotees. For the next thirty years expansionism slumbered or was curbed. The nation was preoccupied with domestic affairs, and expansion seemed to conflict with certain ideals and convictions: Territory separated from the mainland by an intervening ocean is undesirable; the maxim of isolation must be respected; democratic government requires a homogeneous population and would be destroyed by annexation of alien peoples and the maintenance of large armies which distant colonies would require; it is morally wrong and inconsistent with the democratic ideal to subject one people to the rule of another; the United States should concentrate upon the development of a great continental civilization. Shortly after 1890, however, the slumbering sentiment of expansionism awoke, spread, and became so dynamic that the nation was swept beyond its continental limits. Dangers from international complications, dangers to the democratic experiment, were ignored, refuted, or boldly accepted.

How may this new outburst of energy be explained? A correct and precise answer is hardly possible. It is not easy to select from the various influences that seem to have been in operation the specific ones which had most weight. Again the problem is to distinguish between actual motives and alleged motives.

Those who accept the thesis of economic determinism will answer that the "new imperialism" was caused by outward pressure for markets and investment opportunities and by the influence of nationals who had established their residence or invested their money in areas subsequently annexed. No doubt these factors were important. Although investments of citizens of the United States in Samoa and the Philippines were small indeed, these islands were considered as way stations for the vast economic opportunities envisaged in the Far East; and such investments were not only of considerable importance in Cuba, but of still greater significance in the Hawaiian Islands whither a number of Americans had migrated. Moreover, in New York were two editors—Joseph Pulitzer and William Randolph Hearst—who stirred popular passions against Spain largely for the purpose of increasing their subscriptions and hence the economic value of their advertising columns. Yet it is difficult to believe that the economic factor was the sole factor in the new expansionism.

Shortly after 1890 arguments of an emotional or sentimental nature began to be developed in this country to justify another period of expansion. Some of them were old idealisms and rationalizations still expressed in the phraseology of the past. Most of the rest were old conceptions embodied in new symbols with greater appeal to the emotions of a new generation.

The concept of geographical predestination was recalled. Admiral Jeremy Belknap wrote of the Hawaiian Islands in 1893: "Indeed, it would seem that nature had established that group to be ultimately occupied as an outpost . . . . of the great republic on its western border, and that now the

ENTHUSIASMS OF 1898 AND AFTER

time has come for the fulfilment of such a design." Later Representative Charles L. Henry declared that we wanted the islands because they were "more contiguous to our territory than to that of any other nation." Senator Joseph R. Chandler agreed with him, asserting that Nature had made them a part of the defense system of the North American continent. The propinquity of Hawaii to the Philippines was also observed, and it was further asserted that all the "outlying islands in the two oceans" belonged "not to the European but to the American system" because they were nearer to the United States than to Europe. Albert Beveridge was a bit ingenious when he declared regarding the Philippines: "Our navy will make them contiguous." So was the *Boston Herald* when it called up the concept of propinquity and asserted that the Philippine Islands were "our stepping-stone to China." The fact was, however, that the conception of the ocean as a barrier was vanishing. Beveridge announced in September, 1898, that the ocean did not "separate us from the lands of our duty and desire" but rather joined us to them, and Whitelaw Reid declared soon afterward that the Pacific united the American people "with the whole boundless, mysterious Orient." Nature's god was pointing out to them opportunities across the sea.

Nor did the expansionists fail to remember that intensive utilization of the soil was a divine command embracing not only scientific agriculture but an industrial economy as well. The argument formerly used to invalidate the land titles of Indians and Spanish Americans was now employed to nullify the claim of all tropical peoples to political independence. Senator Henry Cabot Lodge wrote in 1895: "The great nations are rapidly absorbing for their future expansion and their present defence all the waste places of the earth. It is a movement which makes for civilization and the advancement of the race. As one of the great nations of the world, the United States must not fall out of the line of march." Captain Alfred T. Mahan envisaged a direct connection between natural right and a higher standard of living: "Thus the claim of an indigenous population to retain indefinitely control of territory, depends not upon a natural right, but upon political fitness, shown in the political work of governing, administering, and developing, in such manner as to insure the natural right of the world at large that resources should not be left idle, but be utilized for the general good." Under American control commodities hitherto neglected or grown and gathered with indifference would be produced: rubber, hemp, tobacco, sugar, and the rest. The expansionists had visions of an economic revolution based upon the effective utilization of Lodge's "waste places of the earth." "They see," said Frank A. Vanderlip, "great development companies formed to cultivate tobacco and sugar by modern methods, others formed to test the riches of unknown mineral deposits, and still others to develop transportation or reap the treasures of the forest." Such men were doubtless influenced by the thesis of John W. Burgess set forth in his *Political Science and Constitutional Law* (1890), by Benjamin Kidd's *Social Evolution* (1894) and *Control of the Tropics* (1898), and by Darwin's "survival of the fittest."

In like manner the expansionists brandished the earlier concept of the law of natural growth. As early as 1897 the *Washington Star* declared that nations like individuals must grow or decay, and Representative Henry R. Gibson was soon asserting that "when God made us a nation, He gave us the right to grow," while Whitelaw Reid warned that a nation which set limits to its development had "passed the meridian of its course," and Professor H. H. Powers invoked "the well-known biological principle that growth is a neces-

ENTHUSIASMS OF 1898 AND AFTER

sary consequence of life; .... without it life cannot possibly persist"; therefore Americans must "instinctively .... want the earth."

Moreover, the arguments of political gravitation, political affinity, and self-defense continued to be used. Hawaii was tending to "gravitate toward political union with this country"; Cuba and the rest of the West Indies must soon "be ours by gravitation"; the guardianship of all the republics of the New World must come to the United States in part by the "force of political gravitation"; Newton's law applied in the political sphere would finally fix the suzerainty of the United States over the entire Western Hemisphere, said the *St. Louis Globe-Democrat* in 1903. The concept of political affinity was confined during this period mainly to Canada and other British possessions in America, but self-defense was given the widest connotation embracing not only proximate but distant lands and far-flung routes of trade as well. The United States had managed to get along for over a century without "volcanic rocks" in the ocean, but now they seemed a vital necessity. Mahan sought to turn the eyes of the nation "outward, instead of inward only," in quest of the country's welfare. His were the views of naval officers, and on the subject of sea-power he was almost a monomaniac.

In this manner old arguments clothed in old phrases were brought forward, but at least two new phrases were invented to emotionalize the modified concepts of the past: "Inevitable Destiny" and "The White Man's Burden." Their influence cannot be measured. It may have been greater than that of all the old rationalizations and idealizations combined. It may have been more potent than crass material interests. The fact that these concepts were so industriously promulgated clearly indicates, at any rate, that those who employed them were confident of their propaganda value even if they were made to serve merely as a cloak to conceal more tangible economic motives. Their examination leads into the realm of political theory and metaphysics.

II

The doctrine of inevitable destiny differs from the arguments of the earlier expansionist period. At that time it was often asserted that the expansion of the United States, whether because of the strife of Europe or because of a political law of gravity, could not be resisted by others. It was rarely asserted that the American people could not restrain themselves, although one of the earlier arguments—omnipotent natural growth—implied as much. But this new apology for expansionism did not declare merely that expansion of the United States could not be prevented by others; it also maintained that the nation itself could not resist the mighty impulse. The people of the United States were caught in the toils of inevitable destiny. It was a curious concept in the land of the free and the strenuous.

Here, then, is a theory of determinism, but there were two types of determinism: One asserted that the inevitabilities of our national life resulted primarily from factors beyond the human will, from external influences, events, and resultant circumstances; the other affirmed that the inevitabilities of national life were produced by subjective factors—instincts, desires, and emotions—which the mass of men could avoid feeling and translating into effective action. The first is *objective* determinism; the second is *subjective* determinism.

Victor Hugo, in describing the French Revolution, expressed the theory of objective determinism. "It seems," he said, "the joint work of grand events and grand individualities mingled, but it is in reality the result of events. Events dispense, men suffer. Events dictate, men sign. .... The great and mysterious writer of these grand pages has a name—God; and a mask—Destiny." The new expansionists expressed similar convictions regarding the course of the United States.

Note carefully the following quotations: "destiny and the vast future interests of the United States"; "the logic of irresistible circumstances"; "bonds of commerce and necessity"; "the policy of annexation is the policy of destiny; and destiny always arrives"; "whether they will or no, Americans must now begin to look outward"; American expansion is "natural, necessary, irrepressible"; the opposition fights against "fate, the stars in their courses, and the inevitable westward march of empire"; "the inexorable logic of events has decreed this annexation"; "the evolution of events, which no man could control, has brought these problems upon us."

Perhaps it will be more interesting to connect some of these mystical assertions with the names of the men who made them. William McKinley said the Philippines came to us "in the province of God" by virtue of "His plans and methods for human progress. .... The march of events rules and overrules human action." Bishop James M. Thoburn attributed the turn of events not to the "deliberate design of the American Government," but "to Providence, another name for God." Charles Denby declared: "Call it destiny, call it the will of God, call it the overruling result of circumstances, call it what you will, it is plain that an overpowering necessity rested upon the commissioners who made the treaty to force on Spain the cession of the islands." John Hay said: "No man, no party can fight with any chance of final success against a cosmic tendency, ...

AMERICA AND THE STRIFE OF EUROPE

against the spirit of the age." Albert Beveridge declared: "The Republic could not retreat if it would..... For the American Republic is a part of the movement of a race,— the most masterful race of history,—and race movements are not to be stayed by the hand of man. They are mighty answers to Divine commands." And Theodore Roosevelt said that the "inevitable march of events gave us the control of the Philippine Islands."

Nevertheless one may recall that certain American leaders met the course of events more than halfway. Roosevelt ordered, contingently, an attack upon the Philippine Islands before the war with Spain began. McKinley, that pathetic "victim of destiny," deliberately sent an armed expedition to the Philippines and made inquiries regarding their economic value before signing the peace treaty with Spain. And Americans seized the government of the Hawaiian Islands five years before they were annexed to the United States. Were these men mere puppets of external events and circumstances? Their opponents would say that they were about as much so as any group of men in history who knew what they wanted and carefully laid plans to seize it. One of their partisans, however, offered this defense: "Statesmanship is the art of seeing where God is going and then getting things out of His way."

But perhaps the nation was a robot of subjective determinism. J. A. Hobson says that the "only direct, efficient forces in history are human motives"; and may not these motives spring inevitably from physiological and psychological urges and impulses? So the expansionists of this period seem to say.

Note this statement from Champ Clark: "Fear and greed are elementary in mankind. If either, and especially if both, or higher motives than either, conspire to make an instinctive impulse of American energy to take Hawaii, we will take it. . . . . The truth is, the premises and predicates of this Hawaiian matter were put into our Aryan blood at the beginning, with the race instinct of migration and its pervading land hunger." And there was yet more from Clark on the borderline of *objective* and *subjective* determinism: "Ralph Waldo Emerson said, 'Hitch your wagon to a star.' When the American flag was made we hitched our national wagon to all the stars, and we have got to go their way. We cannot resist them easily; there is not much American desire to resist." What glorious symbolism! Race instinct hitched to the stars! But Clark now returned to the purely subjective and asserted that the expansion movement was the result of a "longing for distinction which no scheme of government could root out from the minds of the people individually."

Chauncey Depew asserted that an irrepressible emotional force had seized our people—"a colonial possession desire." "It is in the blood, and no power can stop it." Representative Henry R. Gibson developed the theme further: "Wealth, power, and glory are the three greatest objects of human ambition. They are the three things for which the Vikings longed two thousand years ago, ... and these are the three things that have prompted their descendants to brave the seas and storm the lands, following the 'star of empire' as westward it took its way; the old Viking spirit is in the land. It is the controlling spirit of our people. It is bound to have its way. . . . ." Representative William M. Stewart discovered an irresistible growth instinct, a "law of growth" which could not be repressed by the nation or its government. Pure instinct, unreflective and urgent, was the view of Doctor H. H. Powers; "the forces that make our destiny come from deep down in the constitution of things and care little for our yea or nea. . . . . There is not a people living which would not, if pressure were removed, populate the earth" and "acquire universal dominion." Moreover, Powers declared: "The instincts which control . . . . masses of men respond to appropriate stimuli with a regularity that suggests little dependence on argument and deliberation. . . . . The consciousness of power as naturally expresses itself in self-assertion as the consciousness of weakness does in submission. . . . ." Representative Richard Bartholdt asserted: "It is the law of nature, the human longing for change and for the new, the never latent and irresistible force of progress whose mysterious source is nature itself. The western course of the 'star of empire' is one of its most noted manifestations." Some quoted Brooks Adams with approval, and Adams had said: "At the moment of action, the human being almost invariably obeys an instinct, like an animal; . . . . only after action has ceased does he reflect." Others repeated a statement of the British imperialist Seeley: "In a truly living institution the instinct of development is wiser than the utterances of the wisest individual man."

The expansionists possessed the will to believe that all these impulses of common men were good. After the war with Spain was over and the United States had been guilty of what Samuel F. Bemis has described as the "great aberration," Albert Beveridge declared: "If anyone cherishes the delusion that American government will ever be withdrawn from our possessions, let him consult the religious conviction of this Christian people. . . . . Let him, above all, consider history and study our racial instinct. . . . . Our duty of administration of orderly government to weaker peoples will not be abandoned."

"Duty!" "Duty," said McKinley, "determines destiny." But, "Who determines Duty?" asked one of the skeptics. McKinley, who said he had talked with his God about the matter, was ready with an answer: "My countrymen, the currents of destiny flow through the hearts of the people." In other words, Duty and Destiny are the same, and the people unerringly discover them both. Through divine inspiration the American people as a whole always arrive at correct moral judgments. Beautiful romanticism worthy of Jean Jacques Rousseau!

After all, the expansionists of 1898 had but one brand of determinism in essence. Some called it Providence; others called it God or Fate. Whatever its name, this overruling power in the universe controlled both external events and the impulses of the American nation—impulses which were righteous because divinely inspired.

But the anti-imperialists were still doubtful. Like Job they were harassed by the problem of evil. Human affairs seemed to be swayed by a perplexing dualism. The currents of destiny and of duty did indeed flow through the hearts of the people; that was the only place through which they flowed. Yet the hearts of men were inclined toward iniquity as well as toward duty. What if this expansionism resulted from wicked hearts and a false sense of duty? It might be that such expansionist impulses were planted by professors, propagandists, and politicians. Mahan and Burgess, Lodge and Hay, Beveridge and Clark, Pulitzer and Hearst—winged messengers of Divinity! Some were too blind to see their wings.

An uneasy suspicion that the hearts of the sons of Adam were filled with wickedness must have haunted even the most confident. "Unless ye repent, ye cannot enter the Kingdom of Heaven." This passage from Holy Writ had been heard from a thousand pulpits. But the expansionists who had worked so hard to discover these aggressive impulses in the public mind or else to plant them there were equally industrious in their efforts to harmonize them with high moral principles. The nation must have what the expansionists wished it to have, what the nation desired or could be induced to desire, and still preserve its ethical self-respect. In a word, the imperialists were now in desperate need of an exalted moral slogan. To a greater degree than most nations, perhaps, the people of the United States are possessed by an idealism which requires such a slogan. And the slogan was soon found. It was furnished by another resourceful and accommodating Englishman, Rudyard Kipling: "Take Up the White Man's Burden!"

III

Kipling's poem was most timely. At the moment of its publication it was becoming painfully manifest to the expansionists and to the whole nation that the fulfilment of their desires could not be left to Fate or Providence. Force would be required. Already it was being used. It was employed in Hawaii as early as 1893. It was used against Spain in 1898. And now the Filipinos revealed a desire for more than freedom from the yoke of the Spaniards. Their leader, Emilio Aguinaldo, was demanding complete self-government!

This use of force, especially this suppression of the desires of the Filipinos, seemed to be a renunciation of the rights of man which we proclaimed from our cradle. We must not do violence to our principles. We must steadfastly cling to them and satisfy these unerring impulses of righteous hearts at the same time. By an ingenious exegesis Kipling's verse was made to serve the purpose. "An aggressive temper effected a marriage of convenience with humanitarian sentiment."

The expansionists were groping their way toward this solution of the problem before the poem appeared. They could not deny this aggressive temper, this power impulse. Notice of its existence had already been spread over the *Congressional Record* and on the editorial pages of the newspapers. The *Washington Post*, for instance, had stated boldly: "A new consciousness seems to have come upon us—the consciousness of strength—and with it a new appetite, a yearning to show our strength. It might be compared with the effect upon the animal creation of the taste of blood. Ambition, interest, land hunger, pride, the mere joy of fighting, whatever it may be, we are animated by a new sensation. We are face to face with a strange destiny. The taste of empire is in the mouth of the people even as the taste of blood in the jungle. It means an imperial policy, the Republic, renascent, taking her place with the armed nations." The expansionists could not deny the bellicose spirit. They could, however, give it a better name. Mahan called it the missionary spirit. A Senate committee called it paternal love. Lyman Abbott described it as the "new imperialism, the imperialism of liberty." And McKinley, clinging tenaciously to Providence and Duty, said: "God has placed upon this Government the solemn duty of providing for the people of these islands a government based upon the principles of liberty no matter how many difficulties the problem may present."

One of the major difficulties presented, of course, was that of obtaining the consent of the Filipinos to the renunciation of self-government. But the expansionists were already cutting a path around this difficulty. Charles Francis Adams said that children should not be given their first chance to swim in water infested by sharks. Sharks and children!— the children were the Filipinos; the sharks were perhaps of the German and Japanese variety. McKinley also thought of the Filipinos as children for he wrote Andrew Carnegie that their opposition was of slight extent and like the subdued stubbornness of children would soon give way. On another occasion he also remarked: "Did we need their consent to perform a great act for humanity? We had it in every aspiration of their minds, in every hope of their hearts." Such inarticulate yearnings must be satisfied! And in a proclamation to the Filipino dissenters he wrote that while the strong arm of authority must repress disturbances, its fundamental purpose was "to overcome all obstacles to the bestowal of the blessings of good and stable government . . . . under the free flag of the United States." The Americans were not coming as "invaders or conquerors"; they were coming as friends eager to bring them "that full measure of individual rights and liberties which is the heritage of free peoples." So there were two kinds of freedom, the national liberty of self-government and the freedom of the individual. One would be granted, the other withheld. Yet was it not true that the Founding Fathers fought for both at Bunker Hill, Saratoga, and Yorktown?

Some of the expansionists soon discovered an argument that would justify the denial of self-government to the Filipinos. The word "children" was a forecast. Senator Knute Nelson of Minnesota, descendant of the Vikings, now offered the satisfying rationalization. The Filipinos were as yet "unfit for self-government, in the sense that we have it." The granting of independence to them immediately would be an act of "the highest cruelty"—nothing less. Representative Gibson sounded an even more positive note: The world had moved onward to a new policy of advancing civilization and Christianity even against the consent of the governed.

ENTHUSIASMS OF 1898 AND AFTER

Nelson's assertion contained the suggestion of more or less temporary trusteeship; he proposed to give the Filipinos independence when they were "fit for it." Moreover, Senator Joseph Foraker declared: "I do not know of anybody, from the President of the United States down to his humblest follower . . . ., who is proposing by force and violence to take and hold those islands for all time to come." Yet when an attempt was made to commit the expansionists on this point, they were loath to take the pledge.

This reluctance stiffened the opposition of both the anti-imperialists and the Filipino insurgents, and as indignation rose the outcome grew more uncertain. Would the flag be lowered? For a time "moronophobia" helped to keep it aloft. Men were afraid of appearing to play the fool. The European powers, it was contended, would not be restrained by moral scruples regarding Filipino rights and would consider us silly. McKinley warned that we risked becoming the "laughing-stock of the world." Lodge cried, "Humiliation in the eyes of civilized mankind!" But who can be sure that the national emblem might not have been hauled down if the idea of the "white man's burden" had not appeared among the expansionists in the nick of time?

Enter now Senator Beveridge:

[The Filipinos] are not capable of self-government. How could they be? They are not of a self-governing race. They are Orientals, Malays, instructed by the Spaniards in the latter's worst estate. . . . . Mr. President, this question . . . . is elemental. It is racial. God has not been preparing the English-speaking and Teutonic peoples for a thousand years for nothing but vain and idle self-contemplation and self-admiration. No! He has made us the master organizers of the world to establish system where chaos reigns. He has given us the spirit of progress to overwhelm the forces of reaction throughout the earth. He has made us adepts in government that we may administer government among savage and senile peoples. Were it not for such a force as this the world would relapse into barbarism and night. And of all our race He has marked the American people as His chosen nation finally to lead in the regeneration of the world.

Senator Lodge agreed with Beveridge in respect to the political incapacity of the Filipinos. With his presumably vast knowledge of history, the former professor of Harvard affirmed that all human experience was against the possibility of Malays ever learning to act as democrats. The Filipino insurgents were now called by their ethnic name: They were Tagalogs—a word which may have suggested polliwogs to less learned senators. Between the Teutons and the Tagalogs a vast gulf had been fixed—fixed by the hand of Him who had called the universe into existence, given the leopard his spots, given the Ethiopian and the Malay their skins. The United States might now keep the Philippines forever—nay longer: "Forever and a day," said "Uncle Joe" Cannon! And we not only might, we must. In this manner we should attain our full national stature, and the Tagalogs, the Samoans, and the Hawaiians would be blessed.

"Take Up the White Man's Burden!" It was this slogan and the slogan of inevitable destiny that were most employed to justify our movement out across the broad Pacific to the gates of China. And these and other sentimental impulses aroused by energizing concepts joined with strategic and economic interests to carry our empire down into the Caribbean and beyond until we were dominating all the canal zones, ruling five protectorates, and denying the right of revolution throughout Latin America.

IV

The idea of serving humanity by extending the area of freedom was not lost in the midst of the new enthusiasms.

ENTHUSIASMS OF 1898 AND AFTER

The duty of assisting any American people desiring release from European oppression was accepted and proclaimed. McKinley's message of April, 1898, calling for war with Spain referred emphatically to the "cause of humanity .... right at our door." To Representative Charles F. Cochran war with Spain meant a new dedication of America to "liberty and republicanism." Representative James A. Norton said this country must continue to contribute to the realization of the divine purpose "in building up a heritage, erected on the grand foundation principle, the chief corner stone of American institutions, the rights of the people." And Senator Edward O. Wolcott declared that "the war .... must be fought, because it is the manifest destiny of this Republic to stand forever upon the Western Hemisphere [as] a sentinel of liberty." But the concept of the burden of the white man, the emphasis upon order and efficiency, and the notion that the United States must serve as the trustee of civilization in the more turbulent and backward areas of America almost crowded out this democratic sentiment.

Between 1900 and 1913 the United States seemed to be more interested in controlling—one might almost say subjugating—the underdog than in setting him free. "Disorganization and disorder," declared Professor Talcott Williams in 1900, "will not be long permitted in a world grown as small as ours." In another work published by the economist Charles A. Conant in the same year this statement occurred: "The government of adventurers and financial freebooters is coming to an end in Europe, Africa, and Asia, and it may yet be the mission of the United States to bring it to an end in portions of Latin America." In 1899 Theodore Roosevelt had advocated the suppression of the Filipino rebellion in the interest of true liberty, and a few

AMERICA AND THE STRIFE OF EUROPE

months later he had declared: "It is our duty toward the people living in barbarism to see that they are freed from their chains." Already, however, he seemed to be thinking of the rights and opportunities of civilized peoples rather than of the victims of barbarism.

And already the true significance of the "white man's burden" was beginning to be admitted by some of the less sentimental of the expansionists. This phrase which so neatly removed the suggestion of oppression from the word "imperialism" was merely a figure of speech, as Weinberg has pointed out. It was a type of euphemism that may be designated as "onomantithesis," which consists in calling a thing or a characteristic, particularly if it be unpleasant, not by its ordinary name but by its opposite. Thus imperialism, which usually suggests the burdening of the races of color by military subjugation and economic exploitation, was called not the "colored man's burden" but the "white man's burden." Moreover, the real meaning of Kipling's poem, which through a process of wishful exegesis had been overlooked, became somewhat more clear. Senator Ben Tillman, the South Carolina anti-imperialist, perhaps went a little too far when he remarked in 1899 that the verses were not an invitation to imperialism but a warning against it. While hardly meant to be that, the poem nonetheless contained a pervasive element of defeatism. Kipling did not warn men against taking up the burden; he merely warned them against the hope that they could do the heathen much good. "The burden-bearer's aim was the paradoxical one of serving the men of color in order to exalt himself." Strong men, strong nations, must "have done with childish days"; they must attain moral manhood through some heroic deed of strength and force. In short, the burden must be taken up not because of affection for the nominal beneficiary or

ENTHUSIASMS OF 1898 AND AFTER

because of optimism with respect to his political potentialities, but because its assumption was the manifest destiny of athletic men and nations.

Senator George F. Hoar had politely rebuked Senator Beveridge late in 1899 for placing too much emphasis on commercial statistics, but on January 14, 1900, the *Washington Post* boldly declared that empty professions of lofty altruism should be superseded by the announcement that we had "annexed these possessions in cold blood" and intended "to utilize them to our own profit and advantage." A few weeks later Senator Lodge came forward with some reservations. "I conceive my first duty to be always to the American people," he said. "Whatever duty to others might seem to demand, I should pause long before supporting any policy if there were the slightest suspicion that it was not for the benefit of the people of the United States." Giving then the correct interpretation of Kipling's poem, he declared: "A great nation must have great responsibilities. It is one of the penalties of greatness. But the benefit of responsibilities goes hand in hand with the burdens they bring. The nation which seeks to escape from the burden also loses the benefit." And at the Republican National Convention in July, 1900, he said: "We make no hypocritical pretense of being in the Philippines solely on account of others. While we regard the welfare of these people a sacred trust, we regard the welfare of the American people first. . . . . We believe in trade expansion."

In 1901 the liberty of the Cubans was curtailed by the Platt Amendment giving the United States the legal right to intervene in the island for purposes of order and to control certain aspects of their foreign policy. The defenders of the amendment talked little, however, of national interest; they stressed principally our duty to the world. Senator Orville

H. Platt himself emphasized this point, while Representative Townsend Scudder, irritated by the attitude of the Cubans, declared that the United States was "done with nonsense . . . . ; it recognizes alike the dominance of duty and the duty of dominance, wherever it is under contract with mankind to plant civilization, order, pacification, and reasonable liberty."

Cuba was but the first of a series of protectorates set up by the self-appointed trustee. In behalf of the "interests of collective civilization" Colombia in 1903 was deprived of Panama, which the trustee immediately reduced to a protectorate. The Dominican Republic followed next, after a warning to other backward states in America. The Roosevelt Corollary of the Monroe Doctrine, announced in December, 1904, was the expression of a resolution to regulate the conduct of such states with reference to the outside world.

This concept of trusteeship was linked from the outset, however, with defense strategy. For a time European antagonists were virtually forgotten. In 1895 Lodge had alluded to the European powers more or less as friendly rivals in a great civilizing enterprise. But during the Spanish-American War a concert of European governments to restrain the United States was revealed, a movement supposed to have been led by Kaiser Wilhelm II. The enemy appeared once more on the great stage in the form of imperialist and monarchical Germany. Uneasiness on this score was an important reason for the attempt to purchase the Danish West Indies early in 1902, and at the end of that year the joint punitive expedition of Germany and two other European powers against Venezuela caused further excitement. The danger of European intervention was used as an argument late in 1904 and after for Roosevelt's intervention in the Dominican Republic, in spite of the fact that Europe had already entered another epoch of intense strife. The digging of the canal served to emphasize strategic considerations. Philander C. Knox, William Howard Taft's secretary of state, explained his aggressive policy in the Caribbean by asserting that the "malady of revolutions and financial collapse" was "most acute precisely in the region where it" was "most dangerous to us." Thus concern for the interests of collective civilization had been largely substituted for concern for the backward and the oppressed peoples, only to give way to the interests of national strategy—at a time when non-American powers were held in the grip of deadly antagonisms!

V

Material considerations and national self-interest had been stressed too long, however. The plutocratic enemy within the gates had long since been discovered and denounced, the ranks of the Republican party were soon rent in twain, and Woodrow Wilson was summoning the people to a "new freedom." It would have been remarkable if there had occurred no rebirth of enthusiasm for the experiment of the Fathers. Men were forcefully reminded of the original principles and purposes of the nation.

They were also urged to renounce imperialistic tendencies, and this message of October 6, 1913, to the Filipinos was received with acclaim: "We regard ourselves as trustees acting not for the advantage of the United States but for the benefit of the people of the Philippine Islands. Every step we take will be taken with a view to the ultimate independence of the islands and as a preparation for that independence. . . . ." The Democrats also applauded this message of October 27, 1913, to the Latin Americans:

Human rights, national integrity, and opportunity as against material interests—that . . . . is the issue which we now face. I want to take this occasion to say that the United States will never again seek one additional foot of territory by conquest..... We have seen material interests threaten constitutional freedom in the United States. Therefore we will know how to sympathize with those in the rest of America who have to contend with such powers, not only within their borders but from outside their borders also.

But the disciples of the "new freedom" likewise had applauded Wilson when he said near the beginning of his administration:

We hold that just government rests always upon the consent of the governed, and that there can be no freedom without order based upon law and upon the public conscience and approval..... We shall lend our influence of every kind to the realization of these principles..... We are the friends of constitutional government in America; we are more than its friends, we are its champions.

The devotees of democracy with ardor for the cause fanned into flame were eager for the improvement of the system in Latin America. Efforts to extend the area of freedom followed, as futile as they were zealous.

With the passing of Wilson came a flagging of enthusiasm, and economic and strategic interests were admitted with less embarrassment. But the party of imperialism was growing tired of the burden and preparing to withdraw its controls when the champion of the "forgotten man" entered the White House and proclaimed the policy of the "good neighbor." He too invoked the spirit and the ideals of the founders and renounced imperialism in every form. As early as July, 1928, Franklin D. Roosevelt had declared that the time was ripe to "start a new chapter" in the foreign policy of the nation. He asserted:

On that new page there is much that should be written in the spirit of our forbears. If the leadership is right—or, more truly, if the spirit behind it is great—the United States can regain the world's trust and friendship and become again of service. We can .... coöperate .... with every

ENTHUSIASMS OF 1898 AND AFTER

agency that studies and works to relieve the ills of mankind; and we can for all time renounce the practice of arbitrary intervention in the home affairs of our neighbors.

In respect to Latin America both his actions and his words during subsequent years harmonized with this utterance of 1928. Under his administration vested interests were left largely to shift for themselves, and the policy of withdrawal from the Caribbean was continued with greater earnestness and speed. Plans for withdrawal from the Philippines were also further matured. How far his own enthusiasm and that of his followers for democracy and peace would carry the nation into the affairs of the Old World, especially if these sentiments should be reinforced by the fear that antagonists were planning eventually to extend their aggressions to America, remained to be seen. That part of the chapter had not been finished at the beginning of 1938.

EUROPE'S DISCORDS AMERICA'S
ADVANTAGE

CHAPTER VI

EXPANSION: FIRST PHASE

THE purpose of this section is to describe an aspect of American history which has never been portrayed in its larger setting. All the essential facts are known, but the full synthesis is lacking. The conflicts of Europe have not merely disturbed the equanimity of the people of the United States by arousing their sympathies, by interference with their commercial and maritime rights, and by threats of involvement in military strife; Europe's rivalries and wars, both civil and international, have also made it possible for the United States in most respects to assert its will, so far as European governments were concerned, in the affairs of the Western Hemisphere.

I

A harmonious Europe would never have permitted the United States to extend its boundaries and its political dominance from the Appalachians to the Pacific Ocean and from the tropical Caribbean to the snows of Alaska. Without a divided and discordant Europe it is doubtful indeed whether the United States would ever have been born; at any rate, independence could scarcely have been won when it was if England's enemies had not supported the American insurgents in order to humble a powerful antagonist.

By the terms of the Anglo-American treaty of 1783 the boundaries of the new nation were fixed at the Mississippi instead of at the ridge of the Appalachians, partly because England preferred this method of shutting out European

THE AMERICAS IN 1763

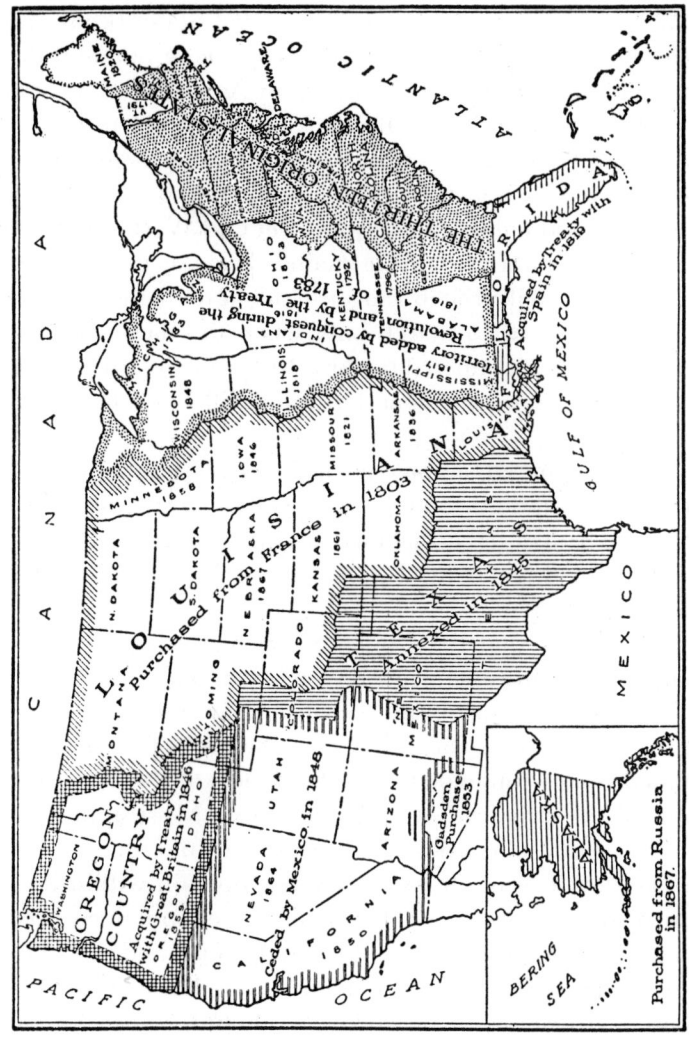

TERRITORIAL EXPANSION OF THE UNITED STATES (1776-1867)

rivals; and within a few years the United States began that career of expansion predicted by prophets of manifest destiny and European political doom in America. Hardly an advance was made without provoking opposition from some quarter of Europe, and as the expansion movement reached its first culmination there was talk of setting up bulwarks of defense and balances of power. Yet Old World resistance was for the most part futile mainly because international conflict and civil strife in Europe made it so. America's god Terminus ceased to march only when the nation became satiated or was hampered by domestic problems. The possible exceptions to this generalization will be noted at the proper time.

Europe entered a long critical period just as George Washington and his colleages were consolidating the United States. The first territorial annexations occurred during the wars of the French revolutionary and Napoleonic era or shortly thereafter.

Spain's fear that the United States might be induced to join England in some aggressive move against the Spanish borderlands was primarily responsible for the first concession. West Florida was reduced to the limits for which the United States contended, and the settlers of the West were granted the privilege of using the lower Mississippi River as well as that of depositing goods near its mouth.

The next cession, a vast territorial domain within itself, was made by Napoleon I, who had scarcely obtained Louisiana from Spain when troubles in Europe and elsewhere caused him to sell it to the United States. His expedition to Haiti was decimated by yellow fever and Negro soldiers, and he was harassed by England with its formidable sea-power. The political authorities in London were not altogether pleased with the sale but they graciously acquiesced

EXPANSION: FIRST PHASE

for the moment, fully realizing that Louisiana was in less dangerous hands.

The Floridas were then annexed piece by piece, with both England and Spain helplessly remonstrating. For a few months during the latter part of the War of 1812 the British thought of depriving the United States of these provinces and Louisiana as well, but Andrew Jackson's victory at New Orleans might have produced a change of mind if the weariness of England had not been sufficient. Later appeals from Spain, ally of Britain now, were of no avail. Conservative British statesmen longed for an era of repose and harmony. They still shuddered when they contemplated what French radicalism and bellicosity had unleashed in Europe a few years before and had no desire to provoke the United States into the republican extravagance of championing liberty, equality, and fraternity in revolting Spanish America. Spain was accordingly advised to make the best of an embarrassing situation: to cede the title to the Floridas for a monetary consideration and obtain as good a bargain as possible with reference to the western boundary of Louisiana. France and Russia, both then seeking the friendship of the United States against some future crisis in Europe, also employed their good offices. The United States not only received the Floridas but was granted whatever title Spain had north of the forty-second parallel in the Far Northwest.

For the next twenty years the eyes of the American expansionists were fixed steadily on Oregon and Texas. They confronted England in both instances. In fact until shortly before 1860 the British were the most formidable opponents of the territorial enlargement of the United States.

John Quincy Adams, secretary of state from 1817 to 1825 and negotiator of the Florida treaty, was among the first of American statesmen to assert the continental destiny of the United States. In a Cabinet meeting of November, 1819, he declared that the world must be

familiarized with the idea of considering our proper dominion to be the continent of North America. From the time when we became an independent people it was as much a law of nature that this should become our pretension as that the Mississippi should flow to the sea. Spain had possessions upon our southern and Great Britain upon our northern border. It was impossible that centuries should elapse without finding them annexed to the United States; .... because it is a physical, moral, and political absurdity that such fragments of territory, with sovereigns .... beyond sea, worthless and burdensome to their owners, should exist permanently contiguous to a great, powerful, enterprising, and rapidly-growing nation. Most of the Spanish territory which had been in our neighborhood had already become our own. .... This rendered it still more unavoidable that the remainder of the continent should ultimately be ours. .... Until Europe shall find it a settled geographical element that the United States and North America are identical, any effort on our part to reason the world out of a belief that we are ambitious will have no other effect than to convince them that we add to our ambition hypocrisy.

By 1824 Russia was ready to recede in the Far Northwest to the line of fifty-four forty, and by 1867 to withdraw entirely from America. The tsars were no friends of England; they looked upon the United States as a possible ally or at least a sea-power which might some day strike down the dread enemy. The British stood firm, however, on their Pacific Coast claims, and in 1846 secured almost half the area between the parallel of forty-two degrees and the southern boundary of Alaska. Since 1823 the European international situation had been less tense, and England, with its control of the seas, ventured at least to oppose the United States to the brink of war.

Meantime the British government was also resisting the southwestward expansion of the United States with almost

EXPANSION: FIRST PHASE

equal stubbornness. In this region official England desired no territory. The purpose was rather to prevent the growth of a rival sea-power and to find in Texas a new source of supply for cotton. The rapid development of America's merchant marine was resented, as was likewise its desire to dominate the Gulf. Britain's blockades might be broken by armed merchantmen, and privateers of the United States swarming from numerous ports might play havoc with British commerce. In English humanitarian circles there existed also the desire to fetter the growth of slavery in Texas as well as elsewhere. The London government, therefore, put forth its utmost efforts, short of war, in order to prevent the annexation of Texas and the further encroachments on Mexico which were sure to result if the absorption of Texas should be followed, as appeared to be certain, by hostilities between the United States and its Spanish-American neighbor. Indeed Great Britain might have gone to war on this expansion issue if France could have been committed and if the Texans had been disposed to co-operate by refusal to join the American Union. The Texans preferred, however, to cast their lot with the United States, and the French government, despite emphatic utterances regarding the need for a balance of power in the New World, was held back by popular dislike of England and popular friendship for the rising nation across the Atlantic. History repeated itself in 1846 when Mexico appealed for Anglo-French aid against its American enemy. In 1848 another vast area was added to the United States.

American politicians thereupon almost disrupted the Union by their violent quarrels over the organization of the new territory. The slavery issue and the mounting bitterness between the North and South had begun to retard the expansionist movement. The outbreak of the Crimean War late in 1853 furnished a golden opportunity which some desired to seize; but the struggle over Kansas interposed. Thereafter it was all but impossible to agree to annex anything. Talk of expansion continued almost as boisterous as before, yet only one small strip of territory, the Gadsden Purchase from Mexico, was acquired between 1854 and 1866. If hostilities had broken out over the Crimea earlier, say in 1849 or even in the beginning of 1853, Cuba and other areas might have been annexed. This, however, is only a conjecture. Cuba was not seized in 1854 or 1855 despite the fact that several prominent leaders seemed to favor the step. During the next five years only southern diplomats and a group of filibusters were actively engaged in expansionist endeavors in warmer lands toward the Equator.

Thus, in the regions considered so far, with the exception of the Pacific Northwest, the European nations, mainly because of strife in their midst, were unable to check the advance of the United States. Such opposition as they offered tended rather to stimulate than to retard the movement, for the desirability of eliminating dangerous neighbors or of anticipating European interference was presented in the United States as a justification for almost every forward step.

II

Other areas were coveted, some of them officially; but they were not obtained during this first period of expansion. In respect to these, European resistance was likewise encountered. Canada may be dismissed with the statement that the British checked the advance repeatedly. Both England and France interfered, not without success, to prevent attempts, which might have failed anyway, to annex the Hawaiian Islands and a part or the whole of the Dominican Republic. For more than a quarter of a

EXPANSION: FIRST PHASE

century they kept watch also over Cuba, proposing tripartite guaranties of Spanish possession or interfering with filibuster raids launched from American ports. After 1854 this vigilance was probably unnecessary. It will be conceded that knowledge of the resolute attitude of these European powers may have caused the United States to postpone its efforts to acquire the island until 1848. But one may reasonably contend that the slavery dispute more than any fear of Old World resistance held the nation back during the Crimean War and the years immediately following.

In Central America sturdy British opposition was encountered as well as that of at least one influential Frenchman who helped to defeat a treaty between the United states and Nicaragua in 1858. The rivalry of England and the United States in the region is a long and complicated story. Interest here is primarily in motives and results.

Washington authorities were concerned mainly in interoceanic transits, but William Walker and other filibusters desired sovereignty over the land. After initial success, however, Walker and some of his companions finally died tragically at the hands of the natives, aided and abetted by the British and by Cornelius Vanderbilt who acted in defense of his proprietary rights across Nicaragua. The fundamental desire of England was to prevent the United States from annexing the region or merely gaining exclusive control of the interoceanic routes; yet many Americans feared that the British cherished larger ambitions, as some of them did. The fact that the London government, which possessed no territory there before 1823, later seized certain strategic points served to confirm suspicions and arouse resentment because of the violation of the Monroe Doctrine. How far the United States would have gone if no European opponent had been met it is impossible to say. Since the national officials revealed small interest in Central America prior to 1846, and since the slavery problem grew ominous after 1850, one may infer that its action would have been limited to the control of the transits.

The British, however, were in no mood to risk the domination of this strategic strip of land by a commercial and maritime rival. Observing the increasing interest of the United States in the Isthmus after 1846, they set to work at once; and in 1849, when the less aggressive Whigs came to power in Washington, English diplomats used the opportunity to tie America's hands without committing themselves to complete abandonment of their restricted territorial ambitions. By the terms of a treaty signed and ratified in 1850 the United States ceded England joint control over all Isthmian commercial routes and agreed not to annex any territory, while Great Britain, although giving a similar pledge of self-restraint, managed to retain Belize (later organized as British Honduras) with vague claims including the Honduras Bay Islands together with a protectorate over the Mosquito Indians occupying parts of Nicaragua and Honduras.

In short, for the purpose of preventing a further violation of the Monroe Doctrine the United States renounced its freedom of action in Central America. But the treaty was soon violently denounced by the Democrats, and by 1853 almost the entire country was in an uproar. British control of Belize and protection of the Mosquitos were a clear breach of a sacred doctrine. British participation in the control of the trade routes was not necessarily such a breach but it might result in violations if the small adjacent states should have to be taken in hand in order to facilitate the utilization and to guard the security of these routes. With the return of the Democrats to power a defiant attitude was

EXPANSION: FIRST PHASE

assumed. Relations between the two Anglo-Saxon nations became bad and then worse, so that by the summer of 1856 they were on the verge of war.

The Crimean problem had been settled by that time, and for the moment relations with France appeared harmonious. For once Europe's strife seemed to be a factor of little consequence. Although the contemplation of future European contingencies may have had some influence, it is doubtful whether such potentialities had much weight at the time. Yet other considerations caused England to pause and finally to recede: commercial relations with the United States and perhaps the dread of war carried on three thousand miles from the home base as well as the anticipation that sectional bitterness might itself stop the American advance.

III

The reflections of British journalists and statesmen during this critical period in their relations with the United States are full of interest. The crisis which reached its culmination early in 1856 began to develop almost eight years before. John H. Crampton, the British minister in Washington, expressed in May, 1848, the belief that suspicion of British designs in America was being deliberately fostered by the expansionists of the United States in order to obtain popular support for aggressive action. Fears on this score did not become extremely intense, however, until after the election of Franklin Pierce.

In a letter of February 7, 1853, to Lord Clarendon, head of the British foreign office, Crampton expressed uneasiness. He said that expansionist senators were "preferring their claims by blowing the coals to the utmost extent of the various pairs of bellows which they" could "bring to bear upon the 'Manifest Destiny' Question." "To anybody unacquainted with the domestic party contests going on here," Crampton continued, "such an outbreak would be inexplicable and alarming, for here they would seem, like a drunken Irishman at a fair, trying to pick a quarrel with everybody they meet. After having for a fortnight talked what they know to be nonsense about the ratification of the Clayton-Bulwer Treaty [namely, the agreement of 1850 regarding Central America] . . . . they are now, as the said Irishman would do to his coat at Donnybrook, trailing the 'Monroe Doctrine' through the Senate, in the hope apparently that somebody will insult them by treading upon it."

Crampton then surveyed the whole problem of American expansion from the British viewpoint. "This matter of Cuba," he said, "is one which involves very serious considerations for us,— . . . . we can no longer avoid looking it in the face and making up our minds as to what we are to do or not to do about it. The question, as you truly observe, involves Peace or War, or, at all events, a risk of war." The British minister thought that England must either remain silent and permit the United States to annex Cuba or else serve notice at once that its annexation would not be allowed. Clearly he was not in favor of the first course and was reluctant to follow the second. In case of hostilities the brunt of war would fall upon England, for while Spanish aid might be counted upon, who could predict what France's disposition would be? "Even if France were with us," he said, "it is clear that by far the greatest part both of the fighting and of the commercial loss would fall to our share."

He suggested that Cuba's fate should be considered "as a part of the more general question of aggression and domination of the United States in every part" of the American continent and asked whether Cuba was "as good a point to make a stand upon as any other." Democratic politicians were asserting that the Monroe Doctrine was a principle of public law from which could be "deduced as a sort of corollary" the right of aggression and domination in the entire hemisphere. "By eternal repetition this so-called doctrine" was "gradually becoming in the minds of the Democracy . . . . one of those habitual maxims which are no longer reasoned upon but felt." Crampton thought that the European powers would "be forced to resist . . . . *somewhere*," and raised the question as to whether the Hawaiian Islands might not be a better issue.

Crampton closed his dispatch, however, by pointing out two factors which would tend to prevent the "aggressive spirit" of the people of the United States from being "carried to extremes"; namely, "Northern and Southern squabbles" and dread of war with England. Every subject tended to degenerate into a quarrel between North and South. The "money-making people" of the United States would fear the commercial consequences of war, and the nation was really unprepared for a military contest with England.

Crampton had defined the issue, and others soon offered their advice. Sir Henry Bulwer declared in March, 1854, that Central America wās rapidly "becoming the most important spot of earth in ye whole world: to us especially with Australia [and] New Zealand in our hands and the Chinese empire falling to pieces." Graham, first lord of the Admiralty, wrote Clarendon on October 24: "We are fast 'drifting' into war with the U[nited] States; and I am afraid that on . . . . the Central American Question we shall not have France on our side; whereas with respect both to Cuba and St. Domingo, France will be disposed to make common cause with us, at least up to a point just short of war. But a rupture between us and the United States is the diversion which Russia anticipates in her favor and anxiously desires. . . . ." Lord Palmerston seemed to be in a rage throughout most of the year. On April 22 he remarked to Clarendon: "These Yankees are such astute bullies and are always trying how far they can go, but they, at least the nation, are far from being as ready and willing to go to war as their negotiators and popularity-hunting orators would wish us to believe." On September 10 he declared that they were not gentlemen but "vulgar-minded bullies." Lord John Russell, on October 31, advised the increase of British naval forces in the Caribbean, and this advice was speedily followed. On November 5 Lord Aberdeen suggested that there was hope of enlisting France "on our side in dealing with . . . . St. Domingo and the transfer of the Sandwich [Hawaiian] Islands." Regarding Central America he suggested cautious avoidance of a quarrel by contriving "to hang up all matters in dispute" through polite negotiations for "some indefinite period."

This cautious advice was adopted, mainly because England was involved in the Crimean War. As early as November 16, 1853, H. W. Addington had remarked to Clarendon: "The shoals of Neutral Rights and Right of Search are quite enough for Great Britain to weather in her relations with her transatlantic children, in the event of an European War, without having any tangible territorial grievance to settle with them into the bargain." British policy was not quite so moderate as Addington advised, despite England's entry into the Crimean struggle at the end of March, 1854; and yet there was a large measure of restraint. Without making any important concessions the British diplomats managed to continue negotiations on Central America for several months, and the London government was careful

EXPANSION: FIRST PHASE

not to raise the issue of maritime rights during the war with Russia.

Nevertheless as the year 1855 drew to its close the situation was becoming "distinctly squally," to use the description of James Buchanan. Angered by the aggressiveness of American naval officers and filibusters, Palmerston advised Clarendon on October 25 to be as firm as he could with Buchanan, who was then minister in London, without making a positive threat. If pressed for an explanation regarding the significance of further increase of English maritime forces in the West Indies, Palmerston was to say that the step was due to the threatening tone of the government and people of the United States. Perhaps indeed he should go even farther and remark to Buchanan that England was better entitled to inquire what the intentions of the Washington government were with reference to Central America. At the end of December, President Pierce's message to Congress threw the whole matter into the field of public discussion and contained besides a complaint regarding illegal recruitments in the United States for the Crimean War.

The Senate proceeded to go over the whole subject in detail, displaying marked hostility to England and distinct unanimity of opinion that the British should be compelled to withdraw from Central America. On March 28, 1856, two days before the signing of the treaty terminating the European war, Pierce added fuel to the flames by dismissing Crampton for encouraging enlistments. Already William Walker had conquered Nicaragua, and as the two Anglo-Saxon nations approached the verge of conflict, the United States recognized the Walker government.

At this most critical juncture, however, a number of British leaders exerted themselves in behalf of peace. Newspapers and opposition politicians as well as the London

Peace Society became active. Both economic and sentimental reasons were urged against war. The value of the cotton trade with the United States was carefully weighed, and it was urged that Mexico and Central America under Yankee rule would be immensely more profitable to England. The suggestion was even made that the British should limit themselves to Suez and permit the interoceanic routes of America to be dominated by their overseas kinsmen.

Before the end of the year the London government evinced a more conciliatory attitude, and British diplomats began to try earnestly to harmonize the interests of the United States and England in America. British holders of Mexican bonds initiated a scheme designed to divert into their coffers a portion of any cash which the United States might pay Mexico for territory, and on October 17 Lord Clarendon signed with George M. Dallas, Buchanan's successor, a convention including important concessions in Central America.

The truculent action of the United States Senate, which refused to approve the agreement without several amendments and thus forced new negotiations, caused the English to waver; but by the end of 1859 a satisfactory solution of the whole problem was reached, and President Buchanan's message of December, 1860, referred cordially to Great Britain. Joint control over the Isthmian trade routes was retained by England, along with Belize, and British withdrawal from Mosquitia was slow; but in other respects opposition to United States expansion toward the south was permanently abandoned.

IV

The outbreak of the Civil War might have furnished the occasion for a reversal of England's new policy, and indeed

EXPANSION: FIRST PHASE

more vacillation occurred; yet there was little real change.[1] For reasons that need not be elaborated here, the London government refrained from intervention. Union and democracy triumphed in the United States, and almost at the same epoch great reforms took place in England which transformed an aristocracy into a system approximating a democracy. Thereafter the clash of political views ceased to be an element of discord between the two nations. Economic competition continued, irritating boundary and fishery disputes occurred, and maritime rivalry would be resumed in the future with the restoration of American seapower; but never again would England be considered an antagonist of the American political experiment. After 1895 conditions in Europe and Asia would cause the British to make positive overtures for American friendship and support.

Shortly before the English government decided to relax its opposition to the expansion of the United States, however, France began to reveal a more aggressive disposition. The new attitude synchronized with the rise of Louis Napoleon to power. His joint interference with Great Britain in reference to Cuba, the Hawaiian Islands, and the Dominican Republic has been noted. He soon began to consider a grander enterprise in Mexico, where European nations were suffering injuries to life and property. He was joined in October, 1861, by England and Spain, which had already decided to reoccupy the Dominican Republic. The reason announced for Mexican intervention was the desire to avenge the outrages suffered by their subjects, but Napoleon had ulterior designs. There were monarchists in

[1] England's policy would have been more consistent if it had embraced a more vigorous opposition to the aggressiveness of France and Spain in America during this period.

AMERICA AND THE STRIFE OF EUROPE

Mexico who desired the country to be ruled by a European prince, and the French emperor was disposed to accommodate them.

He was motivated in part also by a desire to establish a bulwark against the United States. The concept of the balance of power adumbrated by Prime Minister Guizot in 1845 having failed to materialize, the French monarch wished to make another effort. "We have an interest," he wrote General E. F. Forey in 1862, "in seeing the Republic of the United States become powerful and prosperous; but we have no interest in seeing it seize all the Gulf of Mexico, dominate from there the Antilles and South America, and become the sole dispenser of the products of the New World. If the United States should become master of Mexico and consequently of Central America and the pass between the two oceans, there would indeed be no other power in America."

Into the familiar details of the failure of Louis Napoleon's Mexican adventure it is unnecessary to go. Owing to obstacles which will be observed in the next chapter, French troops were finally withdrawn in 1867, leaving the puppet Maximilian to encounter the tragic fate which soon overtook him. The point to be emphasized at the moment is France's inability to erect a barrier against the United States. During the seventy years that followed the French government made no further effort to do so. After the defeat of 1870, the consolidation of Germany, and the establishment of the Third French Republic, it is doubtful whether even the idea was ever entertained. Sharp criticisms of the American policy of the United States often appeared in the French press, but the foreign office took no action. The diplomats had all the problems they could manage in Europe and elsewhere.

EXPANSION: FIRST PHASE

Thus the strife of Europe left the United States a rather free hand in the Western Hemisphere during the decades following the Civil War. But for reasons already alluded to in this volume the expansionist career of America's leading power was interrupted. When it was finally resumed at the end of the century European discords once more proved advantageous.

CHAPTER VII

THE REGULATION OF EUROPEAN CONDUCT IN AMERICA

I

No phase of the foreign policy of the United States has been discussed more than the Monroe Doctrine, and hardly any phase of its policy has been the subject of more confused thinking. Much of this confusion can be avoided if the fundamental motive behind the doctrine is kept in mind. That fundamental motive is the desire to safeguard the security of the nation.

In its original form the Monroe Doctrine contained a list of the types of European activity in the New World that were considered dangerous to the "peace and safety" of the United States. These types of activity as originally envisaged were three in number: (1) the establishment of new colonies in America; (2) the setting-up of European protectorates in the New World; and (3) interference of any kind in the internal politics of American states. In these respects the United States proposed to regulate the conduct of European governments in this hemisphere.

Patient investigation, interesting but often rather irrelevant, has been devoted to the effort to assign major credit for the pronunciamento to this or to that individual. The truth is that like the sentiment of isolationism the feeling expressed by the doctrine was born with the nation. It was merely one of the two complementary principles of American isolation: (1) Keep out of the political affairs of Europe

REGULATION OF EUROPEAN CONDUCT IN AMERICA

and (2) keep Europe out of the political affairs of America. On the part of those who saw so clearly the prudence of the one principle, no great mental exertion was required to perceive the wisdom of the other. The ideas expressed by Monroe in 1823 had been in the atmosphere for forty years. He merely stated what many men, great and humble, had been thinking for a long time. To be convinced of this it is but necessary to recall Hamilton's utterance of 1788 and Jefferson's remarks of 1808. While urging the ratification of the Constitution of 1787, Hamilton exhorted: "Let the thirteen States . . . . concur in erecting one great American system, superior to the control of all transatlantic force or influence, and able to dictate the terms of the connection between the old and the new world!" Instructing agents sent out to communicate with insurgent leaders of neighboring Spanish colonies in 1808, Jefferson declared: "We consider their interests the same as ours, and the object of both must be to exclude all European [political] influence in this hemisphere."

Resentful of the oppressions of the Holy Alliance and deeply attached to their own great experiment which they thought was being menaced by antagonists in Europe, some of the leaders of 1822–23 were on the point of permitting their democratic enthusiasm to outweigh their devotion to isolationism. They wished to take more positive action in behalf of struggling peoples on both sides of the Atlantic. Congressman William Trimble of Ohio revealed the state of mind clearly in March, 1822. Observing the problem in its broadest phase, he pointed out that "all civilized nations were under the dominion of two great social systems— . . . . one . . . . established in the *Occidental*, the other in the *Oriental* [namely, European] world. . . . ." Trimble asserted that the American system had "two aspects, two essential principles—one political, the other commercial." "The first [principle] is known and distinguished," he said, "by written constitutions, representative government, religious toleration, freedom of opinion, of speech, and of the press. The second by sailors' rights, free trade, and freedom of the seas." He then contrasted the American social system with that of Europe. "The political character of that system," he declared, "is aristocracy, monarchy, imperial government, arbitrary power, passive obedience, and unconditional submission. Its commercial character is prohibition, restriction, interdiction, impressment, colonial monopoly, and maritime domination."

Such broad conceptions were widespread in the United States then and before, as already pointed out. The antagonism was clearly seen and dreaded, and the most exalted were advocating a rather aggressive defense. For some time they had been urging the recognition of the revolutionary governments of Spanish America, and now they desired a more active support of the popular cause in Europe. President Monroe sympathized with this more sensitive group, as did Henry Clay and many others. The first draft of Monroe's message of December, 1823, denounced the military suppression of the mass movements of Europe, expressed fervor for republicanism wherever it showed itself, and even advised the recognition of Greece; and more than once in previous years Monroe had been on the point of granting recognition to the struggling Spanish Americans. Cooler statesmen, however, had held him in check. Recognition had been delayed until the spring of 1822, and now these statesmen were trying to persuade him to discard the more defiant parts of his message to Congress.

Among the moderates none has expressed his views so well as John Quincy Adams, who wished to announce a

REGULATION OF EUROPEAN CONDUCT IN AMERICA

maxim of noncolonization by European states in America and to send a private diplomatic discourse on the virtues of democracy to the Tsar of Russia, but who was unwilling to have the repressive policy of the Holy Alliance in Europe denounced in a presidential message. The cosmic atmosphere of the times was clearly revealed in his comments.

.... For more than thirty years Europe had been in convulsions; every nation almost of which it is composed alternately invading and invaded. Empires, kingdoms, principalities, had been overthrown, revolutionized, and counter-revolutionized, and we had looked on safe in our distance beyond an intervening ocean, and avowing a total forbearance to interfere in any of the combinations of European politics. This message would at once buckle on the harness and throw down the gauntlet. It would have the air of open defiance to all Europe. . . . . I did not expect the quiet which we had enjoyed for six or seven years to last much longer. The aspect of things was portentous; but if we must come to an issue with Europe, let us keep it off as long as possible. . . . . If the Holy Alliance . . . . intend now to interpose [in America] by force, we shall have as much as we can do to prevent them without going to bid them defiance in the heart of Europe. . . . . The ground I wish to take is that of earnest remonstrance against the interference of the European powers by force with South America; to make an American cause and adhere inflexibly to that.

The moderates won. Monroe put aside the most defiant phrases of his message, although the final draft did not conceal his sympathies for oppressed peoples everywhere. The European phase of the isolation maxim was upheld and its American phase expanded and emphasized. Both were based upon considerations of national interest, with the problem of security largely in mind. All Europe was warned to keep out of America—democracy's domain. Such interference would be a threat to the peace and security of the United States and—although this factor was not much stressed at the time—would limit its trade opportunities by the extension of the monopolistic colonial system

AMERICA AND THE STRIFE OF EUROPE

II

Thus the Monroe Doctrine was at the beginning primarily a doctrine of national security. Moreover, it has continued to be such in large measure. From time to time, as new types of European activity have been conceived as threats to that security, the doctrine has been expanded so as to embrace these also; and when Japan became a great power the doctrine was applied to the Japanese as well as to the Europeans.

The new types of activity that were listed as being dangerous to national security were the following: (1) the transfer of territory in America from one European government to another; (2) the transfer of territory or sovereignty, even voluntarily, from an American state to a European state; (3) the purchase or lease by European or Asiatic states of naval bases in America; and (4) the employment of force by non-American powers in the collection of damage or contract claims. Activities of the type described under the fourth heading have not uniformly been considered as falling under the prohibitions of the Monroe Doctrine, but they have frequently aroused apprehension because it was suspected that such activities might become a threat to national security.

In the Gulf and Caribbean area, where the security of the United States has been considered most vulnerable, the Monroe Doctrine has been most aggressively applied. In this region a preventive policy—a policy of long-range defense, as it were—has been followed. The government has dominated the region to the extent required (or deemed necessary) to prevent its domination by any other first-rate power. This has been the keynote for more than a century, and the national interest which statesmen have en-

REGULATION OF EUROPEAN CONDUCT IN AMERICA

visaged as being at stake is that of security. The region has been considered most vital to the nation's defense strategy.

At times other motives have operated: land hunger, the desire to promote and protect commerce and investments, the desire to safeguard the lives of nationals, and a degree of eagerness to help the people of the region along the road to progress. But the desire to safeguard national security, supposed to be menaced immediately or remotely by other strong powers, has doubtless been the most prevalent motive and always the one most often asserted.

The broad outlines of the Gulf and Caribbean relations of the United States are well known. The keynote was first sounded by Thomas Jefferson with reference to Louisiana and the Floridas years before the message of Monroe. It was Jefferson's view that these areas bordering on the Gulf of Mexico and so vital to national security must either be retained by weak Spain or transferred to the United States; they must not be permitted to fall into the hands of a stronger power. And they were finally acquired by the United States mainly for the purpose of preventing their acquisition by France or England, although free access to the rivers flowing into the Gulf was another motive.

Land hunger and the fear of European intrusion or domination explain the annexation of Texas, the Far Southwest, and the Pacific Coast. The last two were not a part of the Gulf-Caribbean area, to be sure, but their acquisition vastly increased the strategic importance of this area. Control of the Isthmian routes of interoceanic communication then seemed necessary, and domination of the Gulf and Caribbean region in order to prevent its domination by Europe appeared all the more urgent, for the Pacific Coast and the Far Southwest would have to be defended and, in the new defense strategy, speedy transit across the Isthmus was vital.

AMERICA AND THE STRIFE OF EUROPE

More than a decade before the outbreak of the Civil War the United States began to negotiate for the utilization of the Isthmian routes. The government at Washington interested itself in Panama, Nicaragua, and Tehuantepec, and citizens of the United States became interested in all these and in the Atrato route in Colombia as well. For many years the first three were considerably used but not controlled. England and, to some extent, France were confronted, both of them objecting to the domination of the Gulf and Caribbean by the United States. English opposition in the Isthmian region was so effective that the contest for exclusive control was not resolved in favor of the United States government until the signing of the Hay-Pauncefote Treaty in 1901.

After the Civil War the United States was somewhat reluctant to acquire territory in the Gulf-Caribbean region. It annexed little more than was deemed necessary to make effective its policy of control against the intrusion of other great powers. It annexed Puerto Rico after the war with Spain; bought the Virgin Islands from Denmark, after many years of negotiation, in 1916; and obtained by lease or purchase both naval bases and strips of territory necessary for the construction and control of interoceanic communication across Panama and Nicaragua. The domination of the United States was extended, however, in other ways. Controls of another kind were established and the sovereignty of the nations of the region considerably limited.

All these activities were based for the most part upon conceptions of self-defense, and the Monroe Doctrine, which, let it be repeated, is primarily a maxim of security, was frequently employed to rally national support. In 1904 Theodore Roosevelt announced a special corollary of that doctrine. Advocating a system of aggressive defense, he assumed for the United States a sort of trusteeship of the nations of the Gulf-Caribbean area and proposed to remove all grounds or even pretexts for intervention on the part of non-American powers. With the view of more effectively enforcing the doctrine, he undertook to supervise the conduct of these little nations in their relations with the outside world. In order more efficiently to regulate the activities of Europe in America, he proposed to regulate the conduct of American states in their intercourse with Europeans. In justification of his policy he usually emphasized defense strategy and invoked the shibboleth which had served for almost a hundred years to emotionalize it.

Like some of his predecessors, Roosevelt may have employed the doctrine promulgated by Monroe in order to justify a policy not strictly defensive. Statesmen charged with the grave task of safeguarding the security of their country may become unnecessarily apprehensive under the weight of their responsibility, or they may even be guilty of conjuring up the specter of external menace in order to frighten their constituency into supporting activities directed toward objectives other than national security—territorial aggrandizement, economic advantage, or some "civilizing mission," for instance.

It is probable that the government and the people of the United States have been unduly sensitive with reference to national security. It seems to be a fact that menaces to our security often have been seen or alleged when no real menaces existed. In a *Memorandum* published in 1930, J. Reuben Clark listed with brief comment more than fifty instances of European action or alleged contemplated action "which might be considered or have been considered as falling within the purview of the principles announced by the Monroe

AMERICA AND THE STRIFE OF EUROPE

Doctrine." That many of these instances are purely imaginary or trumped up, there can be little doubt.

European powers have rarely engaged in the types of activity designated as dangerous to the security of the United States even in the most comprehensive interpretations of the Monroe Doctrine. Thoroughly substantiated instances of violation or of a genuine intention to violate that pronouncement are surprisingly few. Evidence now published justifies merely the following meager list to which two or three others might possibly be added: (1) the seizure of the Falkland Islands by Great Britain in 1833; (2) the seizure by the same nation of portions of Central America, especially a part of Honduras, shortly before 1860; (3) the intervention of France in Mexico during the American Civil War; (4) the reoccupation of the Dominican Republic by Spain at the same period; and (5) the transfer of the island of St. Bartholomew from Sweden to France in 1877.

Such are the historical facts. These occupations and acquisitions actually occurred, and they constitute five instances of the violation of the Monroe Doctrine in its broadest scope, only three of which were permanent: the Falkland Islands to which England held a tenuous claim prior to 1823, British Honduras, and St. Bartholomew. Most of the rest remain in the realm of allegation, rumor, or feeble intent. After 1898 the European nations actually lost three of their American colonies, Puerto Rico and the Virgin Islands to the United States and Cuba through independence.

III

Here, then, is one of the striking aspects of modern history. For more than a hundred years the United States has been able virtually to regulate the conduct of European

REGULATION OF EUROPEAN CONDUCT IN AMERICA

powers in America. While Asia has been dominated or carved up into spheres of influence by the European nations, while Africa has been partitioned among them, the New World—with the exceptions noted above—has been largely exempt from Europe's control.

Several explanations may be offered for this singular development: the nationalism and fighting strength of the Latin-American peoples; the preoccupation of Europe in other areas; the remoteness of America; the dread of military encounter with the United States; and the strife of Europe. Among these factors the strife of Europe is of primary importance, emphatically so when linked with the military strength of the United States. The power of resistance possessed by the Latin-American states cannot be dismissed lightly; it was exhibited by Mexico, the Dominican Republic, and the Pacific Coast countries of South America in the 1860's. But these states have lacked dense population, accumulations of capital, order, unity, and technology. At times indeed they have actually provoked or invited European intervention, but such intervention has been sought mainly when the aggression of the United States has been feared. Nor has distance deterred the European powers with reference to other continents, whatever one may think in respect to preoccupations in Asia and Africa. The significant fact—a fact too much ignored by provincial histories of the foreign relations of the United States—is that Europe's strife has been America's shield. Just as European rivalries and enmities helped the United States at birth and permitted the young nation to acquire a vast territorial domain, so likewise have they made it possible for the United States to control the transactions of the states of Europe in the New World. No sector of a divided Europe could afford to risk a conflict across the Atlantic, exposing itself to attack from the rear. This has been the unique fortune of the United States.

It has been little less fortunate that the strongest of these European powers has been opposed to the intervention of the Old World states in America while displaying small disposition to control Hispanic-American politics or seize Hispanic-American territory for itself. England announced in 1823 that it would not annex any part of the region, or view with indifference any seizures by other nations, or permit other powers to interfere by force in the politics of Hispanic America.[1] From that announcement Britain never seriously departed. Minor territorial seizures already noted were made in Spanish America, but on the whole English policy was consistent. Such political interference as the London government engaged in was mainly to counteract the aggressiveness of other nations, including the United States. Even when the expansion of the United States at the expense of the former Spanish colonies could not be prevented, no more than a few strongholds in Central America were occupied by England, all but one of which were later abandoned.

In spite of the comparative weakness of the United States at the time, the nations of Europe failed to help Spain subdue its colonies during the third decade of the past century. France was lukewarm in the matter. It desired to preserve and increase its commerce in America as well as to secure the friendship of the United States, or at least to avoid provoking an Anglo-American alliance. Russia wished to keep on friendly terms with the United States as a counterpoise to

---

[1] This announcement was made both to Jules de Polignac, the French ambassador in London, and to Richard Rush, the minister of the United States. It was soon repeated to Mexico and published in British official documents.

REGULATION OF EUROPEAN CONDUCT IN AMERICA

England. Austria and Prussia were busy with European problems, primarily those of a divided and restless Germany. Above all, England, mainly from commercial motives and jealousy of the other European states, was opposed to such intervention—England with its control of the seas. Even without Monroe's pronouncement intervention might not have occurred. European rivalries were a sufficient obstacle.

For the next thirty years and more Russia continued to court the United States as a makeweight against England; Spain, greatly weakened by domestic troubles, sought to preserve the remnants of its empire against the aggressiveness of the United States; and France and England, never quite free from mutual suspicions, made efforts to prevent the expansion of the United States, as pointed out elsewhere, but scarcely went farther. When France showed some inclination (1835–40) to enlarge French Guiana at the expense of Brazil, Britain exerted decisive diplomatic pressure; and although both France and England took a hand (1838–50) in the domestic politics of the Río de la Plata states, only Frenchmen displayed marked covetousness for dominion in the area, and Britain held these aggressive impulses—apparently not really shared by the French government—completely in check. Both European nations likewise intervened in the Caribbean republics of Haiti and Santo Domingo, but they were motivated in large part by a desire to checkmate the United States, and no controls of a permanent nature were established.

With the coming of the Civil War, France and Spain assumed an aggressive role in America. England, however, while revealing—somewhat inconsistently—little disposition to restrain these powers, reluctantly followed its policy of political aloofness; and Russia continued its overtures for the friendship of the United States in the hope of having in some future emergency an ally able to cope with Britain on the high seas. The stubborn resistance of the Spanish Americans made Louis Napoleon's task difficult in Mexico and frustrated the assaults of Spain both against the Dominican Republic and against the Pacific Coast states of South America. In addition, the French government confronted financial difficulties and political opposition at home as well as a menacing situation across the Rhine. Soon after the suppression of the rebellious states of the American Union, all European intervention in Latin America ceased. Armed forces might have been withdrawn even if the United States had displayed no opposition. At any rate, European intervention terminated before the champion of the Monroe Doctrine was compelled to undertake military resistance.

Followed then a period of calm during which hardly anything occurred to remind the Americans of the critical days of the past. With the development of an aggressive mood in the 1890's came the excitement of a dispute between England and Venezuela regarding the Guiana boundary. For a time the British government, which probably had no intention of any considerable territorial expansion, refused to admit the American pretension to regulate its conduct in America. At the crucial moment, however, the German Kaiser revealed offensive interest in Britain's African affairs, congratulating the Dutch for successful opposition to the Jameson raid from Rhodesia. Vividly conscious of a new and dangerous rival, England decided not to risk a conflict in America. The strife of Europe settled the matter. The boundary dispute was forthwith submitted to arbitration.

Great Britain soon began to seek a complete *rapprochement* with the United States, and within three years the German menace brought dread to America as well as to

REGULATION OF EUROPEAN CONDUCT IN AMERICA

England. Without doubt, however, the Kaiser's designs in the New World were magnified. He too was in search of the friendship of the United States after 1898. He proposed an alliance before the end of that year and thereafter sought assiduously either to win the United States or to keep it from falling under the influence of his most formidable European rivals. With England and Italy he undertook the joint punitive expedition against Venezuela in 1902, but when remonstrances from the United States induced the British to recede he was not long in reaching a decision to withdraw; and it is virtually certain that he had no ulterior political designs either in Venezuela or elsewhere in America. The situation in Europe was too tense to engage in such enterprises across the Atlantic. Nevertheless transatlantic ambitions attributed to the Kaiser were partially responsible for the extension of American dominance into the Caribbean—into Haiti, the Dominican Republic, the Virgin Islands, and Central America. It was in some measure a case of American aggression to forestall apprehended European aggression. Moreover, fear of Germany's intention to violate the principles of the Monroe Doctrine broadly interpreted was perhaps a factor in America's decision to enter the World War. Yet it was only one of several factors, as we have seen.

Shortly after the end of the war the League of Nations, which numbered among its members most of the Latin-American states, showed interest in the settlement of American disputes in accordance with the terms of the League Covenant. The United States displayed uneasiness at once. Coercion of an aggressor in America might result in decided participation in the political affairs of the New World, and the United States was prompt to interpose a polite objection. It proposed also to regulate the conduct of the League in this hemisphere. Mere statement of the Washington government's views was sufficient. The European situation was strained, and the diplomats of Europe were seeking to induce the United States to join the Geneva organization or in some other manner to lend its influence in maintaining European peace and stability.

By 1933 the United States was no longer apprehensive with reference to League efforts to maintain peace among its American members. The rise of the dictators made it most evident that the Geneva institution would entertain no scheme that would even remotely threaten the security of the United States in the New World. The very spread of dictatorship in the Old World, however, caused some uneasiness by the end of 1936, and during the last weeks of 1937 apprehensiveness appeared to increase. Both Franklin D. Roosevelt and Secretary of State Cordell Hull gave expression to the feeling that general disregard of treaties and increasing use of military force were threatening the peace of the world, including America. Moreover, Sumner Welles, assistant secretary, issued a warning to Fascist powers, and several journalists manifested excitement regarding the political fate of Latin America. Newspapers carried headlines, and periodicals contained articles referring to dictatorships—Fascist and what not—in the region. Among the magazines which discussed the subject were *Current History*, *Fortune*, and the *New Republic*.

It was pointed out by the writers that dictators were ruling the majority of the countries to the south; that German trade with them had increased rapidly in recent years; that Italians and Germans were residing in large numbers in Brazil, Argentina, Uruguay, and Chile; and that a system resembling the totalitarian state had been set up in Brazil and Paraguay. With the example of German and Italian intervention in Spain before them, writers for the press were expressing fear of Nazi or Fascist intervention in support of their new fanaticism in South America. In the manner of the ardent democrats of another day, some of the journalists were trying to envisage the problem in its broader setting with dictators substituted for absolute monarchies or military autocracies. And they were beginning to predict that the final battles between dictatorship and democracy would be fought out in America.

Remembering that the United States had never been compelled to take up arms in order to regulate the transactions of Europe in America, the historian was more tranquil with respect to that particular phase of the crisis. Observing the situation with the perspective of more than a century, he felt confident that Europe's strife would continue to shield America. It did not appear that Mussolini and Hitler could ignore France, Russia, and England with its strong navy. Moreover, they had need of their scanty finances at home; it would not be so easy to send recruits and armaments to South America as to Spain; and the people of the area, strongly nationalistic, friendly to the United States, and ardently democratic in spite of departures from the system in practice, were even more able to defend themselves. The chance that the Fascist nations would invade the region or intervene in any other manner there seemed remote. Surely, in view of all these obstacles, they would not dare commit aggressions in this hemisphere. They had all the troubles they could manage in another.

CHAPTER VIII

EXPANSION: SECOND PHASE

I

ACTUATED by the material interests, inspired by the idealisms, and comforted by the rationalizations described in chapter v, the United States began another epoch of expansion in 1898. The energies of a more wealthy and populous nation pressed outward with such mighty force and speed that within twenty years an outlying empire of more than three hundred thousand square miles inhabited by some twenty million people was annexed or controlled. With the exception of the insignificant Virgin Islands, all the annexations, embracing an area of one hundred and twenty thousand square miles and having a population of approximately twelve million, were made within the brief period of two years. As in the earlier era of expansion several of the European nations were not unconcerned, and once more Spain and Spanish America were the beneficiaries or the victims.

From the beginning of the Cuban revolt early in 1895 until the final ratification of the peace treaty between the United States and Spain nearly four years later, the issues that arose between Washington and Madrid were frequently the subject of consideration by the leading foreign offices of Europe. The ardent and boisterous utterances of sympathy by the people of the United States for democratic republics and their scarcely less patent contempt for monarchies continued after the triumph of the great experiment

EXPANSION: SECOND PHASE

over internal rebellion. National attitude was clearly demonstrated on three occasions between 1865 and 1890: in connection with the overthrow of Louis Napoleon in 1870, the downfall of the Spanish king in 1873, and the definite end of the Brazilian monarchy in 1889. It was further displayed in Secretary Richard Olney's instructions of 1895 on the Venezuelan affair, instructions in which he declared emphatically that America was the special realm of popular government, but that democracy was for "the healing" of all nations. And the restored royalty of Spain, when it turned to its neighbors for succor, naturally based its appeal on the political line of cleavage which the French Revolution and the Holy Alliance had so distinctly drawn and which American journalists and politicians had never allowed to be erased. In the name of the monarchical principle and in behalf of thrones everywhere the Spanish monarchy pleaded with the European governments for aid. Diplomats of the Spanish Queen Regent declared that war with the United States and defeat by the jingoistic republic across the Atlantic, accompanied by the loss of the last remnant of a once glorious empire in America, would dangerously strengthen republican agitators in Spain. It might very well lead to the overthrow of the Queen Regent and imperil every royal government in Europe. The support of the French Republic of course would have to be asked on another ground, but this was readily found. If the United States were not vigorously opposed all European colonies in the New World would be seized sooner or later.

For the European nations it was another period of storm and stress. As early as 1893 the American ambassador in London noted that they were watching one another "like pugilists in a ring." The Triple Alliance was already formed and the Triple Entente was in the making. There were bitter rivalries in the Near East, China, and Africa; and England, with no strong and reliable friends on the Continent, was very anxious not to offend the United States. Russia, Germany, and France were in the same mood. Once more Europe's distresses served the United States, which was free to increase its domination in the Caribbean and even to extend its empire out across the Pacific to the neighborhood of China and Japan. Nonetheless, joint European interference might have occurred despite mutual competitions and distrust if France had been a monarchy, if the English sovereign had been as powerful as those across the Channel, and if Russia had been less devoted to the policy of favoring the increase of the power of the United States as a possible weight in the balance against England.

Spanish solicitations were accorded most attention by Austria-Hungary and Germany, but both of these governments hesitated to assume the leadership in a concerted movement to restrain the United States. For some time Austria took the initiative; for a brief period Germany reluctantly tried to lead the way; and in one instance the British ambassador in Washington, almost certainly without instructions, acted as a sort of initiator and master of ceremonies. The subject of the interventionist concert falls naturally into two broad divisions: (1) mediation in the Cuban difficulty and (2) partition of the Pacific islands.

II

The latest Cuban revolt was less than a year old when the United States revealed a new aggressiveness by demanding that England arbitrate its boundary dispute with Venezuela. As soon as it became clear that this question was in process of pacific settlement, Richard Olney, the American secretary of state, who was no doubt moved by the rising

EXPANSION: SECOND PHASE

tide of remonstrance against Spanish colonial policy in the newspapers of his country, offered mediation in the Cuban problem.

While convinced of the good faith and pacific intentions of Olney and President Cleveland, Spain was uneasy with reference to the growing jingoism in the United States, republican agitation at home, and the dangers which the loss of Cuba might entail for the Spanish monarchy. Instead of accepting the co-operation of the United States in the pacification of Cuba, the Spanish government adopted a more vigorous attitude toward the Cuban revolutionists. Washington's mediation, offered on April 4, 1896, was rejected on May 22.

The high officials of Spain then spent the months of June and July in working out a plan to stay the intervening hand of the United States. It was, in brief, a project to prevent American intervention in Cuba by concerted European intervention at Washington. The subject was discussed with the ambassadors of the European courts in Madrid, who appeared to give the plan their benediction, and a memorandum was carefully prepared for submission to the European governments.

The memorandum briefly surveyed the history of the relations of the United States and Spain with reference to Cuba, emphasizing the desire of the United States to annex the island as well as the actions previously taken by the European powers in order to prevent the annexation. It pointed out that the insurrection then in progress would have been suppressed if the insurgents had not received aid and encouragement in the United States, and asked the European foreign offices to lend their joint assistance by supporting the Spanish ambassador in Washington in all his efforts to compel the United States to adopt a more rigid and effective neutrality policy. Because the memorandum was in the form of a circular to be transmitted to all the leading European powers, it contained no reference to the monarchical principle which was not calculated to influence France. Yet the correspondence with the diplomats of the monarchies stressed this political point so emphatically that one who reads the documents is reminded of the Holy Alliance.

Toward the end of July, Cleveland issued a proclamation warning citizens of the United States against engaging in unneutral conduct, but this firmer attitude was not sufficient to satisfy Spain. Cleveland's intentions were good, it was admitted, but more effective action was required; and the elections of November, 1896, might result in the choice of a less friendly government.

Soon after the beginning of August, therefore, the Spanish authorities planned to send the secret memorandum by special agents to the various capitals of Europe. Thereupon it would become the duty of Spain's diplomats abroad to incite the European governments to action. The Spanish colonies in America, other European colonies in America, the Spanish throne, and thrones throughout Europe would all be safeguarded by a collective action against the United States.

It was an interesting, even exciting, plan; but on August 10, 1896, an accident happened. Hannis Taylor, minister of the United States in Madrid, heard of the scheme! Somewhere there was a "leak." It seems almost certain that the secret was revealed by a reporter for the *London Standard* aided and authorized by Sir Henry Drummond Wolff, the British ambassador in Spain. And further information, or at least confirmation of what had been received, appears to have been obtained during a conference with the French ambassador. Taylor demanded forthwith an interview with the Duke of Tetuán, Spanish minister of state.

The conference took place at three in the afternoon of August 10, and according to the account now reposing in the Spanish archives the following dramatic fencing took place during a duel lasting two hours:

The Duke of Tetuán began by remarking that he was glad to accord Taylor a personal interview because he had learned through Señor Wolff that Señor Taylor was disagreeably impressed upon receiving information, through persons the duke would not name, of the existence of a plan under consideration by the Spanish government to obtain diplomatic action from the European powers in the Cuban problem. Tetuán hastened to assure Taylor with greatest emphasis of Spain's full confidence in President Cleveland and Secretary Olney. If Señor Taylor had heard anything to the contrary his doubts should be removed completely when he learned the truth. The projected action had absolutely no reference to the government then in charge at Washington, whatever its relation to the eventualities of the future. He hoped the American minister would keep in close touch with him so that there might be a complete understanding at all times.

Taylor admitted that he had suffered pain upon learning, at first casually and partially and afterward more completely through information and deductions which came to him little by little, of the Spanish government's intentions. The effect of the news was all the more painful because he knew his country well enough to affirm that no other action could arouse such hostility against Spain.

In reply the Spanish diplomat repeated his former assurances. The plan had no reference to the Cleveland government. Uneasiness regarding the future had caused the appeal to the European powers to be considered. Political changes were possible in the United States.

Taylor commented further on the disastrous effects which the joint European diplomatic action sought by Spain would produce. He also remarked that the ambassadors of some of the great powers were no less alarmed than he in face of the certain consequences that would flow from the step that the Spanish government seemed resolved to take.

Tetuán thereupon declared that the ambassadors had expressed no such views to him, but he would not question Señor Taylor's affirmations. Some error must have occurred. Spain had not consulted the European governments directly, but in the course of conferences with their various representatives in Madrid he had received unanimous assurance that any action whatever proposed by the Spanish authorities would be heard with greatest consideration by these governments. He confessed, however, that the British ambassador on the previous day had seemed less tranquil than before.

Insisting on his statement regarding the uneasiness of the ambassadors, Taylor observed that some of them might be playing an ambiguous game; and once more he asserted solemnly that Spain's proposed attempt to obtain European co-operation in the Cuban question would lead to the gravest consequences, because every European intervention in American affairs must offend the United States. He therefore earnestly requested the duke to reconsider the matter and inform him whether Spain's resolution was irrevocable.

Tetuán then intimated that Taylor's complaint was premature, since no written proposal had yet been transmitted to the European governments. He also reiterated his statement that Spanish action was not directed against the Cleveland administration. Whereupon Taylor declared that nei-

EXPANSION: SECOND PHASE

ther Cleveland nor any other chief executive of the United States would ever distinguish between present and future governments in a question that concerned the national interest in the presence of a foreign country, and therefore that the factor of administrative change could not be considered. He then revealed more specific information regarding the attitude of the ambassadors, remarking that both the English and the French diplomats were alarmed by the Spanish plan to ask concerted European intervention.

In response the Duke of Tetuán remarked upon his duties both to Spain and to Spain's neighbors in Europe. He must prepare for future emergencies. The Cuban insurrection might continue beyond March 4, 1897. The coming to power of a new president in Washington with a different, a less considerate, policy might provoke a rupture between the United States and Spain. Even war was conceivable. In these circumstances other nations as well as Spain might be affected, and he was obliged to make the facts in the case known to the European governments before the full crisis arrived.

Taylor hastened to assert that none of the powers of Europe would be disposed to give Spain in such a crisis a degree of co-operation sufficient to produce efficacious results. The United States would be affronted by their action, whatever it might be. And once more he inquired whether it were still possible to suspend negotiations on the plan.

The duke replied that he would not transmit any document on the Cuban question to the great powers without previously notifying Señor Taylor, who might feel confident that so long as nothing further was said to him about the matter nothing of the sort would be sent to the European capitals. Tetuán continued to insist, however, upon the possibility of political change in the United States as well as the necessity which he felt of defining and establishing the attitude of the European governments.

This insistence induced the American minister to agree that the next election in the United States might bring disagreeable consequences. Information from private sources indicated certain victory for William Jennings Bryan, in which case Senator J. T. Morgan of Alabama would become secretary of state. Both men were the worst enemies of Spain! Taylor therefore urged Spain to combine political compromise with military action in order to suppress the Cuban revolution before Cleveland's term expired! As the sincere friend of the Spanish government he requested with utmost earnestness that everything he had said be considered most seriously before taking an irrevocable step with reference to any plan for soliciting European intervention. He hardly knew what means to employ in order to impress upon the mind of the Duke of Tetuán his own strong convictions and the dangers which he foresaw as the result of the action contemplated. He hoped the project would be abandoned entirely.

The duke remarked that the danger to Cuba was undoubtedly grave. Spain, if left alone, could suppress the revolution with its own resources. Unfortunately, however, the solution was not to be found in Havana; it depended on Washington. That had been the reason for initiating the action under discussion. For the immediate future he had no fears, but he could not look beyond March 4, 1897, without deep solicitude. Since negotiations with the European governments proceeded slowly, he was convinced that they should be started early. He would, however, consult the Council of State further, and he promised once more that he would send no document on the matter to the foreign offices of Europe without notifying Señor Taylor.

EXPANSION: SECOND PHASE

The American minister closed the interview by insisting that Spain should not act hastily, but should rather await the issue of the campaign in Cuba, intensified by the dispatch of fresh troops. Assuming a most conciliatory tone, he said he would not send a cable to Washington. He would merely send to his superiors a written report of the interview, a report which would be drawn up in the mildest form in order to avoid any possibility of unfortunate consequences. After both had agreed to give a general account of the conversation to the diplomatic representatives of England and France who were said to be awaiting the results of the conference with anxious interest, Tetuán and Taylor separated.

Taylor did not keep his promise. He sent not only one but two cables to Olney, and a dispatch besides. In these he said that news of Spain's plan was brought to him by a third party and confirmed by the ambassadors of Great Britain and France. He also remarked upon the Spanish fear that the loss of Cuba would mean the end of the dynasty, and noted that Austria-Hungary, whose royal house was related to the Spanish queen, was most apprehensive. He declared in fact that the Austrian ambassador in Madrid had taken a principal part in the conferences concerned with the memorandum. Taylor said further that his first move was to detach the French and the English ambassadors from the project, since he knew that they were prudent, cautious, and afraid of responsibilities. Presumably as one of the results of his efforts these two diplomats soon displayed a desire to prevent the consummation of the Spanish plan. His letter of August 13 concludes thus: The essence of this whole affair "was a secret attempt upon the part of Spain to so unite the European powers to her cause as to enable the combination thus made to dictate to the United States, and to control its actions in reference to the politics of the New World, over which it claimed the right to exercise a supreme influence." In the course of his long interview with the Duke of Tetuán, Taylor seems not to have made any specific mention of the Monroe Doctrine. In his report of his interviews with the diplomatic representatives of England and France, however, he said he assumed a high tone of surprise and indignation and declared that the response to this conspiracy would probably be an order to demand his passport immediately, for the adoption of this Spanish plan would constitute the most offensive violation of the Monroe Doctrine that had ever taken place.

The Duke of Tetuán kept his promise to Taylor in letter but not in spirit. The memorandum was not transmitted to the foreign offices of Europe, but its substance was communicated to them. All appeared eager to assume, however, that Spain had decided to suspend further action for the moment. Some even pretended that Spain of its own accord had decided to defer the attempt to obtain collective intervention at Washington. Gabriel Hanotaux was so anxious to be rid of the affair that he pretended not to have received any information whatever of the ambassadorial conferences which had continued for two months in Madrid! "In brief," said the French minister of foreign affairs to the Spanish ambassador in Paris, "it is a closed incident." Spain's first effort to obtain European aid had failed, but there would be others.

III

In the latter part of 1897 Congress and public opinion in the United States forced the McKinley administration to become more positive with reference to Cuban affairs. On September 18 General S. L. Woodford, who had taken the place of Hannis Taylor, made another offer of mediation.

EXPANSION: SECOND PHASE

Requesting time to consider the matter fully the Spanish government finally rejected this second offer on October 20.

Meantime Spain had turned once again to the European courts. Queen Regent María Cristina communicated with the monarchs of Germany and Austria before the end of September. She appealed to the Kaiser, who was then with Francis Joseph in Hungary witnessing military maneuvers, through her Hapsburg relative. The German Emperor telegraphed the foreign office at Berlin on September 28, suggesting the advisability of intervention either by all the leading European states or else by the Continental powers alone.

The telegram caused excitement. Bernard von Bülow, acting secretary of foreign affairs, recommended caution. France and England might use Germany in order to create friction between Germany and the United States and secure commercial advantages at Germany's expense. The co-operation of Russia and France would be an absolute prerequisite. Another member of the German foreign office pointing out that France would not be willing to serve dynastic purposes advised that Austria, as the most natural advocate of Spain, should be urged to take the lead. The Kaiser later agreed, suggesting that Austria should be persuaded to initiate the concert with the understanding that both France and England should co-operate. He remarked further that protection of the colonial possessions of the European powers against transatlantic ambitions might be made the basis of the general agreement. Evidently the contents of the Spanish memorandum of 1896 were known in Germany! By October 7 Berlin had reached its decision. The German government would go along with the other powers and would try to influence Austria, but it would not itself assume the leadership.

Spain's appeal was made to France early in October. The

French government then consulted Russia and finally presented an answer on November 8. The answer was discouraging. In view of the complicated international situation, France would be disposed to maintain its neutrality in case of a war between Spain and the United States, or at most to suggest arbitration.

At the beginning of December, Austria, feeling certain of the good disposition of Germany and Italy, urged Spain to approach Russia and France again. This advice was followed, but the Russian and French governments said they were willing to do no more than merely advise Spain and the United States to submit their problem to arbitration. Hanotaux told the Spanish ambassador in Paris that France would associate itself with a unanimous collective effort provided this could be agreed upon, but he had great doubt that such unanimity could be secured. In all events he would not refuse to participate if all the European powers should reach an agreement to take conciliatory action at Washington.

The project then entered the quiescent stage only to be revived in the following February, when the policy of the United States became still more energetic. The Spanish government earnestly urged Germany to arrange a joint action "in defense of the monarchical principle, against the republican aggressiveness of America." Germany replied, however, that France was the proper nation to assume the leadership, and France, having been approached for the third time, suggested that Austria should take the initiative. Finally, on March 25, 1898, the Austrian government, responding to pressure from Germany and the frantic pleas of the Spanish Queen Regent, decided to shoulder the burden.

By this time, however, Germany was on the point of asking the pope to lend a hand. On March 26, after consider-

EXPANSION: SECOND PHASE

ing the matter for almost two weeks, the German foreign office had instructed its minister at the Vatican to sound the cardinal secretary of state. Within a few days the head of the Catholic church was attempting to exert his influence through Archbishop Ireland at Washington as well as through the papal nuncio at Madrid. These efforts had little effect in the United States, but the nuncio at the Spanish capital, with the assistance of the foreign diplomats, managed to win Spain's consent to an armistice with Cuba. This consent was given on April 9.

Meantime Austria was engaged in the task of organizing European collective action in Spain's behalf, and by April 6 these efforts had yielded fruit, although Russia and England had moved slowly—England with the understanding that the McKinley government should first be sounded. Touched by the pathetic appeals of María Cristina, Queen Victoria was heartily in favor of restraining the United States. Lord Salisbury, head of the British foreign office, doubted the expediency of such joint action, but finally advised the Queen that England should "not refuse to join in any course taken by all the other" European powers. The particular course he had in mind was a collective note requesting in the name of humanity that Spain and the United States settle their difficulties without war. Such a note, drafted by the ambassadors of England, Germany, France, Austria-Hungary, Russia, and Italy on April 6, 1898, and perhaps partially edited by the American secretary of state, was presented to McKinley on April 7.

Although McKinley's response was as noncommittal as polite, the European powers were optimistic, especially after the Spanish-Cuban armistice of April 9 and McKinley's delay in sending his proposed message to Congress. These diplomats did not know that the Rubicon had already been crossed and that the delay was caused by the desire to allow citizens of the United States time to withdraw from Cuba.

The sending of the war message to Congress on April 11 caused surprise and excitement among the foreign diplomats of Washington and led to a final effort to prevent hostilities, with the Austrian ambassador taking the lead still. On April 14, however, Sir Julian Pauncefote, the British ambassador, perhaps influenced by Queen Victoria, assumed the initiative, presiding over a conference in the English Embassy and editing the first draft of a note which in its final form censured the United States for its aggressiveness in view of the concessions that Spain had made.

Before presenting this second note to the White House, it was, of course, considered necessary to communicate with their superiors back home and obtain consent. This the foreign offices all eventually refused to give. In causing the refusal the attitudes of Russia and England seem to have been decisive. A divided and discordant Europe dared not risk further action. On April 21 the United States and Spain went to war.

The Washington government was probably not aware of what went on in the foreign embassies near the middle of April, but it had complete assurances from its diplomats in Europe that no drastic action would be undertaken by Great Britain and Russia and enough information from the other countries to warrant assuming the risk. Russian diplomats and even the Tsar himself had repeatedly given friendly assurances, and on April 5 Hay wrote from London that the United States could "have the practical assistance of the British fleet" on terms of reciprocity. In connection with the joint note of April 6, Hay cabled that Arthur Balfour, a high official of Downing Street, had assured him that the London government would not propose any steps "which would not be acceptable" to the United States. From France likewise came the report that no "hostile" action would be taken despite French investments in Spain, fears regarding French colonies in America, and the feeling of racial (Latin) affinity for Spaniards; and from Germany, Ambassador Andrew D. White wrote on January 7, 1898:

> On the Continent there has never been a time, probably, when ill will towards the United States has been so strong as at present. Nevertheless, I do not believe that a coalition will be formed against us. The interests of European nations are so diverse, and in many respects so mutually hostile, that it would be very difficult to organize a coalition of them against us. This is the more true, because feeling is more intense about the questions dividing Europe, than it is about those between America and Europe.

IV

The seizure of Manila Bay by the United States fleet raised another subject in which Germany was deeply interested: the distribution of the islands of the Pacific. The history of the previous months was accordingly repeated with one important variation, namely, Great Britain revealed actual opposition to any combination of European governments to prevent the United States from having its way in this region.

During the first weeks of May, German agents in the Far East discovered a disposition on the part of the Filipinos to exchange Spanish domination for a European protectorate, preferably a German. Impressed by this news Bülow communicated with the Kaiser, declaring that the Philippine question was one of the greatest importance, a matter in which Russia and France, as likewise both the United States and England, would be profoundly concerned. "The control of the seas in the end," said Bülow, "may rest on the question of who rules the Philippines, directly or indirectly."

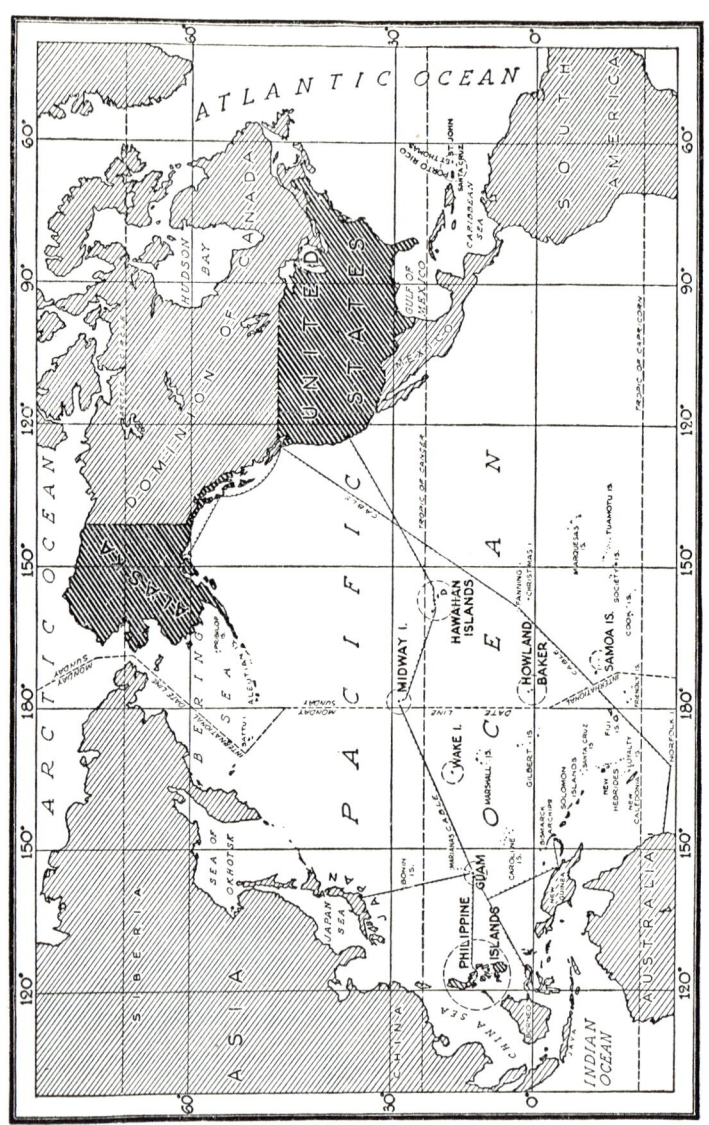

THE ENTRY OF THE UNITED STATES INTO THE PACIFIC

EXPANSION: SECOND PHASE

At the moment the Berlin government did not have sufficient sea-power to retain permanent possession of the islands against the opposition of other countries with large navies. Moreover, encouragement of revolution in the islands would violate the "principle of legitimacy" which formed the basis of German relations with Russia and Austria, and the establishment of a German protectorate might not only cause difficulties with the United States but also provoke a coalition of European powers against Germany. Division of the group among them might be better; the neutralization of the archipelago would be still more acceptable. An attempt should be made to ascertain whether Britain was eager to obtain its share of the Philippines at once or would be satisfied if nobody got anything for the time, and Admiral Diederichs should be sent to Manila Bay to observe the situation and report developments. The Kaiser agreed with Bülow. England should be probed and the naval officer dispatched to the Philippines.

Diederichs arrived at Manila Bay on June 12 with a detachment of the German navy, and friction soon developed between him and Admiral George Dewey. The ambassador of the Berlin government conferred with Lord Salisbury and found him indisposed to discuss the Philippine question. The leading Continental powers were then approached with the idea of neutralization. Spain had suggested to Germany, France, and Russia that they assume control over Manila, and the Spanish governor-general had gone so far as to urge Diederichs to receive the city in deposit. Bülow found, however, that the neutralization proposal was not warmly received at Paris and St. Petersburg.

It was then decided to get in touch with the United States and advocate a general redistribution of the islands of the Pacific. Ambassador T. von Hollenben was instructed accordingly. He was told that Germany desired "naval stations in East Asia." He was also told to broach the idea of a *rapprochement* between Berlin and Washington. Germany, and perhaps Germany alone of all the great powers, would be willing to back the territorial demands of the United States in the Far East. France and Russia were opposed to the establishment of another great nation in the region, while England was not accustomed to trouble itself for the sake of a friend. Ambassador Paul Hatzfeldt was also ordered to confer with John Hay in London. Fearing an alliance between the United States and England—the same fear had been expressed earlier in Madrid—the German foreign office pointed out that an American understanding with Germany would be worth more than one with Great Britain, for Germany's territorial demands would always be more modest owing to limited financial resources and a critical location in the heart of Europe.

Hatzfeldt replied at once that Hay was most friendly with England and very taciturn. It was likely that little would be gained by an interview with such a man; Hay would immediately communicate any German proposals to the British government. Hatzfeldt therefore advised that negotiations for an understanding with the United States should be opened instead with the American ambassador in Berlin.

Hollenben's dispatches from Washington were scarcely more satisfactory. The political parties, he said, had no fixed program in the Pacific; the administration, however, was more disposed than the politicians, he thought, to comply with German desires. He urged that negotiations regarding the commercial differences between the two countries should be initiated at once in order to remove all grounds for friction; and he warned that the seizure of any

EXPANSION: SECOND PHASE

Spanish possession by Germany would be considered an unfriendly act.

Meantime the acting secretary of the German foreign office had engaged in a long conversation with Ambassador White. This Berlin high official, who did most of the talking, went over the whole subject of recent German-American relations. Germany, he said, deserved more credit than any other power for the observance of correct neutrality in the war then being waged, for Germany was the only nation that had been tempted to take a different course. To the German admiral alone had Manila been offered in deposit. Upon Germany alone had rested the responsibility for the decision with reference to European intervention in the war. And in maintaining this friendly attitude the Kaiser had been compelled to disregard the sentiments of his people. While the Germans were not exactly Hispanophile, they were, nevertheless, not friendly toward the United States. Their attitude could not be explained entirely by sympathy for the Spanish monarchy, or by the feeling that the attack on Spain was unjustified, or even by commercial competition. Their unfriendliness was to be accounted for in no small measure by grievances in the colonial sphere. The negotiation of the recent treaty for the annexation of the Hawaiian Islands—the annexation resolution was signed by McKinley on July 7, 1898—was in itself not a cause of resentment, but the German people were disappointed when the United States did not thereupon cede its claims on Samoa to Germany. The German government, however, begrudged America neither the fruits of its victory nor its increasing importance in the world. Quite on the contrary, Berlin authorities were willing to support the United States in the peace negotiations, provided that the Washington government would not oppose Germany's modest colonial aspirations, which merely embraced full possession of the Samoan and the Caroline Islands together with maritime bases in the Philippines and perhaps in the adjacent Sulus.

The acting head of the Berlin foreign office then proposed what almost amounted to an alliance. The history of the world during the next century, he declared, would be determined in a large measure by an understanding between the United States and Germany at the close of the Spanish-American War. If the United States should take a hostile stand and form an alliance with Grest Britain, this would lead to a coalition of France, Russia, and Germany, and a feverish enlargement of fleets. Thus the United States itself would be forced to maintain large armaments after the end of the war. On the other hand, a German-American agreement would promote peace and disarmament, since war would be unlikely so long as Germany through a friendly understanding with the United States could avoid joining England on the one side, or Russia and France on the other. Only by such a *rapprochement* with Germany could the United States without military expenditures and without jeopardizing its own peculiar institutions fully realize its colonial ambitions.

White, who for cultural reasons was kindly disposed toward Germany, listened with sympathy to the utterances of Acting Secretary Baron von Richthofen and was scolded by the Washington government for the few friendly remarks he made with reference to Germany's desires. Perhaps German high officials soon learned of this. At any rate they soon discovered from other sources, and particularly from Hay, that the United States was not in a mood to satisfy Germany.

The German officials also concluded, however, that the Washington government desired no more than a naval station in the Philippines. Acting on this conclusion the neutralization project was again revived, but when Hatzfeldt interviewed Salisbury on the subject he found the British diplomat so unfavorable he dared not reveal that his action had been authorized from Berlin. Already British statesmen had been publicly suggesting English good will toward America and the desirability of an alliance. And on July 28 Hay had cabled: "British Government prefer to have us retain Philippine Islands, or failing that, insist on option in case of future sale."

Germany, not yet fully understanding the ambitions of the United States, secretly turned to Spain with inquiries regarding the Philippines, the Sulus, the Carolines, and other South Sea Islands, as well as Fernando Po and the Canaries. When Baron Richthofen learned, however, that the Spanish-American peace protocol of August 12 placed the fate of the Philippines in the hands of the peace commission, hope of acquiring this group almost vanished and diplomatic activity was directed principally toward the Ladrones and the Carolines, with some talk of a naval base in the Sulus or the Philippines. In September the Spanish government finally signed a secret agreement to sell Germany the Carolines after the war with the United States had been finally terminated, and promised to give Berlin favorable consideration in any future disposal of other Spanish insular possessions. The secrecy of these negotiations resulted from the desire to avoid irritating the United States as well as from the fear that the ambitions of England and other powers might be aroused.

During the sessions of the Spanish-American peace conference at Paris, October 1, to December 10, 1898, the Spanish government made at least two more appeals for European support against the demands of the United States.

But these were likewise futile; even the Kaiser felt that such a hope was preposterous. German diplomats were then trying to obtain the Sulus on the theory that they were not a part of the Philippines and to prevent the United States from acquiring Wake Island or a part of the Carolines.

Between December, 1898, and June of the following year, Germany obtained from Spain for the sum of twenty-five million pesetas not only the Caroline and the Pelew Islands but the Mariannes, except Guam, as well. These acquisitions necessitated further negotiations with the United States, but the whole problem was settled by the middle of 1899. The United States failed to acquire a cable station in the Carolines, but Germany likewise failed to obtain any bases either in the Philippines or in the Sulus, which went to the United States along with the Philippine Archipelago and Guam. Moreover, on January 17, 1899, an American man-of-war seized Wake Island in spite of the German contention that it belonged to Germany's Marshall group.

On August 31 Berlin also proposed the partition of the Samoas which had been causing friction between the United States, Germany, and England for several years. Welcoming an opportunity for release from an "entangling venture," the Washington government eagerly considered the proposal. London also viewed the proposition with favor, and before the end of the year this problem was solved. The United States obtained Tutuila, Germany received the rest of the Samoan group, and England was granted compensation elsewhere by the Germans themselves.

The first great outburst of the new expansionism in the United States was over and then there was a brief pause. The strife of Europe had permitted the United States to

EXPANSION: SECOND PHASE

achieve its objectives not only in America but far away in the Pacific where England stood in the background urging it to stay—England the great unallied sea-power in bitter rivalry with Germany and profoundly distrustful of Russia.

V

Throughout this critical four-year period the growing nation across the Atlantic was courted by the European governments, each in its own way. The Old World balance of power was unstable and each was striving to improve its position. It was England, however, whose courtship made the greatest impression.

Germany, whose conduct was too aggressive and somewhat misrepresented by British diplomats and journalists, emerged as the enemy. Practically every influential statesman was soon talking of the German menace. The three men who had most to do with the shaping of the foreign policy of the United States during the next six years were Theodore Roosevelt, John Hay, and Henry Cabot Lodge. All three distrusted and disliked Germany.

Hay, who had been in London during the Spanish-American War, was the most hostile and suspicious of all. On July 27, 1898, shortly after an interview with Hatzfeldt, he wrote Lodge:

.... The jealousy and animosity felt towards us in Germany is something which can hardly be exaggerated. .... They want the Philippines, the Carolines, and Samoa—they want to get into our markets and keep us out of theirs. They have been flirting and intriguing with Spain ever since the war began and now they are trying to put the Devil into the head of Aguinaldo [the Filipino chief]. .... There is to the German mind something monstrous in the thought that a war should take place anywhere and they not profit from it.

When one of the European powers, probably Russia, sounded Hay, who was then secretary of state, with reference to joint representations to England regarding the treatment of the Boers, he replied on January 4, 1900, that the traditions of the nation precluded any such action. A few days before he had made a similar statement to Holleben, but had added that he believed the "continued existence of the British Empire" would be advantageous. Holleben had asked whether if England were called upon to strip herself of troops for the South African war she would be able "to count upon the United States as a friend." In November, 1901, in connection with the discussion of a joint expedition to China to exact indemnity for the Boxer uprising and to maintain order, Hay declared: "I would rather, I think, be the dupe of China than the chum of the Kaiser."

Lodge was scarcely less passionate. On March 30, 1901, he asserted in a letter to his dear friend Theodore that the German Emperor had moments when he was "wild enough to do anything." On June 3, 1905, he wrote Roosevelt that the Kaiser was "unstable, crazy for notoriety—not to be trusted."

Roosevelt also was not without grave distrust, although at times he had rather intimate relations with William II. On March 27, 1901, Roosevelt remarked to Lodge: "The Germans regard our failure to go forward in building up the navy this year as a sign that our spasm of preparation, as they think it, has come to an end; that we shall sink back, so that in a few years they will be in a position to take some step in the West Indies or South America which will make us either put up or shut up on the Monroe Doctrine." This view no doubt expressed his attitude for most of the remainder of his life. On May 15, 1905, after Wilhelm had been helpful in Roosevelt's efforts to restrict and shorten the Russo-Japanese War, the strenuous American complained to his friend Cabot that the Kaiser was "so jumpy, so little

EXPANSION: SECOND PHASE

capable of continuity of action, and therefore so little capable of being loyal to a friend or steadfastly hostile to an enemy," that he was not fully to be trusted.

Thus stood Germany in the minds of American political leaders[1] after the close of the Spanish-American War: a country ruled by an impulsive and pugnacious monarch surrounded by a military autocracy, a prosperous nation looking for wider markets, an ambitious nation searching for colonies, naval bases, and coaling stations—searching for them everywhere, even in America, in spite of the Monroe Doctrine, which the Germans considered an obstacle that they were determined to remove. Statesmen at Washington thought Germany desired Margarita or other Venezuelan territory, harbors off the coast of Lower California, Curaçao, Dutch Guiana, the Danish West Indies, the Dominican Republic, Haiti—anything and everything. Yet Germany really coveted above all else the friendship and support of the United States against dreaded European antagonists, or at any rate devoutly hoped that the United States would never join England.

This now seems so clear to the historian that he is astonished at the distrust and apprehensions of the statesmen of a generation ago. To them, nevertheless, the menace, however they may have exaggerated it in order to win popular support for extending the American empire down into the Caribbean, may have had substance and reality. Because of this and other motives already described in chapter v they soon continued the expansionist movement begun in 1898.

Theodore Roosevelt's Latin-American policy was vigorous if not ruthless. He forced the Platt Amendment upon Cuba, thereby reducing the country to the status of a pro-

[1] Elihu Root also shared the sentiments of Roosevelt, Hay, and Lodge.

tectorate. He acquired the Panama Canal Zone by shielding and perhaps indirectly fomenting the secession of Panama from Colombia. He then established a protectorate over the new state of Panama. He took charge of the Dominican Republic by means of military coercion and subjected its finances to rigorous control. He proclaimed a new corollary of the Monroe Doctrine by which he asserted the right and duty of the United States to regulate the conduct of certain Latin-American states in their relations with Europe. Insisting on peace in the five republics of Central America, he sought to promote it by having them sign peace agreements, set up institutions for the pacific settlement of international disputes, and renounce the right of revolution.

For the most part William Howard Taft continued Roosevelt's policies. He retained the three protectorates of the Roosevelt administration and continued to deny the right of revolution in the five nations of Central America. He forced a de facto protectorate upon Nicaragua and negotiated a canal treaty with the puppet government in that republic, but neither action was approved by the United States Senate. By negotiations known as "dollar diplomacy" he attempted to obtain control of the customs—i.e., of most of the public finances—of other countries of the Caribbean.

While Woodrow Wilson's policy had a different tone and a somewhat different motivation, it was hardly less aggressive. He signed the treaty which legalized the protectorate over Nicaragua and ceded the United States a lease over the Nicaraguan canal route. By armed force he established a more drastic control over the Dominican Republic and almost obliterated the sovereignty of Haiti. He raised no objection to negotiations which might have reduced Costa

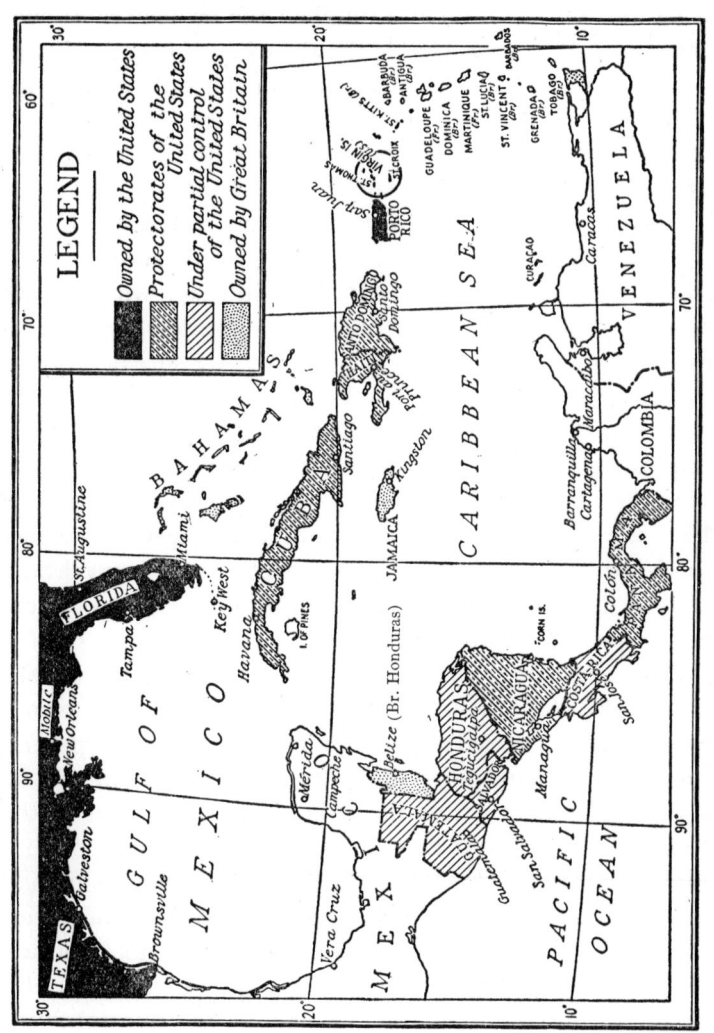

THE UNITED STATES IN THE CARIBBEAN (1898–1933)

Rica to a protectorate and retained the protectorates over Cuba and Panama. Under the doctrine of constitutionalism he denied the right of revolution not only to the five states of Central America but to all the rest of Latin America. He expanded the empire of the United States to its utmost limits—he, the apostle of the "new freedom."

At those limits the empire remained until Herbert Hoover began to contract it. Under him the withdrawals were effected piecemeal and almost surreptitiously, without any fundamental change in the political philosophy, unenthusiastically and even reluctantly under the pressure of hostility to former policies both in the United States and in Spanish America. Came then Franklin D. Roosevelt with the enthusiasm of strong convictions, almost with tumult and shouting. By the end of 1937 all the outposts occupied since 1901 were abandoned save Puerto Rico, the Canal Zone, the Virgin Islands, the Nicaraguan lease, and a naval base or two, and preparations were made to surrender political control in the Philippines.

During all the second period of this new epoch of expansion the European governments, occupied with international strife, exercised no restraining influence. They passed through crisis after crisis and were in no condition to take a hand in affairs across the Atlantic in opposition to the United States. What they had tried to do in 1896–98 but stimulated the movement, parts of which some of them may actually have approved. The advances were made with Europe in mind at almost every step. It is possible that the recessions were made also in part for a similar reason. Latin America must be kept friendly against possible interventions of the League of Nations in American affairs, and emphatically so against any intrusions of the Fascist powers.

THE UNITED STATES AND THE PEACE
OF EUROPE

CHAPTER IX

THEODORE ROOSEVELT AND THE PEACE OF EUROPE

I

IN POINTING out that Europe's discords have often proved advantageous to the United States the writer has not meant to suggest that the American people should rejoice because of such strife. They have never done so. On the contrary, they have always lamented the unhappy situation, however greatly they have rejoiced because of their remoteness from the fields of carnage. Nor was their first concern with the peace of Europe caused in any marked degree by the realization that its wars might draw them in. The early pacifists and many of the later ones were motivated largely by humanitarian considerations. They wished to free their brothers across the Atlantic from the scourge of war. And the same was true in the main of the political leaders of the United States. They never viewed Europe's strife with cold indifference no matter how willing some of them may have been to take advantage of it to increase national commerce, domain, and power. None of them ever suggested that the United States should foment suspicion and conflict among the European states or that it should stand aloof solely or even in part because nothing should be done to change a situation which could be utilized to serve national interests. Of the three outstanding American statesmen who interested themselves in the peace of Europe, one was actuated almost entirely by idealistic motives, another largely so, and the third in part by such considerations.

It is a singular fact that one of the most militaristic presidents of the United States sought to distinguish himself in the role of peacemaker. Yet this fact is not difficult to explain. Theodore Roosevelt was keenly sensitive to popular sentiment, intensely interested in international affairs, and eager for action on a world-stage. On three important occasions he attempted to make a contribution to the peace of the Old World, and although as in the case of several of his other activities his influence was hardly so great as he proclaimed it to be, there is little doubt that it was felt.

II

The Permanent Court of Arbitration at The Hague, established in fulfilment of the terms of an agreement signed by the peace conference of 1899, was on the point of death because of inaction and lack of prestige. Baron de Constant, a French internationalist who had been present at the Hague assembly, conferred with Roosevelt in February, 1902, at the very moment when the court seemed most lifeless. He had come to Washington mainly for the purpose of revealing to the strenuous president the large part he might play in world-politics.

Introduced to Roosevelt by Jules Cambon, the French ambassador, the Baron began the conversation with a challenge. "You are a danger or a hope in the world," said Constant, "according as you advance toward conquest or arbitration, toward violence or justice. It is believed that you are inclined toward violence." Roosevelt asked how the world might be convinced that this was not true. "By giving life to the Hague Court," was the Frenchman's response. He then went on to assert that the leading statesmen of Europe were boycotting the court and deliberately letting it die.

President Roosevelt took up the challenge immediately. On the very day that he had the conference with Constant he instructed Secretary Hay to find some issue which the United States could submit to the Permanent Court. The Pious Fund controversy with Mexico was found to be an appropriate subject and was soon referred to that tribunal. Moreover, a few months later Roosevelt used his influence to induce some of the leading European powers to submit their claims against Venezuela to the same court, which possibly owes its survival to the American president. Andrew Carnegie, then rapidly becoming an outstanding champion of world-peace, thereupon wrote Roosevelt a flattering letter: "The world took a long step upward," said the wily Scot, "and Theodore Roosevelt bounded into the short list of those who will forever be hailed as supreme benefactors of men."

Roosevelt was not immune to such high compliments, and numerous pacifists at home and abroad soon entered into a sort of sacred conspiracy to push him forward. The Interparliamentary Union, organized in Paris in 1889 for the purpose of promoting international harmony, met for the first time on American soil—in St. Louis—in the summer of 1904; and important among its proceedings was a resolution requesting Roosevelt to call another Hague conference in behalf of world-peace. The members of the Union were cordially received at the White House, where the American chief executive returned a favorable answer to their appeal.

The peace advocates prepared the ground for the world's second peace conference with amazing industry; but the assembly of 1907 proved a greater disappointment than

AMERICA AND THE STRIFE OF EUROPE

its predecessor. Attended by delegations from almost all the nations of the earth, the conference spent the major portion of its time discussing the laws of war, not the laws of peace. "Of the ten conventions that were in the end adopted, every single one concerned the technique of war." Among other things they dealt with the use of bombs in attack on harbors, the use of balloons, the right of capture at sea, and the subject of prize courts. The German delegation defeated a proposal for a permanent treaty of arbitration sponsored by the Americans, while the British stood their ground against the American effort to limit the scope of war by expanding the rights of neutrals. The conference could do nothing with the armament problem except merely to urge the governments to give it serious consideration. "A few crumbs were tossed to peace lovers, such as the resolution condemning the forcible collection of debts . . . . ; and the chief victory, an improved formula for the permanent court of arbitral justice, later disintegrated completely in the fingers of the diplomats to whose tender mercies it was entrusted." A peace conference deteriorated into an assembly where tacticians fenced for advantages in the conduct of the next war!

After airing their discouragements the advocates of peace could only solace themselves with the thought that great movements usually have small beginnings. At least the peace movement had become official, and statesmen of the world were beginning to participate in it. The pacifists promised themselves that there should be another conference and hoped that its work would be more substantial.

III

Meantime Roosevelt had been trying to promote European peace in other ways. He had, in his opinion, prevented the Russo-Japanese War from involving other nations, and he had certainly hastened its termination. He had also helped to deal with the Moroccan Crisis of 1905–6. He had in fact been waging peace with great vigor.

In 1911 he remarked to a German friend that the United States because of its strength and its geographical position was becoming more and more the earth's balance of power. This thought was not new to the dramatic New Yorker at that time. He had already acted on it while president.

Twice between 1904 and 1906 he had intimated to a restless Europe that any nation which dared grasp an opportunity to profit by the existing disorder would have to reckon with the most positive opposition of the United States. Convinced that the United States held the scales in Asia as well as in Europe and could tip them either way, he acted on this conviction and made America's influence in world-affairs felt.

Ascending a lonely peak he thoughtfully scanned the Pacific, its shores, and the regions beyond, and supposed he pierced the mysteries of the world's great thereafter. He promptly reached the conclusion "that human welfare would best be served by the preservation in Asia of a balance of power in which Russia and Japan would be left face to face to moderate each other's actions." By making use of the American balance of power he localized the Russo-Japanese War, or thought he did, and brought it to an end before either nation exhausted the other. By wielding the balance a second time he saved Europe, or believed he saved it, from a general war growing out of the first Moroccan Crisis. In both instances he was convinced, or said he was, that he had preserved the peace by threat of force, by the compulsion of prospective sanctions.

More than ten years later, reasoning from the experiences

of this earlier period at a time when Europe was in the midst of its terrible catastrophe, Roosevelt declared that if he had been president in 1914 he would have prevented or localized the World War. "If I had been president," he said, "I should have acted on the thirtieth or the thirty-first of July, as head of a signatory power of the Hague treaties, calling attention to the guaranty of Belgium's neutrality and saying that I accepted the treaties as imposing a serious obligation which I expected not only the United States but all other neutral nations to join in enforcing. .... I believe that .... the American people would have followed me." He was sure that this step would at least have averted a general war.

IV

The war between Russia and Japan, which began in February, 1904, was essentially a contest for the control of northeastern Asia. "As soon as this war broke out," said Roosevelt later, "I notified Germany and France in the most polite and discreet fashion that in the event of a combination against Japan to try to do what Russia, Germany, and France did to her in 1894 [they deprived Japan of the fruits of victory over China and reaped some of the harvest for themselves], I should promptly side with Japan and proceed to whatever length was necessary on her behalf." He was writing to Cecil Spring Rice, and he admitted that he knew England would also support Japan.

Recently published documents from the archives of Paris and London contain no indication that Roosevelt went so far as to declare that he would aid the Japanese in case of a European combination against them. The diplomatic correspondence does reveal, however, that Roosevelt repeatedly used his influence to keep the war from spreading. The whole tendency of his efforts was to assure Japan a free hand in dealing with Russia.

In fact, despite occasional apprehensions regarding future ambitions of the Japanese, Roosevelt's sympathies were on their side throughout the war. Referring to Russia's defeat at Port Arthur on January 2, 1905, he wrote to his son:

> For several years Russia has behaved very badly in the Far East, her attitude toward all nations, including us, but especially toward Japan, being grossly overbearing. We had no sufficient cause for war with her. Yet I was apprehensive lest if she at the outset whipped Japan on the sea she might assume a position well nigh intolerable toward us. I thought that Japan would probably whip her on the sea, but I could not be certain; and between ourselves—for you are not to breathe it to anybody—I was thoroughly pleased with the Japanese victory, for Japan is playing our game.

"Japan is playing our game." This expression may have contained a double meaning. He might have alluded to the possibility that Nipponese success would prevent Russia, perhaps followed by other European powers, from closing the door of commercial and investment opportunity against Americans in China. Or he may have meant to suggest that defeat of Russia would prevent that country from disturbing the peace of Europe in the near future. Or again he may have had in mind both the open door and European peace.

Roosevelt evinced active concern in the war from beginning to end, and the pacifists of the United States soon began to urge him to offer his mediation. They pointed out that he might become a world-figure by taking the problem in hand, and later they supplied evidence of war weariness among the people of both belligerents. They likewise pointed out that further loans to either by international bankers would be hazardous. John Hay appears to have been touched by their appeals, but Roosevelt was little influenced by them. Indeed, he wrote an English friend that he felt the "heartiest scorn" for men who, "whether from folly, from selfishness, from shortsightedness, or from sheer cowardice, rail at the manly virtues and fail to understand that righteousness is to be put before peace even when, as sometimes happens, righteousness means war."

The fact is, he needed no prodding from the peace advocates. He had tried both directly and indirectly to prevent the outbreak of hostilities; afterward he repeatedly urged all the leading powers to employ their diplomatic influence in behalf of peace. He did not actually assume the task of peacemaker in dead earnest, however, until requested to do so by Japan on May 31, 1905. Meantime both France and Germany had urged peace upon Russia and perhaps upon Japan; only the English held aloof out of scrupulous regard for the sensitiveness of their Oriental ally.

It was on June 8 that Roosevelt made his formal offer of mediation to both belligerents, an offer which both accepted immediately. On August 9 the representatives of the two nations met Roosevelt at Portsmouth, New Hampshire, where after much warning and cajoling, and after many appeals to Germany, England, and France for aid, he finally succeeded in inducing the antagonists to sign a treaty of peace. The document was dated September 5, 1905.

On the whole, the peace terms were favorable to Japan. Yet the Russians feigned such expanded elation that the Nipponese felt aggrieved. They felt aggrieved notwithstanding the fact that shortly before the peace conference met at Portsmouth, Roosevelt had given Japan pledges both startling and unprecedented. Without consulting the United

States Senate, Roosevelt promised Japan, through W. H. Taft at Tokio, not merely a free hand in Korea in return for a disavowal of aggressive intentions against the Philippines; he also proffered other commitments that made the United States virtually a secret member of the Anglo-Japanese alliance. And according to a press dispatch published on October 14, 1937, Viscount Kentaro Keneko, one of the negotiators of the Portsmouth treaty, asserted that Roosevelt urged him to go home and tell the Japanese authorities to proclaim an Asiatic Monroe Doctrine! The general effect of such commitments, although they were made with the avowed purpose of maintaining peace in Europe and Asia along with equal commercial opportunities in the Chinese Empire, was to align the United States with Japan and against Russia in Eastern Asia—Russia the traditional friend with ulterior motives of employing the United States against England. But Russia probably did not know enough of this transaction to be deeply offended, and the more favored Japan was likewise the more aggrieved.

At the cost of the displeasure of both belligerents, Roosevelt had made his contribution to the peace of Europe. He had shortened a war and perhaps had localized it, although one cannot be certain of course that other European nations would have entered the conflict even if Roosevelt had exerted no pressure upon them.

V

Before the Russo-Japanese War terminated, the European powers faced a crisis in Morocco, and once more Roosevelt interested himself in the peace of Europe. Joseph Bucklin Bishop, a devoted biographer of the strenuous president, has summed up the contribution of Roosevelt as follows: "It is a diplomatic secret that President Roosevelt is entitled to the credit of arranging the important Algeçiras Conference of 1906 and dictating the terms on which war between France and Germany, with the possible involvement of England as the ally of France, was averted."

Bishop rested his case entirely upon a long letter of Roosevelt's to Whitelaw Reid, ambassador of the United States in London, a letter that purports to give in full the secret negotiations by which the American chief executive imposed his will upon France and Germany and thus preserved the peace of Europe. Bishop says this lengthy letter is "historical material of the first interest and value," but at least one reliable historian, John H. Latané, felt that it is "a highly self-conscious document, written not for Whitelaw Reid but for posterity."

Never a very modest man indeed, Theodore Roosevelt sometimes displayed an imperfect memory or a tendency to exaggerate his role to the brink of misrepresentation. There is not here the slightest wish, however, to deny him a hearing. In brief, his version of the affair is as follows:

On March 6, 1905, Speck von Sternberg, the German ambassador in Washington, asked Roosevelt whether America would join Germany in advising the Sultan of Morocco to reform his government, and in promising the Sultan that, if he would do so, the United States and Germany would support him in any opposition he might make against the attempts of France to gain exclusive control over Morocco. Roosevelt replied that he could not see his way clear to interfere.

Between April 5 and May 29, Germany made several more appeals to Roosevelt, pointing out how German national honor and national interests were involved and urging Roosevelt to use his influence in behalf of a general conference of the interested parties. The American president was especially requested to persuade England to agree to a conference.

During most of this period Roosevelt was on a bear-hunt in Colorado. He still felt that he ought not to become involved in the matter, but he authorized Taft, who was acting as secretary of state in Hay's absence, to ferret out England's attitude, if this could be done without arousing suspicion, and communicate it to Germany.

When he returned to Washington he found Speck and Jules Jusserand, the French ambassador, much concerned lest Germany and France should go to war over Morocco, and by the middle of June he began to fear that war might actually occur if he failed to take action. He therefore urged France to agree to a conference, promising that the United States would participate in it and that the American delegation would strongly oppose unjust action on the part of Germany. France soon agreed to such an international assembly, informing Roosevelt that his advice had been responsible for the concession.

Roosevelt at once wrote the Kaiser a congratulatory letter, declaring that France's agreement to the conference was a diplomatic triumph of the first magnitude for Germany. He also wrote Speck to the same effect, reviewing his own actions with reference to the Moroccan question. Roosevelt had spoken to France rather than to England, he said, because he thought it useless to try to deal with England—useless because England in case of war would profit by the destruction of the German fleet and the loss of German colonies, no matter what happened to France. Let Germany be satisfied with France's acceptance of the conference proposal and in a spirit of conciliation arrange the program with France in advance.

AMERICA AND THE STRIFE OF EUROPE

But Germany and France could not agree on the agenda, and Roosevelt had to offer his good offices again. He made the following proposal in substance: "The two governments agree to go to the conference with no program, and to discuss there all questions in regard to Morocco, save of course where either is in honor bound by a previous agreement with another power." This proposal was accepted by both nations. The Kaiser was in fact so grateful that he gave Roosevelt a promise: In any difference of opinion between France and Germany arising during the conference he would be ready to support the compromise recommended by the American president.

Nor could France and Germany agree on the place where the conference should be held, and, besides, the Kaiser objected to one of the French delegates. Whereupon Roosevelt poured oil on the troubled waters once more and both Berlin and Paris thanked the mediator profusely.

The conference finally assembled in Algeçiras, in southern Spain, on January 16, 1906, with an American delegation present. The discussions were long and heated, and the final convention was not signed until April 7. Still exerting constant pressure upon Germany, Roosevelt practically compelled the Kaiser to accept the terms upon which the eventual agreement was reached.

Such is Roosevelt's account of his work as peacemaker. Most of the documents necessary to verify his story are now available. They indicate that while he magnified the importance of his part in the affair his version is in many respects correct. The gravest defect is the slight account which he takes of the complicated European forces at work during the Moroccan Crisis. According to him, Roosevelt spoke, and Berlin and Paris required no other considerations to make them obey. His self-esteem was increased by the polite conventionalities with which the European diplomats answered his proposals. Two notable instances of this relate to what he asserted to be his prime achievements in the imbroglio.

In the first place, Roosevelt's only support for his thesis that he caused France to accept Germany's demand for a conference consists of a quotation from a diplomatic note in which the French government stated that its acceptance was due to Roosevelt's influence. He had indeed told Jusserand on June 25, 1905, that he intended to warn Sternberg that the world would not "understand or pardon wars entered into for frivolous reasons," and that in case of war the support which would be brought to the aid of France would be "very formidable." But France's courteous acknowledgments of Roosevelt's efforts must not be taken too seriously. Frenchmen must have been fully conscious of the American tradition of isolation. The Moroccan Crisis was a European crisis, and the forces which impelled France to agree to the conference were probably European forces in the main. They were the same forces which had overthrown a French foreign minister in June, 1905: the aggressive attitude of Germany and the somewhat more conciliatory spirit of the new French cabinet. When Théophile Delcassé was replaced by Maurice Rouvier on June 6, 1905, French opposition to the Moroccan conference began to weaken. Moreover, the Paris government practically knew it was assured of a majority at such an assembly. For England and Spain had definitely promised their diplomatic support, Italy had recognized French aspirations in Morocco since 1900, and Russia, although still involved in the last stages of the war with Japan, was France's ally. But Roosevelt's narrative takes little account of this European situation. He would have one believe that his support alone, chivalrously accorded to France, made that nation courageous enough to accept the risks of a conference.

In the second place, Roosevelt makes it appear that he forced the Kaiser to accept the basic features of the American plan of settlement by hints that the United States would aid France in case of war and by a threat to publish diplomatic correspondence that would discredit Germany. Speck's published reports of his conversations contain no indication, however, that he was conscious of being threatened, nor is there any convincing evidence in the German documents that the Berlin government was frightened by the prospect of publication. The vigorous warning which Roosevelt told Jusserand he was going to give Sternberg seems to have been concealed in polite language indeed. There was no reference to unpardonable wars undertaken for frivolous reasons and no reference to "very formidable" aid for France. The letter which he sent Speck on June 26, 1905, to be transmitted by telegraph to Berlin merely declared: "I feel .... it would be most unfortunate even to seem to raise a question about minor details, for if under such circumstances the dreadful calamity of war should happen, I fear that his high and honorable fame might be clouded." If Germany's attitude at the Algeçiras Conference became more conciliatory during its last few weeks, it was perhaps largely because on March 3, 1906, a certain vote indicated that she was in a hopeless minority. After that, William II confronted the necessity of a graceful retreat or war. As for Roosevelt's contribution of a plan which became the basis of the final agreement, the truth is that contrary to the general impression given by his biographers the final act of settlement differed in many respects from the proposals of the strenuous American.

But this is not to assert that Roosevelt had no influence

in the adjustment of the Moroccan question. With the prestige which he possessed as the chief executive of a powerful nation, he was one factor in effecting the decision in favor of a conference, in determining where the conference was to be held, and in the final results achieved. Yet he was not the sole or perhaps even the decisive factor. He tried to employ what influence he had in behalf of peace when no immediate material interests of his nation were at stake, but his influence was in all probability less important than he alleged. In some measure, large or small, he helped to preserve the peace of Europe—temporarily.

VI

Roosevelt's interest and activities with reference to European peace after he ceased to be President of the United States cannot be stated with finality. His papers in the Library of Congress are not accessible after 1909.

He did almost as much as any other man to involve the United States in the World War. His statement in regard to what he would have done in the summer of 1914 if he had been in the White House has already been quoted. He would have shaken his fist at the Kaiser and warned him not to cross Belgium. He thought this would have been sufficient. But he would have taken the United States into the war against Germany if the warning had not been heeded.

This is what he said he would have done in a letter which he wrote on October 3, 1914. Yet in August and September of the same year he was sounding a different note. Indicating that the Berlin government had acted no worse than most other nations had repeatedly acted in the past, he refused to pass judgment on Germany. He said: "I am not now taking sides one way or the other as concerns the violation or disregard of these treaties. . . . . It is certainly eminently desirable that we should remain entirely neutral. . . . . I am sure the sympathy of this country for . . . . Belgium is very real. Nevertheless, this sympathy is compatible with full knowledge of the unwisdom of uttering a single word of official protest unless we are prepared to make that protest effective. . . . ." It was not until more than two months after the invasion of Belgium that he decided to announce he would have taken a bold stand if he had been in the White House at the end of July, 1914. Would his decision have been any more rapid if he had actually been president?

Soon after the opening of the year 1915, however, he began a vigorous and steady drive to involve the United States in war with Germany. The political tendency of this drive was to force Woodrow Wilson to adopt a far-reaching preparedness program and a firmer attitude toward Germany. Wilson's war messsage of April, 1917, was probably the only Wilsonian utterance that ever delighted Theodore Roosevelt, who had favored declaring war on Germany almost two years before.

Did Roosevelt favor a League of Nations and the entrance of the United States into such a league? The evidence now available does not support an unequivocal answer; nor does it indicate that Roosevelt's position was unequivocal.

For assistance in terminating the Russo-Japanese War he received the Nobel Prize, and in an address before the Prize Committee at the Norwegian capital in May, 1910, he suggested a world-association of nations in behalf of peace. On that occasion he not only recommended the signing of arbitration treaties, the extension of the work of the Hague Tribunal, and an agreement for the limitation of naval armaments, but declared with his customary emphasis that "it would be a master stroke if those great Powers honestly bent on peace would form a League of Peace, not only to keep the peace among themselves, but to prevent, by force if necessary, its being broken by others."

He joined in 1916 a private organization in this country known as the League to Enforce Peace, but this may have been with the view of boring from within and militarizing that organization. And it is asserted that at the end of November, 1918, he endorsed in general the idea of an international league. Yet in an address of the previous September he declared that it was wrong to "supplant nationalism by internationalism," and Roosevelt's ablest biographer has ventured to predict that had Roosevelt lived—he died early in January, 1919—"he would have joined the battalion of death that killed the League of Nations" so far as the United States was concerned.

Such was Roosevelt's career as peacemaker. His method was the method of diplomacy backed by force. He wielded a weapon which he described as the balance of power, and perhaps wielded it successfully on two occasions. But he also resuscitated the Hague Court and sponsored the second Hague Peace Conference. He relied primarily on fear instilled by physical force, but he also relied somewhat on moral suasion. And in his later years he was seldom able to rise above bitter partisan considerations.

CHAPTER X

BRYAN AND THE PEACE OF EUROPE

I

For the first time in the nation's history, on March 4, 1913, a confirmed pacifist took charge of the State Department in Washington. He was the idealist in world-politics, one of the most eloquent dreamers any nation ever produced, a man whose matchless voice had stirred millions of people for twenty years. In many respects, as Merle Curti has remarked, the story of William Jennings Bryan's crusade against war is pathetic. Because he was devoted to universal peace he worked diligently for it and experienced fleeting joy in his supposed achievements. Yet he fought in one war and was in a measure responsible for the treaty inaugurating American imperialism; lived to see Europe plunge into history's most destructive war; was unable to prevent his own nation from joining in the slaughter; helplessly looked on while his country turned its back upon the League of Nations, an organization which in his opinion represented the world's brightest hope for peace; and at his own request was buried with military honors in the national cemetery at Arlington.

His aversion to bloodshed, his conviction that war was contrary to the Christian religion, his belief that there was a better instrument than force for solving vital international problems, came to him gradually. "The seeds of his pacifism were sown in his boyhood; the Spanish-American War, and, more particularly, the imperialism which seemed to result from it, marked an important step in its development; and finally, his visit to Tolstoy in 1903 quickened and confirmed his faith in love as an effective alternate force."

Bryan was deeply religious, and the lesson that all men are brothers was taught at his mother's knee. At the early age of nineteen he seems to have envisaged universal brotherhood as the goal of nations and the golden rule as the chief means of attaining it. At that time he wrote a young friend that clanking armor, glittering steel, and the gory field of battle had no charm for him. While the years that followed were busy years in which he was struggling to establish a law practice and build up a political reputation, he never forgot the precepts of his boyhood. He cherished them and they became the cornerstone of his pacifism.

Thus founded on Christian ethics, "Bryan's philosophy of peace was nourished by faith in American individualism and popular government." He thought that the behavior of nations and the behavior of individuals were precisely analogous. Angry individuals could be prevented from fighting by keeping them apart until their grievances could be investigated and their controversies calmly discussed. It should be possible to deal with nations in the same way. Closely associated with this personalistic point of view was his faith in the essential nobility and sanity of common men. He was convinced that the spread of democracy throughout the world would put an end to war. He considered militarism and popular government incompatible, and believed that most wars were instigated by monarchies, aristocracies, and plutocracies. He was sure that the burden of war always fell on the masses, and he had no doubt that the people, with democracy tending everywhere to replace other political systems, would soon be able effectively to protest against being slaughtered in the interest of the privileged few.

AMERICA AND THE STRIFE OF EUROPE

Since the basic sources of his pacifism were shared by millions of other Americans, Bryan's philosophy of peace was not original. In one important respect, however, he was original. He was the first high official in the United States to attempt to put his pacifist faith into practice. "He was a pioneer among statesmen in taking up the work of the earlier peace advocates" and trying to "translate it into terms of political action."

Yet his pacifism had definite limits. In the late 1890's, when the inflammatory propaganda for war with Spain swept the nation, Bryan "enthusiastically waved a Cuban flag at a Jeffersonian banquet." He declared that the United States should intervene in Cuba despite the grave probability that intervention must mean war. "Far from attempting to stem the popular clamor, Bryan blessed it." Democratic zeal, or rather humanitarian sentiment, overcame his devotion to peace. "His voice was the voice of the frontiersman speaking for self-determination, for popular sovereignty; it was the cry of the leader of an oppressed agrarian population sympathizing with the struggling underdogs on neighboring soil." "Humanity demands that we should act," he said eloquently. "War is a terrible thing and cannot be defended except as a means to an end, and yet it is sometimes the only means by which a necessary end can be secured. . . . . War is the final arbiter between nations when reason and diplomacy are of no avail."

Evidently Bryan did not know the facts. He did not have access even to the facts in McKinley's possession during the first days of April, 1898. Diplomacy had already won practically all that was asked of Spain, and reason could have avoided the war if reason had not been blinded by the passionate agitations of Hearst, Pulitzer, and the politicians.

Yet Bryan favored war and even went to war—this man

for whom military trappings had no charm at the age of nineteen. Wearing the "new uniform on which his wife had tearfully stitched the necessary insignia," he took command of his regiment, "flashing his sword into the sunlight of a hot July day." He was now a crusader. He was not betraying his principles: "He had never condemned a holy war."

Nonetheless his conscience disturbed him—those maternal precepts, those lessons taught him in the Sabbath schools, the teachings of Jesus. And was this a holy war after all? He was haunted by fears, not of battle but of the political consequences of battle. Instead of bringing freedom to Cuba this conflict might end in the enslavement of the Filipinos and the increased power of the party dominated by the plutocracy. He soon began to wonder whether it were not better for him to be in the civil arena combatting this new menace.

The war drew to its close. A peace treaty involving the acquisition of colonies and new responsibilities of world-power was before Congress. It had to be approved by the lower house, of which he was then a member. And Bryan not only voted for the treaty but urged other Democrats to give their approval! He wished to avoid prolonging the war, he said. He wished to carry the issue of imperialism, sister of war and mother of navies, directly to the people. On that issue and those of the tariff and free silver taken from his platform of 1896 he fought his second great political battle and lost.

The Spanish-American War and its aftermath strengthened Bryan's pacifism. "He had learned that a war for a just principle, a holy war, might easily become a war of conquest; that it might strengthen militarism and navalism, enrich the industrial and financial classes against which he had been struggling, and turn attention from the domestic problems he had at heart." Seeking compensation for his political defeat and the victory of imperialism and navalism, he turned more energetically toward the problems of peace.

In the winter of 1902–3 he visited Count Leo Tolstoy in Russia—Tolstoy, the man who had declared "all war whatever" to be "unnecessary murder, cruel, futile, and senseless." This noted Russian taught that peace could be attained "not through arbitration tribunals, but only through the refusal of men to support . . . . war and preparation for war." A dreamer and a mystic, "Tolstoy further insisted that love alone could conquer force and violence. No war could be just, because force itself was an expression of the lowest animal passions in man—passions which could be checked by 'inner explorations of self' and by rational observance of the divine law of love in every human relation."

After a long interview, Bryan came away more convinced than ever that Christ's doctrine of love and brotherhood could solve every human problem. But he could not accept the Russian's doctrine of anarchistic opposition on the part of the individual to what he regarded as morally unjustifiable behavior on the part of governments. Such a doctrine might be correct under a monarchy; it could not be harmonized with Bryan's democratic theory. His faith in the people and in their agent, the state, made it impossible for him to subscribe to the thesis of war resistance in all circumstances. Nevertheless he considered Tolstoy the moral titan of Europe, hung the Russian's portrait in his home, and frequently quoted from his writings.

Returning to America, the Great Commoner began forthwith to deliver moving addresses on peace and to write articles on the subject in his daily newspaper. For almost a quarter of a century this was to be his main avocation. In the big tabernacles and on the Chatauqua platforms he reached millions of people. After the harvest season whole families migrated to town from the surrounding farms, often bringing tents and provisions with them. Under the scorching canvas of the great pavilions tired women in calico and gingham fanned themselves and nursed their babies; tall, gaunt men—failures and half-failures—were thrilled by what the speaker said; self-conscious youth and even children felt the spell of his melodious voice. Fortified against the heat by a pitcher of iced water and a palm-leaf fan, the great orator swayed and exalted his rural audiences with his grim earnestness, pointed anecdote, and happy humor. As a popularizer of the ideal of international peace and human brotherhood he was indeed the Peerless Leader.

II

As early as 1905 Bryan began to direct his peace efforts toward the world's rulers. In February of that year he urged President Roosevelt to negotiate treaties by which every international dispute, without any exception whatever, should be submitted to the Permanent Court at The Hague. In the following October he presented the same idea to a group of Japanese statesmen.

In July, 1906, he attended the conference of the Interparliamentary Union in London. Here one of the most important subjects to be discussed was the draft of a general treaty of arbitration. Bryan moved to amend the document as follows:

> If a disagreement should occur between the contracting parties which, in terms of the arbitration treaty, need not be submitted to arbitration, they shall, before declaring war or engaging in any hostilities, submit the question in controversy to the Hague Court or some other impartial international tribunal for investigation and report, each party reserving the right to act independently afterwards.

AMERICA AND THE STRIFE OF EUROPE

He supported his amendment with one of those eloquent appeals so characteristic of the great orator in his prime. He fairly swept the conference off its feet. He declared that his proposal was in harmony with the draft-arbitration treaty and more important even than the treaty itself. Certain questions affecting the honor and integrity of nations were considered outside the jurisdiction of courts of arbitration. Yet it was just these questions which most endangered international peace. It was the purpose of his plan to deal with such questions. The impartial tribunal to which they would be submitted would investigate the facts. If the facts could be separated from the question of honor, the chances were a hundred to one that both the facts and the question of honor could be settled without war. Moreover, the investigation would give time for calm consideration. Man excited was a very different animal from man calm. Issues between men and nations ought not to be settled by passion but by deliberation and reflection. If the hand of war could be stayed until conscience could assert itself, war would become far more remote. "When men are mad they swagger around and tell what they can do; when they are calm they consider what they ought to do." Finally, this impartial investigation of questions supposed to affect the honor or integrity of nations would give time "to mobilize public opinion for the compelling of a peaceful settlement..... Public opinion is coming more and more to be a power in the world."

With slight modifications Bryan's amendment was speedily adopted. He took London by storm, and visitors poured in upon him. He discussed his peace plans with both King Edward and the English prime minister, who heard him with great sympathy. He felt he had at last won the ear of the world. Thereafter he discussed arbitration and tribunals of investigation in season and out of season.

After doing more than any other man to elevate Woodrow Wilson, who was to become the founder of the League of Nations, to the presidency of the United States, Bryan became secretary of state. He was perhaps the first pacifist in history to hold such an exalted office.

He lost no time in putting into execution his designs for universal peace. He laid plans for a third conference at The Hague as well as for a centennial celebration of Anglo-American peace which would impress other nations by the example of two great peoples settling their difficulties during a century by pacific means. Moreover, before the end of April, 1913, he summoned the diplomatic representatives in Washington and proposed the negotiation of treaties committing the signatory parties to submit all questions without exception to an investigating commission and to abstain from hostilities until the commission's report had been made. A year would be allowed for the investigation and as a period for "cooling off." By July 24, 1914, twenty-two treaties were signed, and eventually eight more were added to the list. The Secretary was hopeful, and his great heart was overflowing. He sent to his Nebraskan newspaper, the *Commoner*, an editorial on "The Dawn of a New Era, the Coming of the Prince of Peace."

But already an Austrian prince had been assassinated, and within two weeks a stupendous war was raging. It was as if fate itself had placed Bryan in high office at a time when the whole world was repudiating pacific methods of settling disputes and thinking only of appeal to the sword. Yet he must have been comforted by a statement in a letter which he received from Cecil Spring Rice in October: "It may be that some people at first spoke lightly of your idea.

AMERICA AND THE STRIFE OF EUROPE

No one who has studied the diplomatic history of the events leading to the present disastrous war will speak lightly of your idea again. For it is abundantly manifest that even one week's enforced delay would probably have saved the peace of the world."

III

Now that war had broken out, Bryan directed his energies toward two objectives. He offered mediation to the belligerents, and he made desperate efforts to keep the United States out of the maelstrom.

He clung tenaciously to the hope of bringing the struggle to a speedy end. On August 4 and 5, 1914, he sent an offer of mediation to the leading belligerents. The offer was politely but firmly refused. Yet Bryan was not discouraged. "If you will examine the five answers received," he wrote Wilson on August 28, "you will be reminded of that passage in the Scriptures which says they all with one accord began to make excuses. Each one declares he is opposed to war and anxious to avoid it and then lays the blame on someone else." Bryan went on to suggest that mediation should be proposed again at the first opening, and since all the combatants had declared that they regretted the war and had been opposed to it, the new offer should contain quotations from their very mouths.

At the instigation of Oscar Straus, who claimed to have positive information of Germany's desire for peace, another proffer of mediation was made on September 7. When this proved equally futile, Bryan advanced the idea of a just peace without victory, a concept which Wilson later made his own. Urging the president to persevere in his peace efforts and declaring that the world was looking to the United States to lead the way, Bryan remarked:

BRYAN AND THE PEACE OF EUROPE

> Both sides seem to entertain the old idea that fear is the only basis upon which peace can rest. It is not likely that either side will win so complete a victory as to be able to dictate terms, and if either side does win such a victory, it will probably mean preparation for another war. It would seem better to look for a more rational basis of peace. . . . . The most potent of all influences for the promotion of peace is the substitution of friendship for hatred. . . . .

Bryan urged Wilson to make a third offer of mediation at once, but the president delayed.

Shortly afterward Bryan began to consider a personal visit to Berlin and London for the purpose of trying to terminate the war, but Colonel Edward M. House was selected for the mission instead. The secretary of state then gave encouragement and aid to the private efforts of Jane Addams and her associates, who soon met women from other nations at The Hague in the hope of finding a way to mediate and in order to prepare for a just and durable peace. He also urged Andrew Carnegie to make an appeal to the Kaiser, with whom Carnegie was personally acquainted.

After his resignation from the State Department on June 7, 1915, for reasons to be noted on a subsequent page, Bryan again thought seriously of undertaking a peace mission to Europe but abandoned the plan because of unpleasant publicity and lack of any proper organization to send him. At the Democratic National Convention in St. Louis in July he wept at a recital of the victories of peace, and as late as December, 1916, almost, if not actually, in tears, he remarked to a minister of the Gospel that the failure of the Federal Council of Churches to dispatch him as a peace emissary was the deepest disappointment of his life. At that moment in fact he was considering a mediatory project of his own.

One offer to engage in such a mission, however, he reluctantly declined. In Detroit, Michigan, an auto magnate and philanthropist was dreaming his dream of conciliation and adventure. He would charter a ship, gather on board a galaxy of savants and pacifists, and take the matter straight to the kings of Europe. Bryan was in Detroit in September, 1915, consulting with Henry Ford, and of course was invited to join the peace-ship crusade. But the project was so ridiculed that the Commoner became cautious. He decided to wait until he could see how the expedition made out. Nevertheless he stood on the dock and smilingly blessed the pacifists as the good ship "Oscar II" steamed away from New York. Ford's effort turned out indeed to be a sort of children's crusade—quite as futile, but less disastrous, since all the crusaders finally found their way back home. "Only when news came that Ford had abandoned his colleagues at Christiania did Bryan cancel his passage for The Hague," where "he had half promised to meet the crusaders."

When Congress convened in December, 1916, Bryan was on hand to work in the interest of peace. A few days later, when Wilson sent a note to the belligerents asking them to state their war aims and peace terms, Bryan congratulated him heartily. Indeed, he did more. He got in touch with the German ambassador and urged this diplomat to plead with the Kaiser to state specific and reasonable terms. He also begged David Lloyd George, the British premier, to obtain his government's consent to peace negotiations. "There is no dispute that must necessarily be settled by force," Bryan reiterated. "All international disputes are capable of adjustment by peaceful means. . . . . Do not, I pray you, by refusing an exchange of views assume the responsibility for a continuation of the unspeakable horrors of this unparalleled conflict. Your decision may mean life and death to millions." But once more his exertions were barren. A few weeks later the United States entered the war.

BRYAN AND THE PEACE OF EUROPE

This solemn step was finally taken by the Wilson administration in spite of Bryan's assiduous efforts to prevent it. He had opposed war loans to the governments of the Triple Entente, he had favored warning Americans against traveling on belligerent ships, he had urged a more correct neutrality to be effected by a more vigorous defense of American rights against England and by some method of getting food through to Germany—he had done everything he could to keep the nation from being drawn into the tragic struggle. He had even resigned from the State Department and imperiled his political future when he thought that the "Lusitania" note would lead directly to war with Germany. "I go out into the dark," he said.

War did not result immediately, as is well known. Yet there was an unmistakable drift, and Bryan, as a private citizen, kept up his fight. Traveling thousands of miles by rail he addressed large audiences all over the country, denounced the preparedness movement, combatted Taft's League to Enforce Peace, and explained in detail his plan for keeping out of the conflict. He urged that Germany be given the benefit of one of his peace treaties, which Berlin had accepted in principle. Let the dispute be submitted to a commission; think the matter over for a year! Let the people speak! Submit the question of peace or of war to a popular referendum! The voice of the inert but peace-loving masses should not be muffled by the clamor of special groups whose greed led them to arouse the martial spirit. Bryan also kept in close touch with members of Congress and tried until the last to prevent them from voting to enter the war.

But he was fighting for another lost cause. This Presbyterian elder was foreordained to frustration and futility. He was trying to apply the principles of Christianity in a perverse age. After an overwhelming majority had voted for war, he acquiesced in accordance with the dictates of his political philosophy. "Please enroll me as a private and assign me to any work I can do," he wrote the president. Bryan bought liberty bonds, contributed to the Red Cross, and helped stir the patriotism of the recruits.

But he soon turned his mind once more to the peace of Europe. He hoped he might be appointed as a member of the American peace commission and prepared himself industriously with that in view. Wilson, however, preferred others. Although Bryan did not approve all the terms of the League Covenant, he nevertheless favored the entrance of the United States into the League and the World Court. Later he advised the cancellation of the war debts, pointing out that such a step might be used as a lever to secure the reduction of armaments.

In 1925 he made his last contribution to the cause. He submitted an essay in the contest for the Bok peace prize. It was largely a repetition of his old formulas in which he had never lost faith. "His draft," says Merle Curti, "distinguished between justiciable and non-justiciable disputes. The former were to be submitted to the existing international court; the latter, without exception, were to be referred to commissions of enquiry. All legal and moral obligation to use force in carrying out the decisions was repudiated. . . . ." He still clung to his belief that men were reasonable except in moments of anger. Yet he added that "nations might, by international agreement, refuse loans and commercial intercourse to governments that began war without first submitting the dispute to the court or the commissions of inquiry." In no instance, however, save actual invasion, was war to be declared except by popular referendum. The plan also "emphasized the necessity of development of peace sentiment through meetings, discussion of the causes and cure of war, extension of woman suffrage throughout the world, and the naming of highways in such manner as to suggest peace."

Bryan's plan, submitted under a pseudonym, failed to win the prize. He then sent it to President Coolidge and Secretary Kellogg. "My heart has been in the peace movement for nearly a quarter of a century," he explained to the head of the State Department. Three months later the Peerless Leader was dead.

Both Bryan and Roosevelt endeavored, each in his own way, to help preserve the peace of Europe. Each had his remedy for Europe's strife. Bryan thought that the Old World needed more of the gospel of democracy and pacifism as well as better instrumentalities for effecting peaceful change. Theodore Roosevelt insisted that it needed America's Big Stick and balance of power. Having full confidence in the sanity and essential goodness of men, especially common men, Bryan thought that the reign of democracy would result in the reign of peace. Believing that national and international harmony could be attained only through the operation of inner restraints based upon habit and assent, he tried to develop a popular emotional attachment to peace and sought to preserve it by means of impartial commissions of investigation, judicial procedure, calm discussion, and compromise. He was loath to employ menace or direct coercion through military force or economic pressure. He did not favor the extensive use of sanctions of any kind, although he admitted that there were times when force was necessary as a last resort in order to exact justice or punish injustice. Because he preferred the inner restraints of custom, conscience, and reasoned assent, he made no reference to the balance of power as a device for the maintenance of peace. Theodore Roosevelt was a man of a totally different type with different convictions. While not entirely rejecting Bryan's milder methods, he was inclined to place the emphasis on force or menace. He relied more on the effectiveness of fear than on the efficacy of moral restraints. He was energetic and imposing rather than gentle and persuasive. He was more a militarist than a pacifist.

Woodrow Wilson, whose contribution to the peace of Europe must now be discussed, was something of a combination of Bryan and Roosevelt. He preached Bryan's gospel of peace and popular rule, but he rested his stern faith also upon the armies of the Lord.

CHAPTER XI

WILSON AND THE PEACE OF EUROPE

I

THE activities of the United States as peacemaker in Europe during the World War era fall into two definite periods: the first, in which as a quasi-neutral nation it made overtures for mediation, and the second, in which as a belligerent it acted as the mentor of the powers with which it was associated and tried to shape the final terms of peace. Aside from the preliminary work of a confidential agent sent to Europe prior to the outbreak of hostilities, the Washington government made five distinct efforts to bring about peace before finally entering the war, namely, in August and September, 1914, in the first half of 1915, and at the beginning and the end of 1916. The second period—the period of participation as a belligerent—was signalized by the evolution of the Fourteen Points as the basis of permanent peace, by the armistice based largely thereon, and by the final peace negotiations at Versailles. The offers of mediation made in August–September, 1914, have already been considered, and those of late 1916 alluded to, in connection with the activities of Bryan.

Wilson was ardently devoted to peace but lacked the simple faith of the Great Commoner. He did not possess Bryan's firm confidence in the efficacy of mere treaties of arbitration and conciliation as preventatives for European strife. Owing to his more exalted position and because the world considered him somewhat more practical, Wilson had

AMERICA AND THE STRIFE OF EUROPE

greater prestige as peacemaker than Bryan ever enjoyed. For a brief dramatic moment indeed he seems to have stood as a majestic figure—the hope of a weary and harassed world. But this grand moment was quickly followed by the tragic denouement in which the late allies once more waved aloft the banners of nationalism, cast aside ethical and even prudent considerations, and entered a mad scramble for pawns, indemnities, and guaranties. In the end the idealist was repudiated by the nations he came to save—and by the nation that sent him. In a large degree his hopes, labors, and disappointments were shared by a quiet little Texan who was then a millionaire living in New York.

Wilson came to the presidency not without forebodings regarding European affairs. He knew that only by the sheerest of margins, perhaps, had general European wars been averted during the Moroccan crises of 1905-6 and 1911 and in connection with the Balkan imbroglio of 1912-13. He was aware of a tension which augured ill for European peace.

The President called into consultation his trusted friend and adviser the quiet Texan, Colonel Edward M. House. He remarked to the Colonel that the situation was more intense than it had been for years and asked whether something could not be done to direct the attention of European statesmen to the "dangers breeding in their midst." It appears that House had already been thinking the matter over and had come to the conclusion that a friendly understanding which might preserve the peace of the world could possibly be reached between England, Germany, France, and the United States. During a visit to Europe in the summer of 1913 he had not only arrived at this conclusion but had decided that the German Kaiser, whom he considered probably the foremost ruler in Europe, must be won over sooner or later if this ideal of peace were to be achieved. House now laid his plan before Wilson and received his indorsement. It was then and there decided—December 12, 1913 —that House should visit Germany at the earliest convenient date and interview the Kaiser on the question of international peace and the practicability of a sort of league of common interest between the United States and the leading European powers. If the Kaiser appeared interested the Colonel was then to proceed to London. His mission was to be kept strictly secret.

On May 16, 1914, Colonel and Mrs. House took passage on a German liner bound directly for Hamburg. Before the end of the month he was busy interviewing the important officials of the German government. Some of the members of the foreign office were not unresponsive, especially Alfred Zimmerman; but the heads of the military machine were less amenable. This was true especially of Grand Admiral von Tirpitz, minister of marine. To House's plea for a reduction of armaments in the interest of peace, Tirpitz countered by stoutly defending Germany's maintenance of a strong army and navy in order to put fear into the hearts of Germany's enemies. "The situation is extraordinary," the Colonel wrote Wilson on May 29, 1914. "It is militarism run stark mad. Unless some one acting for you can bring about a different understanding there is some day to be an awful cataclysm. No one in Europe can do it. . . . . It is an absorbing problem and one of tremendous consequence. I wish it might be solved, and to the everlasting glory of your administration and our American civilization."

On June 1 House had an interview with the Kaiser at Potsdam, where a grand military festival was being held. House found the German Emperor much less prejudiced against England and much less belligerent than Tirpitz.

AMERICA AND THE STRIFE OF EUROPE

The Kaiser said he wanted peace but complained that Germany was menaced on every side. He remarked, however, that England, America, and Germany were kindred peoples and should be drawn closer together. House then pointed out that the German monarch was arousing the hostility of England by increasing his navy; whereupon the Kaiser replied that Germany was entitled to a navy commensurate with her growing power and importance, that she must have one to defend her commerce, and that it must also be large enough to cope with the combined sea-power of France and Russia. House then revealed to him the purpose of his mission. The United States wished to help preserve the peace of Europe, and House was the special agent of President Wilson. He had come to Germany because he desired to see the Kaiser first. Later he would sound France and England. House left Germany not completely satisfied, yet not entirely discouraged.

Since Paris was in the midst of a cabinet crisis, House did not bring up the matter of peace while there. After a week of observation he proceeded to London, arriving on June 9.

In London he interviewed the leading British statesmen, including the foreign minister, Sir Edward Grey. He was told that he could count on England's co-operation and that the foreign secretary was even then casting about for some method of getting in touch with the Kaiser without offending France and Russia, who were Britain's allies. When House suggested, however, that Grey go along with him to see the Kaiser at Kiel, the foreign secretary made no response. Aware that House had promised the German Emperor to report to him the result of his visit to the British capital, Sir Edward requested the Colonel to advise the Kaiser of England's pacific sentiments and her desire for a better understanding among the nations of Europe.

WILSON AND THE PEACE OF EUROPE

On July 7 House wrote William II a long letter. He told him that while in Paris he had reached the conclusion that the French had given up all idea of revenge for the loss of Alsace-Lorraine, and that his high hopes on visiting England had not been disappointed. He begged the Kaiser to make a favorable response so that another forward step might be taken in the cause of peace. He then waited for two weeks in the hope of receiving an answer to his appeal and of returning to Germany, possibly in company with Sir Edward Grey. But no reply came, and on July 21 he sailed with his wife for America.

House was at sea only two days before Austria sent the fateful ultimatum to Serbia. By the time the Colonel landed at Boston the die had been cast. Thousands of German soldiers were soon pouring into Belgium. Twelve years later the Kaiser from his place of exile confided to an American journalist that the visit of Colonel House "to Berlin and London in . . . . 1914 almost prevented the World War." But in August, 1914, only Wilson and House knew that a mission which may have promised so much had ended in frustration.

House was not hopeless after the failure of the mediatory offers of August and September, 1914. He soon began to confer with the diplomatic representatives of the belligerents in the United States and in the course of a few months came to the conclusion that if he were again in Europe he might be able to work out the bases of peace. He even ventured to hope that Germany would evacuate and indemnify Belgium. Wilson seems to have left the whole matter largely to House's judgment, and after a brief interview with the President on January 12, 1915, it was definitely decided that the Colonel should undertake another mission to Europe.

AMERICA AND THE STRIFE OF EUROPE

On January 30 he set sail from New York on the British vessel "Lusitania." The credentials which Wilson had given him made it clear that he was not to engage in an official attempt at mediation. He was represented merely as a friend of the American chief executive qualified to serve as an intermediary through whom the belligerent nations might exchange views relative to peace terms and to methods by which future wars might be avoided. It was a stormy voyage, and as the great Cunard Liner entered the danger zone, its captain, perhaps not unknown to Colonel House, ordered the American flag to be raised.

At the very time that he arrived in England the German government was inaugurating a new submarine policy. A war zone about the British Isles was proclaimed, in which after February 18 enemy merchant vessels were to be sunk without warning and without regard for crews and passengers. Neutral passengers and ships were warned against entrance into the zone, especially if belligerent vessels continued to raise neutral flags. The new policy evoked a protest from the United States, accompanied by a warning to England against making use of the American flag.

All this complicated the situation for the Colonel. And he was further embarrassed by a letter which he received from Alfred Zimmerman in which the undersecretary of the foreign office stated that it would not be feasible to ask an indemnity for Belgium because such a request would be bitterly resented by the German people. House was sorely perplexed, for some of the interviews which prompted his mission abroad had been based upon the assumption that Germany would evacuate and indemnify Belgium—so at least the Colonel thought. He decided to tarry a while in England before crossing over to the Continent.

During the next few weeks he got in touch with as many

Englishmen as possible whose influence he considered of any importance in the cause of either immediate or permanent peace. He had tea with some, lunch or dinner with others, and dozens of private interviews. He found the King more bellicose than Grey or Lord Bryce, while Lord Curzon wished to dictate peace in Berlin regardless of how long it might require to get there. Some of them advised House not to go to Germany until the British forced the Dardanelles, which they thought they could do in three or four weeks. He set out, however, on March 11, 1915.

He stopped in Paris on the way and had interviews with the French minister of foreign affairs and various members of the foreign-office staff. The outlook for a reasonable peace in Paris was even less encouraging than in London. With the recent triumph of the Marne, the spirit of revenge revived and hovered like an ugly specter over the cause of peace.

He reached Berlin on March 19 in a blinding snowstorm. He found the high officials cordial to him personally but growing increasingly bitter toward the United States because Americans were selling munitions to the nations of the Triple Entente. He also found the civil and military officials at variance with each other, and the civil authorities divided among themselves. No one was ready to listen to any proposals for the cessation of hostilities. But since the Germans were threatened by a shortage of food, House managed to obtain a sympathetic discussion of the possibilities of a partial restoration of neutral trade.

Returning to England near the end of April, he finally persuaded—or thought he had persuaded—Grey and the British government to allow foodstuffs to go into Germany provided the latter would agree to discontinue the use of submarines and asphyxiating gases. The Colonel was now most enthusiastic. On May 19 he sent a feverish note to James W. Gerard, ambassador of the United States in Berlin, requesting him to submit the proposal to the German government. The Berlin authorities refused to accept this compromise, and righteous indignation filled House's soul. Already, on May 7, the "Lusitania," on which he had been a passenger four months before, had been sunk by a German submarine with dire consequences to American travelers. When he sailed for America on June 5, 1915, his mind was made up regarding the course his country should take. There was nothing to do but work out the details of a formula upon which the United States should enter the war on the side of England and France. But there were still pacifists at home.

When House reached Washington he found Wilson in a mood for more drastic action. Germany had not given a satisfactory answer to his protest against the sinking of the "Lusitania," and Americans were suffering from the policies of both belligerent groups. The President was thinking of making an open demand for a peace conference and stating that the United States would support the group which would agree to terms that gave fairest promise of securing Europe from the threat of militarist aggression. If America should come into the war in this fashion it would come as a crusader for peace. Wilson decided to send House to Europe once more to investigate the possibilities of this plan.

The Colonel reached London on January 5, 1916, and managed after three weeks to get some idea of the peace terms that England might be willing to accept. He then proceeded to Berlin, where the experiences of his previous visit were repeated: a cordial reception, gracious interviews, a stout defense of German conduct, interest in the outcome of the war, a firm denial of any responsibility in its origins, and a desperate determination to triumph over the enemy and exact indemnity. No longer an impartial peacemaker, House proceeded to France, where he accomplished nothing, and in a few days returned to London. There, on the anniversary of the birth of George Washington, he and Sir Edward Grey attached their signatures to a significant memorandum. Briefly its terms were the following:

As soon as Grey should inform him that the time was opportune, the American chief executive would call a conference to put an end to the war. If England and her allies accepted the convocation and Germany and hers did not, the United States would enter the war on the side of the Triple Entente. If the conference met and failed to make peace, the United States would likewise join the Entente as a belligerent. In either case, Germany and the other members of the Triple Alliance would have a new enemy! The major items in what House and Grey considered a fair peace agreement were listed thus: the restoration of Belgium, the transfer of Alsace-Lorraine to France, a maritime outlet for Russia, and compensation elsewhere for territorial losses suffered by Germany.

With this precious memorandum tucked away in his baggage the Colonel sailed for America on February 25. On March 7 Wilson accepted the Grey-House understanding after inserting two "probably's": In the event that the members of the Triple Alliance declined a conference, the United States would *probably* enter the war on the side of the Triple Entente; and the United States would *probably* join England and its allies in case the conference assembled and failed to make peace. The dice were clearly loaded against Germany, unless Wilson's "probably's" were inserted with something more than Congressional opposition in mind.

AMERICA AND THE STRIFE OF EUROPE

Nothing came of this agreement. Futile correspondence between House and Grey finally convinced Wilson that we must "judge for ourselves" when to intervene. The Allies would welcome America's entrance into the war, since its boundless resources were sorely needed. But they preferred to have America enter on the submarine issue. If the United States came in on a grievance of its own rather than with a purely idealistic program, the Allies felt they would have more freedom in determining the eventual terms of peace. An associate with less idealistic motives might prove more congenial. In the late summer of 1916 the Washington government considered retaliation against British blacklisting of certain American exporters.

As soon as the political campaign of 1916 was out of the way, Wilson directed his attention once more to the problem of peace. He decided to draft a note to each of the belligerents urging them to outline the specific objectives for which they were fighting. In the final dispatch, which was dated December 18, 1916, Wilson said:

Never yet have the authoritive spokesmen of either side avowed the precise objects which would, if attained, satisfy them and their people that the war had been fought out. The world has been left to conjecture what definite results, what actual exchange of guaranties, what political or territorial changes or readjustments, what stage of military success, even, would bring the war to an end.

It may be that peace is nearer than we know; that the terms which the belligerents on the one side and on the other would deem it necessary to insist upon are not so irreconcilable as some have feared. . . . .

The President is not proposing peace; he is not even offering mediation. He is merely proposing that soundings be taken in order that we may learn, the neutral nations with the belligerent, how near the haven of peace may be for which all mankind longs with an intense and increasing longing.

Germany was the first of the belligerents to reply to Wilson's appeal, but the reply was not specific. The German foreign secretary merely suggested that his government was ready to begin direct negotiations through delegates to a peace conference on neutral soil. The later replies of the Allied Powers were hardly more concrete and satisfactory. On January 31, 1917, the German government sent in a less indefinite description of the peace terms which it would be willing to accept, but on the same date came the announcement from Berlin that unrestricted submarine warfare would be resumed on February 3. Its resumption on that day led to an immediate severance of diplomatic relations between the United States and Germany, and on April 6 America entered the war. This ended the first phase of Wilson's work as peacemaker.

II

The immediate occasion of the entrance of the United States into the war was the vindication of American rights against Germany. But resentment because of the ruthless employment of the submarine was probably not the sole motive that prompted Wilson's course. Nor was it urgent economic pressure alone. Quite sincerely, perhaps, Wilson placed the issue upon a different plane, whatever may have been the motives of some of his advisers. In his mind it was a war, in some respects defensive, to end all war by means of a just peace and the spread of the principles of democracy —"for the right of those who submit to authority to have a voice in their own governments, for the rights and liberties of small nations, for a universal dominion of right by such a concert of free peoples as shall bring peace and safety to all nations and make the world itself at last free."

Wilson had already been contemplating for months the bases of a permanent peace. He now turned to the task more energetically than ever. In September, 1917, he set up a commission of experts to advise him on every angle and phase of possible peace terms. It was composed of some of the outstanding scholars of the country—a "brain trust," if you please!

By the beginning of 1918 he was ready to state in general terms the conditions of that permanent peace which had become his major objective. On January 8 he went before Congress for that purpose, and his message contained what has become widely known as the Fourteen Points. They were his prelude to peace. For the convenience of the reader they may be reduced to seven: (1) open covenants of peace openly reached; (2) freedom of the seas; (3) removal, so far as possible, of economic barriers and the establishment of equality of trade conditions; (4) reduction of armaments to the lowest point consistent with domestic safety; (5) the self-definition of peoples, colonials as well as others; (6) the evacuation of numerous territories; and (7) a general association of nations for the purpose of guaranteeing, by force if necessary, the political independence and territorial integrity of all states, great and small alike.

These terms became in large measure the basis of the Armistice of November 11, 1918, and Wilson was determined that the final treaty of peace should embody them. It was for the purpose of making these ideals prevail that the President sailed for Europe on December 4. As he walked the deck of the "George Washington" he felt keenly the weight of responsibility that pressed down upon him—felt the great burden and had his misgivings. At least this was the report of a drama-loving journalist. One evening Wilson said, or was alleged to have said, to George Creel: "It is to America that the whole world turns today, not only with its wrongs, but with its hopes and grievances. . . . . All of these expectations have in themselves the quality of terrible urgency. There must be no delay. It has always been so.

WILSON AND THE PEACE OF EUROPE

People will endure their tyrants for years but they will tear their deliverers to pieces if a millennium is not created immediately. Yet you know and I know these ancient wrongs, these present unhappinesses, are not to be remedied in a day or with the wave of a hand. What I seem to see—with all my heart I hope that I am wrong—is a tragedy of disappointment."

The enthusiastic applause which greeted him on the other side probably drowned this foreboding for a time. At Brest and at Paris there were great ovations. Flags fluttered everywhere, bands played, airplanes zoomed above, and the streets for miles were packed with waiting people. Hearts were filled with emotion and many eyes were moist. For three days the peacemaker was feted, honored, and entertained; and since the delegates from the other nations had not arrived, he decided to visit England and Italy in order to explain his plans to the people. On December 26 he reached London, where he was met by members of the royal family and by the entire cabinet. As he rode with the king in the royal coach through the leading thoroughfares of England's capital, he was greeted by great crowds waving and cheering. He explained his peace principles in addresses in London and in Manchester. He then proceeded to Italy, where he was acclaimed by similar crowds—men, women, children, soldiers—surging along the streets, waving flags, and shouting "Viva America! Viva Wilson!" The Italian press described him as the "best loved man in the world." When he had gone, bronze tablets were struck off to commemorate his visit and streets were named in his honor.

Wilson was profoundly impressed. His confidence in the people was strengthened. He had spoken to them from the depths of his heart; had laid before them his dreams and plans for peace. He thought they had given him and his ideals a vote of confidence. Flushed with triumph he envisaged himself as the leader of a world-constituency. With such backing he would establish justice, freedom, peace!

But the people had other leaders also—men who appealed to other motives, to the spirit of fear, venegance, and self-aggrandizement. Wilson failed, as the world knows and laments, to establish a just peace. The treaties framed during the course of the next few months were in many respects quite unjust. Along with the chaotic aftermath of war, along with a terrific economic depression, they produced the Europe of 1932 and following. But they would have been much worse except for the influence of the American peacemaker, and men might today be witnessing a far different Europe if even his modified plans had been followed through. He succeeded in persuading the European diplomats to agree to a League of Nations with sanctions, but also with devices for effecting peaceful change in international arrangements.

Returning to America he encountered far more bitter defeat after a campaign which completely broke his health. The world was not ready to accept his program. Its leaders seemed blind or perverse and obstinate; its people were confused and impotent. After a lingering illness he passed from the scene.

He felt until the last that he could have led the nations into the promised land if only his own had been willing to follow him. "This nation," he wrote in January, 1920, "entered into the war to vindicate its own rights and to protect and preserve free government. It went into the war to see it through to the end, and the end has not yet come. . . . . The world has been made safe for democracy, but democracy has not been finally vindicated. . . . . This, in my judgment, is to be the great privilege of the democracy of the

United States, to show that it can lead the way in the solution of the great social and industrial problems of our time. . . . ." In his last public address he complained bitterly that we had "turned our backs upon our associates and refused to bear any responsible part in the administration of peace."

And we had for a time. From his death in February, 1924, until the summer of 1928, no American statesman concerned himself seriously with the strife of Europe, actual or potential. The nation continued its policy of isolation which Wilson had so deeply deplored. Nevertheless the pacifists and internationalists of the United States kept up their interest and their work, until finally, near the end of 1927, Frank B. Kellogg, secretary of state under the Coolidge administration, began negotiations for a world-peace agreement. The Briand-Kellogg Pact of August 27, 1928, soon signed by more than sixty nations, was the result. It was not a document of tremendous importance perhaps, but it won the Nobel Peace Prize for another American.

As interpreted by Kellogg and his successor, Henry L. Stimson, the pact represented a return to the views of W. J. Bryan. By its well-known terms the signatory powers renounce war as an instrument of national policy and pledge themselves to settle all international disputes by pacific means. The agreement contains no provision for sanctions, either economic or military. Its Republican proponents envisaged no sanctions at all save the sanction of adverse public opinion against any nation that dared break its pledge. But they insisted that public opinion was the most powerful of all sanctions. In an address of August 8, 1932, Secretary Stimson said:

> The Briand-Kellogg Pact provides for no sanctions of force. It does not require any signatory to intervene with measures of force in case the

AMERICA AND THE STRIFE OF EUROPE

pact is violated. Instead it rests upon the sanction of public opinion, which can be made one of the most potent sanctions of the world. . . . . Its efficacy depends upon the will of the people of the world. . . . . If they desire to make it effective, it will be irresistible. Those critics who scoff at it have not accurately appraised the evolution in world opinion since the World War.

How like Bryan in his implicit faith in the sanity and gentleness of the human race, in his belief that popular sovereignty was spreading and that the rule of democracy must bring world-peace! Yet democracy was already losing ground, and public opinion failed to hold at least three armed nations to the pledges of the Paris Pact during the next five years.

As the strife of Europe increased, the United States evinced more and more concern and somewhat greater disposition to co-operate, until the summer of 1935, when with wavering uncertainty and growing apprehension the nation shifted its position once again toward extreme isolation, shifted and doubted the wisdom of its course. It stood like a giant Hamlet, tragic and perplexed. Until world public opinion became more effective, what leader should it follow—an eighteenth-century Washington or a twentieth-century Wilson?

CHAPTER XII

THE PLIGHT OF THE ISOLATIONISTS

SHORTLY after midnight, on April 5, 1917, Claude Kitchin of North Carolina, floor leader of the House of Representatives, arose and made an impassioned appeal to a tense audience. Profoundly impressed with the gravity of the situation, he declared:

> My conscience and my judgment, after mature thought and fervent prayer for rightful guidance, have marked out clearly the path of my duty, and I have made up my mind to walk it. . . . . I have come to the undoubting conclusion that I should vote against this [war] resolution. . . . . Whatever the future, ... I shall always believe that we could and ought to have kept out of this war.

Kitchin suggested how we might avoid involvement:

> Great Britain every day, every hour, for two years has violated American rights on the seas. . . . . She has not only denied us entrance into the ports of the Central Powers but has closed to us by force the ports of neutrals. She has unlawfully seized our ships and our cargoes. She has rifled our mails. [She has black-listed our firms.] She has declared a war zone sufficiently large to cover all the ports of her enemy. She [has] made the entire North Sea a military area— . . . . [filled] it with hidden mines and told the neutral nations of the world to stay out or be blown up. We protested [in vain; then we yielded]. No American ship was sunk, no American life was destroyed, because we submitted and did not go . . . . [into the North Sea]. We kept out of war. We sacrificed no honor. We surrendered permanently no essential rights. We knew that these acts of Great Britain, though in plain violation of international law and of our rights on the seas, were not aimed at us. They were directed at her enemy. They were inspired by military necessity. Rather than plunge this country into war, we were willing to forego, for the time, our rights. I approved that course then; I approve it now.
>
> Germany declares a war zone sufficiently large to cover the ports of

her enemy. She infests it with submarines and warns the neutral world to stay out, though in plain violation of our rights and of international law. We know that these acts are aimed not directly at us but intended to . . . . cripple her enemy, with which she is in a death struggle. We refuse to yield; we refuse to forego our rights for the time. We insist upon going in.

In my judgment, we could keep out of the war with Germany as we kept out of the war with Great Britain, by keeping our ships and our citizens out of the war zone of Germany as we did out of the war zone of Great Britain. And we would sacrifice no more honor, surrender no more rights in the one case than in the other. . . . .

But we are told that Germany has destroyed American lives while Great Britain [has] destroyed only property. [I reply that] Great Britain destroyed no American lives because this nation kept her ships and her citizens out of . . . . [England's] war zone which she sowed with hidden mines.

Although the question was clearly answered in the negative in Wilson's war message of four days before, Kitchin went on to ask:

. . . . Are we quite sure that the real reason for war with Germany is the destruction of lives as distinguished from property, that to avenge the killing of innocent Americans and to protect American lives war becomes a duty?

He then alluded to our recent relations with Mexico, pointing out that Mexican bandits had raided American towns and "shot to death sleeping men, women, and children in their own homes," but that we did not go to war to avenge these deaths. We merely sent an armed expedition into Mexico to hunt down and punish the bandits. And when the "soldiers of Carranza, of the Mexican government which we had recognized, met our soldiers, shot the American flag from the hands of an American soldier, shot down . . . . our soldiers, and Carranza, instead of disavowing the dastardly act, defiantly approved and ratified it," we did not go to war with Mexico to avenge the destruction of

THE PLIGHT OF THE ISOLATIONISTS

American lives and the insult to the American flag. "We were willing to forego our rights," said Kitchin. "I approved that course then; I approve it now." Why could we not, why should we not, forego for the time being the violation of our rights by Germany, as we had done in the cases of England and Mexico?

> War upon the part of a nation is sometimes necessary. . . . . But here no invasion is threatened. Not a foot of our territory is demanded or coveted. No essential honor is required to be sacrificed. No fundamental right is asked to be permanently yielded. . . . . No national policy is contested. . . . . Here the overt act, ruthless and brutal though it be, is not aimed directly at us. . . . . The whole aim and purpose and effort are directed at a powerful enemy.
>
> The House and the country should thoroughly understand that we are asked to declare war not alone to protect American lives and American rights on the high seas. We are to make the cause of Great Britain, France, and Russia, right or wrong, our cause. We are to make their quarrel, right or wrong, our quarrel. We are to fight out . . . . a difference between the belligerents of Europe to which we . . . . are utter strangers. . . . .

The speaker who made these remarks was not pro-German, nor were there any German or Irish voters in his district. He was an American one hundred per cent. Yet, in spite of this and an even abler speech by Robert M. La Follette in the Senate, only six senators and forty-nine members of the House agreed with Claude Kitchin on that fateful night, and some of these were from sections with heavy Irish and German votes.

If he had been living exactly twenty years later he would have observed a decided shift toward his point of view. And the shift was based upon what was conceived to be the lessons of history. Lawmakers had become historians. They had examined into the causes of the World War. They had also investigated the causes and manner of our involvement. On some points they were in agreement; with reference to others almost every lawmaker had become his own historian.

The majority of both houses of Congress appears to have reached an agreement on three subjects: (1) The belligerents in the last war can not be divided neatly into the righteous and the wicked; (2) the United States will have great difficulty in determining the guilty and the innocent in the next European war; and (3) even if it were possible easily to distinguish between them, it were better for the United States to remain aloof and let the European nations settle their own problems. It is probable that the majority would also have displayed sympathy for the view that the entrance of the United States into the World War in April, 1917, was an error.

On the causes and the manner of our involvement the lawmakers differed. Some were convinced, after bankers and munition merchants had been investigated, that our participation was the result of the plots of certain demons whom they described as capitalists and war-traffickers. Some concluded that we had been drawn into the conflict by an imprudent aggressiveness in defense of our rights as a neutral, or at any rate by an unequal insistence upon those rights as between the English and the Germans, after having been seduced by clever British diplomats and propagandists who then as later confidently expected "every American to do his duty." Others still believed that we entered the war largely for the laudable purpose of shielding the world from German militarism and defending and promoting the cause of democracy and peace. But some members even of this last group, this group of idealists, were probably willing, although with some reluctance, to make two rather damaging admissions: The German menace was magnified and the effort in behalf of democracy and peace was largely futile.

THE PLIGHT OF THE ISOLATIONISTS

Yet this group is still resolute and hopeful, and the isolationists will have to keep their eyes on them. Such men have dynamic ideas and a sort of messiah complex. They are still convinced that the democratic way of life is superior to any other and are willing to go to war in order to defend their contention. They believe that the principles of democracy have made this nation great and unique. They ardently desire that these principles may encompass the earth. They are also devotees of peace and ready to fight for it. They hold the fervent conviction that this nation has a mission in the world.

In former days men of similar convictions were the prophets of "manifest destiny," of "inevitable destiny" and of the duty of white men to assume the burden of giving order and progress to the mixed and primitive and colored races of the earth. They were largely responsible for extending our boundaries from Florida to California and Oregon. They were likewise largely responsible for expanding our political control down into the Caribbean and out across the Pacific to the borders of China. Such men tend to become the makers of history, whether good or bad.

Who can be certain that individuals of this type were not responsible for our involvement in the World War? Examine the records of the men of influence in this country, even including the powerful bankers, and you will find that most of them were hostile to the German "military autocracy" from the very outset. Impartiality between the belligerents was rare in the Wilson administration. Perhaps the only strictly neutral man in Wilson's cabinet was W. J. Bryan, who held the same democratic creed but was restrained by pacifism and by a lack of conviction that the principles to which he was devoted were actually threatened or could be served by taking sides in the war. And Bryan resigned in June, 1915. Next to Bryan in his determination to maintain an impartial attitude and follow a strictly neutral course was Wilson himself. But Wilson was weakened almost to paralysis by Page and House and Lansing, all pro-English. Political friends and political enemies played upon a mind, heart, and will already half convinced, until the President finally capitulated and became a crusader. He became a crusader for political principles, principles which the nation was accustomed to cherish and willing to defend when they were thought to be in peril.

The United States entered the World War in 1917 in part to punish Germany for what was conceived to be a breach of good faith and a violation of our rights. But Kitchin was probably not in error when he suggested that this was not the only or even the most important motivation. The nation was in a crusading spirit.

Between August, 1935, and April, 1937, however, this same nation was firmly resolved to follow a twofold motto: Keep the Americas out of war and keep war out of the Americas. Disagreements occurred with reference to the method of attaining these goals, especially that of keeping the Americas, and particularly the United States, clear of an Old World conflict, a task which was generally admitted to be a very difficult one. A few contended that the only way to keep the United States out of war would be to keep war out of the world, while the majority argued that strict isolation would be the surest means of arriving at this pacific objective for America.

But with reference to the appropriateness of this twofold resolution of keeping the Americas out of war and of keeping war out of the Americas, there was no argument in this country. Perhaps at no time in its history was the United States more determined to avoid involvement in war.

THE PLIGHT OF THE ISOLATIONISTS

It was with this purpose in mind that Congress adopted three so-called "neutrality" measures within less than two years. And it was with the same end in view that the second Roosevelt called together the peace conference which was held in Buenos Aires in December, 1936.

The three neutrality enactments represented a victory, although not a complete victory, for the isolationists; but at the Buenos Aires Peace Conference the spirit of isolation probably was borne down by the spirit of internationalism. Sixteen of the twenty Latin-American states were members of the League of Nations and bound by the pledges of the League Covenant with reference to sanctions against the aggressor nation.

Between August of 1935 and the end of April of 1937 the isolationists were, nevertheless, in the ascendancy in the United States. Although they were probably not unwilling to have the United States participate actively in plans for preventing the independent American states from engaging in wars among themselves, they evinced a sort of storm-cellar attitude toward potential wars in Europe. They displayed a spirit of indifference or hopelessness with reference to Europe and the rest of the world quite unlike Theodore Roosevelt, Wilson, Bryan, and certain other pacifists of another day.

During this period of anxiety we were able to observe four courses, any one of which the United States might choose in case of an Old World conflict: (1) An active policy which seeks to determine and to punish the aggressor. This policy was rejected by the lawmakers because of the fear of an erroneous decision or on account of the feeling that the non-American world should be left to solve its own problems. (2) The traditional policy of neutrality, which attempts to define the rights of neutrals with the view of enforcing them. This too would be a positive policy. But the members of Congress, apparently on the point of abandoning the old and vigorous struggle for the rights of neutrals, refused to adopt this policy. Lawmakers seemed to feel that the attempt to defend our rights as a neutral caused our involvement in 1917. (3) Abstention from any commitment in advance, leaving the conduct of our policy toward the belligerents in the hands of the president and the secretary of state until the time came to accept or reject a resolution to enter the next European war. Congressmen and senators were not willing to do this. They apparently believed that bankers, war-traffickers, militarists, foreign propagandists, and the world-service brigade had converted or coerced Wilson in 1917; they were afraid that another president would develop illusions of world-leadership. (4) A policy which would neither attempt to discriminate among the belligerents nor undertake to enforce the rights of neutrals as previously defined, but rather would renounce these rights temporarily and endeavor to limit contacts with the war zones. This fourth course was the one which the national lawmakers were disposed to follow in general, although they left the president considerable discretion—probably more than many of them desired.

The "neutrality" legislation as revised by Congress in April, 1937, and signed by the President on May 1, was in part mandatory and in part discretionary. The following acts are automatically prohibited when the President proclaims a state of war to exist between two or more foreign states: (1) export of "arms, ammunition, and implements of war" to belligerents or to neutrals for transshipment to belligerents; (2) purchase or sale of government bonds or other long-term obligations of belligerents; (3) solicitation of war contributions; (4) transport to belligerents or to neutrals for transshipment to belligerents of arms, ammunition, and

THE PLIGHT OF THE ISOLATIONISTS

implements of war in vessels of the United States government or its citizens; (5) travel by citizens of the United States on belligerent vessels; (6) the arming of merchantmen belonging to the United States or its citizens.

These six automatic or mandatory prohibitions are clearly based upon historical conceptions regarding the causes of our involvement in the World War. They are designed to shield the nation against the investment bankers and the merchants of lethal weapons. They are also intended to avoid the raising of the issue that furnished the occasion for our entrance into the war against Germany: the destruction of American lives on the high seas by the belligerents. Prior to the break in diplomatic relations with Germany on February 3, 1917, German armed forces were responsible for the death of some 179 citizens of the United States on the high seas, and of these only 3 were traveling on an American vessel; 166 were on British vessels, of whom 128 were on the "Lusitania," and 10 were on those of Italy. Between February 3 and April 6, 1917, when the United States declared war on Germany—an intention which became quite evident soon after February 3—the German government was responsible for the loss of 83 more American lives. Of these, 18 were on belligerent vessels, all save one on British vessels; 64 were traveling on our own vessels; one on a Norwegian, that is to say, a neutral boat.

Our complaint against Germany on this score, previous to the severing of diplomatic relations, arose, therefore, largely as a result of the travel of American citizens on belligerent merchantmen, some of them armed merchantmen or ships traveling under naval convoy. The lawmakers of 1937 were determined that this cause of involvement should not arise again. (Bryan may have nudged Claude Kitchin as they watched these proceedings from the Elysian fields, for both had favored an embargo on loans, arms, and munitions, and both had insisted that citizens of the United States should be warned against taking passage on belligerent vessels.)

These, then, were the mandatory provisions of the "neutrality" legislation of April–May, 1937. What of its discretionary phases? The President has authority, at his discretion, to prohibit the following acts: (1) transport on an American vessel to a belligerent state of any commodity whatever that he may designate; (2) export of any goods to a belligerent until after "all right, title, and interest" has been transferred to a foreign government or agency; (3) use of ports of the United States as a base of supply for belligerent ships; and (4) use of such ports by foreign submarines or foreign armed merchant ships except in accordance with the strictest regulations of the President. And subsequent events revealed that the President's authority to proclaim the existence of a state of war could be used with wide discretion: Nations found that war could be waged without a formal declaration, and the President seemed disposed to let them proceed with hostilities without announcing his discovery that war had actually begun. Finally, in the application of all the provisions of this law to a state in the throes of civil war, the President is permitted broad discretion.

In allowing the national chief executive to exercise his judgment in these matters, the members of Congress were influenced by at least two considerations. A few doubtless hoped that within the range of these provisions the President might in some way find it possible to support one belligerent or the other in the interest of European peace or national policy. Many more hoped to avoid the economic distress of

THE PLIGHT OF THE ISOLATIONISTS

isolation in case of a general European or Asiatic war. They doubtless knew that drastic embargoes would cause dire distress. The United States is by no means so self-contained as some of our isolationists seem to suppose. Normally, some 10 per cent of our commodities are exported. In 1914 we produced 18 commodities which depended on foreign markets for more than 10 per cent of their sales, and in 1929, 24 of our products were dependent to the extent of more than 10 per cent of their sales on foreign countries. In many instances the percentages of the total production of commodities that found an outlet abroad ranged from 18 to 60: cotton, tobacco, wheat, lard, rosin, turpentine, copper, kerosene, typewriters, heavy machinery, and so forth. And this is only one side of the picture, for imports also must be considered. We must import, for instance, coffee, tea, bananas, cocoa, sugar, rubber, raw silk, and sisal hemp; we depend almost entirely on foreign sources for 8 minerals: antimony, chromite, manganese, nickel, tin, asbestos, potash; and we are partially dependent on foreign sources for 11 others.

Clearly this road to freedom from war would require rigid discipline and Spartan fortitude. In 1936 partial compensation had been sought in Latin America, but the Latin Americans refused to commit themselves to drastic embargoes which made no discrimination between aggressor and victim and tended to cut them off from the markets of Europe. They were bound by pledges to the League and they feared economic distress.

Will this so-called "neutrality" legislation enable the United States to keep out of the next European war? If it can be enforced, perhaps it may.

There are many, however, who believe that the United States is bound to be involved again. They obtain their arguments largely from history. They point out that the

AMERICA AND THE STRIFE OF EUROPE

United States was drawn into the Napoleonic wars and into the World War, the only general European wars that occurred during a century. Most of this group contend that since the United States is certain to be involved eventually, the Washington government should therefore actively participate in efforts to prevent war, even to the extent of putting "teeth" in the Kellogg-Briand Pact or joining in the League sanctions at the risk of war. They contend that we should continue to engage in wars to prevent wars, until wars have actually been prevented. They are the idealists again, but they contend that they are also realists. And they may be, since not a few idealists are.

It is not difficult for the historian to indicate how we might have avoided the War of 1812. Most historians would now agree, perhaps, that this war would likely have been evaded if an expansionist group had not developed in Congress at the critical moment of our contest for the rights of neutrals, and if the opening of the Latin-American markets had not nullified the effects of our embargoes. This expansionist group of 1812, although resenting the violation of our commercial rights by the British, desired to go to war mainly for the purpose of seizing Canada and the Floridas. If it had been possible to control the expansionists at that juncture, the United States might have kept clear of the conflict in Europe.

The historian can also indicate a way in which the United States might have kept out of the World War. This way was suggested by Bryan and Kitchin. It is also suggested by the recent "neutrality" legislation. The United States might have avoided being drawn in by setting up an embargo on loans and preventing its citizens from traveling on belligerent vessels. Relaxation of British restrictions on our commerce with neutrals might even have been effected by

THE PLIGHT OF THE ISOLATIONISTS

means of a threat to retaliate through an embargo on arms, ammunition, implements of war, and possibly raw materials. If the actual application of such an embargo against Great Britain had become necessary and if this had brought us to the verge of war with England, then we could have desisted in time to avoid war. In that case, however, it would have been necessary to yield to Germany on the question of Germany's submarine-infested war zone about England.

The United States might have been able to avoid the war if this policy could have been adopted and enforced. It might have been impossible, however, to carry out such a policy in this country, despite the fact that Wilson won the election in 1916 mainly because his partisans could tell the people that he had kept us out of war and could lead them to believe that he would continue to do so. The execution of such a policy would have required the dismissal of Lansing and Page and a break with Colonel House. It would have required a determined stand against all those who desired to profit from an increased or even a normal foreign trade. It would also have required the conviction that Germany was bound to be defeated in the end, or that the success of Germany would not constitute a threat to the security of the United States, of democracy, and of world-peace. Those who held the opposite view—the exalted champions of the political faith—would have been more difficult to control perhaps than the economic group, and the two would have coalesced.

Here are these idealists again, these men with explosively dynamic ideas and a keen sense of the purposes of destiny, these makers of history! When the interests and ideals of the nation converge or seem to converge, when these ideals are exalted to the status of cosmic conceptions, and when practical operations of these cosmic conceptions are deemed to be threatened, Americans, like most other men, are ready to fight. That is what occurred in this country between 1914 and 1917. It may also occur during the next European war.

This writer thinks he can hear the voices of the prophets now. He thinks he has not entirely ceased to hear them since 1917, although at times they were very faint. The idealists have continued to work. They were the important influence back of the Briand-Kellogg Pact, and they wish to endow that pact with means of enforcement. They are insisting that we participate in the League sanctions. They contend that traditional neutrality is immoral and cowardly. They declare that there are just wars and unjust wars and that it is not difficult to distinguish between them. They behold wicked rulers running riot, menacing peace, menacing democracy. Dictators who have renounced and ridiculed our faith are threatening the tranquillity of the whole world, they say, and the security of our political system. And the idealists will have the backing of exiles from Germany and Austria supported by friends powerful in finance who have possession of facilities for molding American public opinion.

This writer thinks he has heard a messiah-like voice issue from one who resides in the White House and roams widely. It came over the ether waves from Buenos Aires on December 2, 1936; and it said:

> Three centuries of history sowed the seeds which grew into our nations; the fourth century saw those nations become equal and free and brought us to a common system of constitutional government; the fifth century is giving us a common meeting ground of mutual help and understanding. Our hemisphere has at last come of age. We are here assembled to show it united to the world. We took from our [European] ancestors a great dream. We offer it back as a great unified reality. . . . .

THE PLIGHT OF THE ISOLATIONISTS

.... In expressing our faith in the western world, let us affirm:

That we maintain and defend the democratic form of constitutional representative government.

That through such government we can .... provide a wider distribution of culture, of education, of thought, and of free expression.

That through it we can obtain a greater security of life for our citizens and a more equal opportunity for them to prosper.

That through it we can best foster commerce and the exchange of art and science between nations; that through it we can avoid the rivalry of armament, avert hatred, and encourage good will and true justice.

That through it we offer hope for peace and a more abundant life to the peoples of the whole world. . . . .

[Let the inhabitants of the American nations] make it clear that we stand shoulder to shoulder in our final determination that others who, driven by war madness or land hunger, might seek to commit acts of aggression against us will find a hemisphere wholly prepared to consult together for our mutual safety and our mutual good.

The voice also spoke at Chicago on October 5, 1937; and it said:

Without a declaration of war and without warning or justification of any kind civilians, including women and children, are being ruthlessly murdered with bombs from the air. In times of so-called peace ships are being attacked and sunk by submarines without cause or notice. Nations are fomenting and taking sides in civil war in nations that have never done them any harm. Nations claiming freedom for themselves deny it to others.

Innocent peoples and nations are being cruelly sacrificed to a greed for power and supremacy which is devoid of all sense of justice and humane consideration. . . . .

There must be positive endeavors to preserve peace. America hates war. America hopes for peace. Therefore, America actively engages in the search for peace.

From a banquet table in Nashville, Tennessee, on the evening of June 3, 1938, another voice rang out. The accent and quality were different but the sentiments were the same.

AMERICA AND THE STRIFE OF EUROPE

Solemn contractual obligations are brushed aside with a light heart and a contemptuous gesture. Respect for law and observance of the pledged word have sunk to an inconceivably low level. The outworn slogans of the glorification of war are again resounding in many portions of the globe. Armed force, naked and unashamed, is again being used as an instrument of policy and a means of . . . . aggrandizement. It is being employed with brutality and savagery that outrage and shock every humane instinct. . . . .

Some nations, at least, maintain their devotion to the principles of international law, resting, in turn, upon the foundation of co-operation, justice, and morality. I can wish for our country no more glorious course than to be a leader in devotion to these principles and in service of their preservation and advancement. . . . . There was never a time in our national history when the influence of the United States . . . . was more urgently needed than at present—to serve both our own best interests and those of the entire human race. . . . .

The search for national isolation springs from the counsel of despair. . . . . Not through a sudden and craven abandonment of our national traditions nor through attempts to turn our backs upon our responsibilities as a member of the family of civilized nations can we advance and promote the best interests of our people.

It is my firm conviction that national isolation is not a means to security, but rather a fruitful source of insecurity. For, while we may seek to withdraw from participation in world affairs, we cannot thereby withdraw from the world itself. . . . .[1]

Do these not remind us of the voices we heard in 1917? Who can resist such appeals? Who in the midst of a crisis can convince himself that they ought to be resisted? Claude Kitchin and his fifty-five were borne down by the hosts of the leaders in 1917. Men of ideals follow messiahs; they have always followed them. Men with vested interests will follow them too, especially when interests and ideals converge. This is the plight of the isolationists.

---

[1] This quotation is taken from the address of Cordell Hull before the Tennessee Bar Association. The paragraph order has been changed by the present writer.

CRITICAL BIBLIOGRAPHY

CRITICAL BIBLIOGRAPHY

The materials bearing upon the relations of the United States and Europe are immense and varied. Not even *all the important printed* sources and secondary authorities upon which the present work is based will be included here. The main purpose of this brief Bibliography is to describe those which have proved most suggestive to the author and which may be used to check the accuracy of his facts and the soundness of his central concept. The majority of the secondary works listed contain bibliographies and footnote citations to sources of information. Compilers of bibliographies on the foreign relations of the United States have had their burden greatly lightened by the recent publication of a masterly *Guide to the Diplomatic History of the United States* by Samuel F. Bemis and Grace Gardner Griffin (Washington, 1935). For the study of America and the strife of Europe, pages 733–36 and 756–79 of this guide are of supreme importance. They deal with catalogues, directories, and collections of newspapers, and contain a list of the writings of American statesmen and diplomatists. Perhaps they justify the omission of such data for the most part from this Bibliography. In searching for the motivations of the foreign policies of the United States it is also important to examine the records of debates in Congress, which have not been sufficiently emphasized in the Bemis and Griffin guide: the *Annals*, the *Register of Debates*, the *Globe*, and the *Record*.

I. SOURCES

BAKER, RAY STANNARD, and DODD, WILLIAM E. *The Public Papers of Woodrow Wilson.* 6 vols. New York and London, 1925–27.

Volumes III–VI are invaluable for the foreign policy of this able internationalist.

AMERICA AND THE STRIFE OF EUROPE

British Documents on the Origins of the War. Ed. G. P. GOOCH and HAROLD TEMPERLEY. 11 vols. London, 1927–37.

Concerned with the background of the World War, these documents throw considerable light on the European relations of the United States since 1889, especially with reference to the Pacific and Caribbean areas.

Die grosse Politik der europäischen Kabinette, 1871–1914. Ed. JOHANNES LEPSIUS, ALBRECHT MENDELSSOHN-BARTHOLDY, and FRIEDRICH THIMME. 40 vols. in 54 vols. Berlin, 1922–27.

Among other things, this collection contains diplomatic correspondence regarding many phases of German-American relations. Volumes XIV–XXI, dealing with Pacific affairs, the Spanish-American War, the Russo-Japanese War, Caribbean questions, and the first Moroccan Crisis, are especially useful.

Documents diplomatiques français (1871–1914). 17 vols. Paris, 1929—.

Similar to the German and English collections listed above; compiled and published by a special commission appointed by the French ministry of foreign affairs. For the book of which this Bibliography forms a part, these documents are important mainly because they include correspondence bearing upon the Russo-Japanese War and the Moroccan Crisis of 1905–6.

GODSHALL, WILSON LEON. *American Foreign Policy: Formulation and Practice.* Ann Arbor, 1937.

A compilation of selections from sources—mainly presidential messages and diplomatic correspondence—this large volume has proved most useful in the preparation of the present work.

GWYNN, STEPHEN. *The Letters and Friendships of Sir Cecil Spring Rice.* 2 vols. Boston and New York, 1929.

Spring Rice was a distinguished Englishman who probably had great influence over Roosevelt, Hay, and Lodge, developing their friendship for England and especially their distrust of Germany.

HASSE, ADELAIDE R. *Index to United States Documents Relating to Foreign Affairs, 1821–1861.* 3 vols. Washington, 1914–21.

Properly this work should be listed under guides, but that classification has been excluded from this Bibliography. During most of the period covered by Miss Hasse, published correspondence on the foreign relations of the nation was scattered through an immense number of United States public documents. The Hasse index is therefore most useful as an aid to research, emphatically so for the present volume, since it also locates materials in the

CRITICAL BIBLIOGRAPHY

Congressional Globe. For the periods before 1828 and after 1861 the diplomatic correspondence of the United States has been assembled in special collections: for the earlier by Francis Wharton and Blair and Rives; for the later by the United States government in the well-known annual volumes entitled *Diplomatic Correspondence* (1861–1868) and *Foreign Relations* (1869—). See Bemis and Griffin for a description of these compilations. See also the works by William R. Manning described below.

The Intimate Papers of Colonel House. Ed. CHARLES SEYMOUR. 4 vols. Boston and New York, 1926–28.

The "inside" details of Woodrow Wilson's grave concern with the peace of Europe, arranged as a narrative by the editor. Colonel House's self-confidence was amazing and his views often differed more than he realized from those of the chief executive whom he served as special agent and confidential adviser. Like Page and Lansing he was pro-English.

LANSING, ROBERT. *The Peace Negotiations: A Personal Narrative.* Boston and New York, 1921.

The comments of a rather bewildered diplomat, one of the representatives of the United States at the Versailles Peace Conference of 1918–19.

———. *War Memoirs of Robert Lansing.* New York: Bobbs-Merrill Co., 1935.

A most impressive revelation of the unneutral attitude of a secretary of state during the two and a half years preceding the entrance of the United States into the World War.

MANNING, WILLIAM RAY. *Diplomatic Correspondence of the United States concerning the Independence of the Latin-American Nations.* 3 vols. New York, 1925.

———. *Diplomatic Correspondence of the United States: Inter-American Affairs, 1831–1860.* 8 vols. Washington, 1932–37.

Invaluable collections for the study of the relations of the United States with Europe as well as with Latin America. No student of American diplomacy can afford to ignore them. The second work is still in progress; two or three more volumes will appear.

RICHARDSON, JAMES D. *A Compilation of the Messages and Papers of the Presidents.* Washington and New York, various editions.

This familiar source is listed here because of its importance in the study of the ideology of the foreign policy of the United States. For the first section of the volume now presented it was indispensable.

AMERICA AND THE STRIFE OF EUROPE

SAVAGE, CARLTON. *Policy of the United States toward Maritime Commerce in War.* 3 vols. Washington, 1934–36.

A carefully classified publication setting forth in convincing manner the difficulties encountered by the United States in its efforts to assert its rights as a neutral in times of general European wars.

Selections from the Correspondence of Theodore Roosevelt and Henry Cabot Lodge. 2 vols. New York, 1925.

These two men largely shaped the foreign policy of the United States for several years after 1898. Their letters to each other reveal some of their motives and rationalizations, particularly their distrust of the Kaiser.

SHOTWELL, JAMES T. *At the Paris Peace Conference.* New York, 1937.

Afterthoughts and diary of a member of Wilson's "brain trust," in which the Calvinistic Wilson is said to have been rather severe toward Germany.

UNITED STATES SENATE. *Hearings before the Special Committee Investigating the Munitions Industry . . . . Pursuant to S. Res. 206. . . . .* 73d Cong., Parts I–XXXV. Washington, 1934–37.

Parts XXV–XXXV, which should be examined with discretion, throw a flood of light on the manner of our involvement in the World War.

II. SECONDARY AUTHORITIES

ADAMS, EPHRAIM D. *British Interests and Activities in Texas.* Baltimore, 1910.

———. *Great Britain and the American Civil War.* 2 vols. London and New York, 1925.

———. *The Power of Ideals in American History.* New Haven, 1913.

Valuable works of a competent and conservative scholar. The first two throw light on the attempts of England to prevent the annexation of Texas and on the British attitude during a grave crisis in American domestic affairs. The author is very friendly toward the mother-country, and the first volume should be read in connection with the works of Justin H. Smith described below. The third of Adams' works here listed is especially useful because of the chapters on manifest destiny and nationalism.

The American Secretaries of State and Their Diplomacy. 10 vols. New York, 1927–29.

This large reference work on the foreign relations of the United States, edited by Samuel F. Bemis, suffers from a number of minor defects but is

CRITICAL BIBLIOGRAPHY

nevertheless invaluable. It contains contributions from some of the best scholars in the United States.

ANDERSON, EUGENE NEWTON. *The First Moroccan Crisis.* Chicago, 1930.

Probably the most satisfactory discussion of the subject. Professor Anderson gives some attention to Roosevelt's part in the affair. See Hale's contribution described below.

ARNETT, ALEX M. *Claude Kitchin and the Wilson War Policies.* Boston, 1937.

An illuminating discussion of an attractive statesman who opposed the entrance of the United States into the World War.

BAKER, RAY STANNARD. *Woodrow Wilson: Life and Letters.* 6 vols. Garden City, 1927–37.

A great work by one of America's ablest journalists and the authorized biographer of the founder of the League of Nations; based on primary sources and written with sympathy, but virtually without prejudice. The role of Colonel House in international affairs diminishes with the appearance of each volume after the fourth. Two or three more are yet to be published. Perhaps nothing better of its kind has ever been written in the United States.

―――. *Woodrow Wilson and World Settlement.* 3 vols. New York, 1922.

Much inferior to the masterly work described above, these volumes must be read with caution. Nevertheless they are one of the best publications on the subject.

BAXTER, JAMES P., III. "The British Government and Neutral Rights," *American Historical Review,* XXXIV (1928), 9–29.

―――. "Some British Opinions as to Neutral Rights," *American Journal of International Law,* XXIII (1929), 517–37.

Two articles on the period of the Civil War in the United States written by a scholar with a first-class mind.

BEARD, CHARLES A. *The Idea of National Interest: An Analytical Study of American Foreign Policy.* New York, 1934.

―――. *The Open Door at Home.* New York, 1935.

Two very stimulating books by one of America's foremost thinkers; most helpful in the preparation of this work.

BEMIS, SAMUEL F. *Pinckney's Treaty: A Study of America's Advantage from Europe's Distress.* Baltimore, 1926.

A most suggestive work by an outstanding specialist in the relations of the United States and Europe.

AMERICA AND THE STRIFE OF EUROPE

BISHOP, JOSEPH BUCKLIN. *Theodore Roosevelt and His Time Shown in His Own Letters.* 2 vols. New York, 1920.

An enthusiastic biographer who assumed that Roosevelt was as mighty as the Rough Rider thought he was; useful, however, in spite of this.

BORCHARD, EDWIN, and LAGE, WILLIAM POTTER. *Neutrality for the United States.* New Haven, 1937.

A forceful presentation of a definite point of view. The authors believe that the United States could and should have kept out of the last great war, and that it should undertake to enforce its rights as a neutral in the next one.

BRANDENBURG, ERICH. *From Bismarck to the World War: A History of German Foreign Policy.* Trans. ANNE E. ADAMS. London, 1927.

A thorough work on the subject, with paragraphs on the relations of the United States and Germany during the period.

CLARK, J. REUBEN. *Memorandum on the Monroe Doctrine.* Washington, 1930.

This monograph published by a lawyer in the diplomatic service is valuable for its presentation of more than fifty violations, or alleged or apprehended violations, of the Monroe Doctrine. No attempt is made to ascertain the facts, but a disposition is shown to renounce the Roosevelt Corollary.

CLINE, MYRTLE A. *American Attitude toward the Greek War of Independence, 1821–1828.* Atlanta, 1930.

A work illustrating how democratic fervor added to a devotion to the classics tended to cause the United States to depart from the sacred maxim of isolation.

COX, ISAAC JOSLIN. *The West Florida Controversy, 1798–1813.* Baltimore, 1918.

The standard work on the subject, heavy but sound.

CURTI, MERLE. *The American Peace Crusade, 1815–1862.* Durham, 1929.

———. *Austria and the United States, 1848–1852.* ("Smith College Studies in History," Vol. XI, No. 3.) Northampton, 1926.

———. *Bryan and World Peace* (*ibid.*, Vol. XVI, Nos. 3–4). Northampton, 1931.

———. "George N. Sanders—American Patriot of the Fifties," *South Atlantic Quarterly*, XXVI (1928), 79–87.

———. *Peace or War: The American Struggle, 1636–1936.* New York, 1936.

CRITICAL BIBLIOGRAPHY

———. " 'Young America,' " *American Historical Review*, XXXII (1926), 34–55.

Nothing has been more illuminating in the investigation of the subject of the United States and the strife of Europe than the writings of Curti. His style is good and he knows the meaning of his facts. These works of his demonstrate the emotional conflict between isolationism on the one hand, and democratic and pacifist zeal on the other. My chapter on "Bryan and the Peace of Europe" is based largely on Curti's study of the Peerless Leader

CURTIS, EUGENE N. "American Opinion of French Nineteenth-Century Revolutions," *American Historical Review*, XXIX (1924), 249–70.

Further illustration of the conflict between isolationism and democratic enthusiasm.

DENNETT, TYLER. *Roosevelt and the Russo-Japanese War*. Garden City, 1925.

A book to be read with caution and in the light of subsequent publications of diplomatic documents, but the best work on the subject.

———. *John Hay*. New York, 1933.

A judicious and competent biography of an influential diplomat. Hay was ambassador to England during the Spanish-American War and secretary of state under Theodore Roosevelt.

DENNIS, ALFRED L. P. *Adventures in American Diplomacy, 1896–1906*. New York, 1928.

A most useful and valuable work, but this volume must be read with the understanding that its author is pro-English and decidedly anti-German. As yet there is nothing better for the period.

DULLES, FOSTER RHEA. *America in the Pacific*. Boston and New York, 1932.

For present purposes this book is helpful because it traces the development of American interest in the Far West and the Pacific Area.

ETTINGER, AMOS A. *The Mission to Spain of Pierre Soulé, 1853–1855*. New Haven, 1932.

Important for its revelation of the desire of certain American leaders for the annexation of Cuba and of the extent to which they were willing to go in order to achieve their objective. Multiple archival research has greatly improved the volume. The efforts of England and France to preserve Cuba for Spain are fully revealed.

AMERICA AND THE STRIFE OF EUROPE

FARRAR, VICTOR J. *The Annexation of Russian America to the United States.* Washington, 1937.

A sound and cautious monograph evaluating the motives for the sale and the purchase of Alaska.

FERRARA, ORESTES. *Tentativas de intervención europea en América, 1896–1898.* Havana, 1933.

———. *The Last Spanish War.* Trans. WILLIAM E. SHEA. New York, 1937.

These are two editions of the same excellent work, the best thing in print on the subject, written by a brilliant Italo-Cuban. Much of my eighth chapter is based on this small volume.

GAZLEY, JOHN G. *American Opinion of German Unification, 1848–1871.* ("Columbia University Studies in History, Economics and Public Law," Vol. CXXI.) New York, 1926.

More evidence of democratic sympathies in the United States, but sympathies modified and deflected by other currents of sentiment. This monumental survey of the press throws light on American attitude toward popular movements in France and Hungary as well as in the Germanies.

GRATTAN, C. HARTLEY. *Why We Fought.* New York, 1929.

One of the first impressive evidences in the United States of a revisionist view with reference to American entrance into the war against Germany; but economic factors are probably overemphasized.

GRIFFIN, CHARLES CARROLL. *The United States and the Disruption of the Spanish Empire.* New York, 1937.

Deals with the period from 1810 to 1822, illuminating some obscure phases of the subject and showing how democratic fervor clashed with isolationism supported by considerations of economic, territorial, and strategic self-interest.

HALE, ORON JAMES. *Germany and the Diplomatic Revolution: A Study in Diplomacy and the Press, 1904–1906.* Philadelphia, 1931.

Supplements Anderson's work listed above, adding some information on the relations between Roosevelt and Wilhelm II in respect to the Russo-Japanese War and the first Moroccan Crisis.

HAZEN, CHARLES DOWNER. *Contemporary American Opinion of the French Revolution.* Baltimore, 1897.

This is an examination by a competent scholar of the attitude of Americans at home and their diplomats abroad. On the whole, sympathies were decidedly with the French revolutionaries, although their extravagances caused an unfavorable reaction after 1792.

HENDERSON, GAVIN G. "The Diplomatic Revolution of 1854," *American Historical Review*, XLIII (1937), 22–50.

——. "The Pacifists of the Fifties," *Journal of Modern History*, IX (1937), 314–41.

Two articles describing the peace sentiment in England and the manner in which the Crimean War tended to unsettle the old balance of power in Europe. The second should be examined along with Curti's *American Peace Crusade* listed above.

HENDRICK, BURTON J. *The Life of Andrew Carnegie.* 2 vols. New York, 1932.

——. *Miscellaneous Writings of Andrew Carnegie.* 2 vols. New York, 1933.

The biography and writings of an Anglophile industrialist and pacifist prepared by a noted American journalist. Carnegie was a well-meaning amateur in world-politics, the man who furnished the sinews of the later peace movement in the United States.

——. *The Life and Letters of Walter Hines Page.* 3 vols. Garden City, 1922–25.

The ambassador to England who paralyzed Wilson's efforts to assert the maritime rights of the United States against Great Britain, Page was another amateur with the noblest impulses. This is a good biography.

HIBBEN, PAXTON. *The Peerless Leader: William Jennings Bryan.* New York, 1929.

Probably the best biography of the great Commoner, the section on his diplomacy being written by C. Hartley Grattan, with too little emphasis on Bryan's pacifism. This phase of his career is better treated by Curti.

HILL, HOWARD C. *Roosevelt and the Caribbean.* Chicago, 1928.

Although a good dissertation, this work is by no means the last word on Roosevelt's Caribbean policy.

HOWE, GEORGE F. "The Clayton-Bulwer Treaty," *American Historical Review*, XLII (1937), 484–90.

Describes the restiveness of the United States under a treaty which tended to prevent its domination of the canal zones, the agreement of 1850 with England.

AMERICA AND THE STRIFE OF EUROPE

KEIM, JEANETTE. *Forty Years of German-American Political Relations*. Philadelphia, 1919.

A good preliminary study of growing friction between the United States and Germany. Written before the publication of the war documents by the governments of the great powers, the monograph is now out of date in several respects.

LALLY, FRANK EDWARD. *French Opposition to the Mexican Policy of the Second Empire*. ("Johns Hopkins University Studies in Historical and Political Science," Ser. XLIX, No. 3.) Baltimore, 1931.

Dr. Lally contends that domestic opposition had nothing to do with Louis Napoleon's withdrawal from his Mexican enterprise; partisan opposition was virtually silenced after 1864.

LUTHIN, REINHARD H. "St. Bartholomew: Sweden's Colonial and Diplomatic Venture in the Caribbean," *Hispanic American Historical Review*, XIV (1934), 307–24.

Deals with a little-known violation of the Monroe Doctrine broadly interpreted. This small Caribbean island was transferred to France in 1877.

MCCAIN, WILLIAM D. *The United States and the Republic of Panama*. Durham, 1937.

This volume is a detailed account of the relations of the United States with one of its protectorates—a thorough monograph by an able young scholar.

MARRARO, HOWARD R. *American Opinion on the Unification of Italy, 1846–1861*. New York, 1932.

This work deals with impulses to go crusading, impulses arising from economic interest and popular sympathies for the oppressed, but held in check by clashing sentiments; an illuminating study.

MILLIS, WALTER. *The Martial Spirit*. Boston and New York, 1931.

A helpful discussion of the causes of the Spanish-American War, with perhaps a little too much emphasis on the martial spirit.

———. *Road to War: America, 1914–1917*. Boston and New York, 1935.

Again the author probably lays undue stress on economic forces and war propaganda. Both of his works, however, have decided merit.

MOREL, E. D. *Morocco in Diplomacy*. London, 1912.

A rather popular study valuable for present purposes chiefly because it contains on pages 252–302 an English version of the agreement reached at Algeçiras on April 7, 1906.

CRITICAL BIBLIOGRAPHY

Munro, Dana G. *The United States and the Caribbean Area.* Boston, 1934.

A fairly satisfactory general account, rather patriotic, based upon published sources only.

Nevins, Allen. *Henry White: Thirty Years of American Diplomacy.* New York, 1930.

This biography of a minor American diplomat is helpful but not in all respects thorough. Like Hay and Page, White was an Anglophile. The highest points of his career were his participation in the conferences of Algeçiras and Versailles. Nevins accepts Roosevelt's exalted conceptions of his influence in world-politics.

Nicolson, Harold. *Portrait of a Diplomatist.* New York, 1930.

A biographical sketch of Sir Arthur Nicolson, the most influential British representative of Algeçiras—the man who dominated the conference.

Normano, J. F. *The Struggle for South America.* Boston and New York, 1931.

This very suggestive survey deals mainly with the recent period and considers ideology as well as economic forces.

Notter, Harley. *The Origins of the Foreign Policy of Woodrow Wilson.* Baltimore, 1937.

A significant contribution to the ideology of Wilson in relation to the place of the United States in world-affairs. World-leadership for constitutional democracy, social justice, and peace was his central concept, and this concept was born shortly after 1900. He was an ardent and often militant crusader; he "loved a good fight."

Owsley, Frank L. *King Cotton Diplomacy.* Chicago, 1931.

Based upon an amazing amount of research and written in a somewhat uneven style, this large volume has been too much disparaged by the critics. It is by far the best work on the foreign relations of the Confederate States of America, and it is not likely to be superseded in this generation.

Parish, John C. *The Emergence of the Idea of Manifest Destiny.* Los Angeles, 1932.

This small pamphlet is a valuable contribution to the genesis of the expansionist movement in the United States.

Parks, E. Taylor. *Colombia and Its Relations with the United States.* Durham, 1934.

Important for present purposes because it deals with the canal diplomacy of the United States and the influence of investments of American citizens upon foreign policy.

AMERICA AND THE STRIFE OF EUROPE

PERKINS, DEXTER. *The Monroe Doctrine, 1823–1826.* ("Harvard Historical Studies," Vol. XXIX.) Cambridge, 1927.

———. *The Monroe Doctrine, 1826–1867.* Baltimore, 1933.

———. *The Monroe Doctrine, 1867–1907.* Baltimore, 1937.

The author of these volumes is the outstanding authority on the subject which he treats. They are the result of industrious investigation in the archives of the great powers, perhaps with insufficient attention to the printed sources and secondary works in the United States and Latin America. His contributions have been of great service to the author of the study now offered to the public.

PRATT, JULIUS W. "The Collapse of American Imperialism," *American Mercury*, XXXIII (1934), 269 ff.

Suggestive as a contribution to a subject which needs further investigation.

———. *Expansionists of 1812.* New York, 1925.

———. *Expansionists of 1898.* Baltimore, 1937.

Two significant volumes by a penetrating scholar. The first affirms the influence of land hunger on the outbreak of the War of 1812; the second emphasizes the part played by politicians, publicists, and journalists in creating a new expansionist impulse in the American nation.

PRINGLE, HENRY F. *Theodore Roosevelt: A Biography.* New York, 1931.

The most satisfactory account of the life of this amazingly active personality.

RIPPY, J. FRED. "The Buenos Aires Peace Conference of 1936," *South Atlantic Quarterly*, XXXVI (1937), 171–79.

An attempt to view this conference in its larger setting.

———. "The Initiation of the Customs Receivership in the Dominican Republic," *Hispanic American Historical Review*, XVII (1937), 419–57.

A consideration of the motivating factors in Theodore Roosevelt's Caribbean policy.

———. *Latin America in World Politics.* 3d ed. New York, 1938.

The latest edition of the first effort to survey international rivalries with respect to the region during the period since 1808.

———. *Joel Roberts Poinsett.* Durham, 1935.

Portrait of an apostle of democracy and liberty whose zeal was not appreciated in some quarters of Latin America.

CRITICAL BIBLIOGRAPHY

———. *Rivalry of the United States and Great Britain over Latin America (1808–1830).* Baltimore, 1929.

A study of democracy versus monarchy, of the championship of freedom of the seas against British domination of them, and of the efforts of England to prevent the expansion of American power and influence; a work based upon research in the archives of Washington and London.

———. "The United States and the Establishment of the Republic of Brazil," *Southwestern Political Science Quarterly,* III (1922), 1–15.

Further revelation of sympathy for kindred political forms, this article examines the American attitude toward the overthrow of Dom Pedro II in 1889.

———. *The United States and Mexico.* 2d ed. New York, 1931.

European influences as well as idealizations and rationalizations of leaders in the United States are weighed. The *Congressional Globe* was carefully scanned by the author for expansionist apologies, as was likewise the *Record* of the Wilson period and after.

RIPPY, J. FRED, and DEBO, ANGIE. *The Historical Background of the American Policy of Isolation.* ("Smith College Studies in History," Vol. IX, Nos. 3–4.) Northampton, 1924.

The first effort to trace the genesis of this important policy. Chapter i of the volume now presented is based largely on this monograph which contains a Bibliography and ample citations to sources.

RYDEN, GEORGE HERBERT. *The Foreign Policy of the United States in Relation to Samoa.* New Haven, 1933.

A thorough treatment of an embarrassing international entanglement in the Pacific Area.

SCHIEBER, CLARA E. *The Transformation of American Sentiment toward Germany.* Boston and New York, 1923.

An account of the rise of the concept of the German menace in the United States.

SCROGGS, WILLIAM O. *Filibusters and Financiers: The Story of William Walker and His Associates.* New York, 1916.

The standard work on an extravagant phenomenon, with some attention to British counter-operations in Central America.

SEYMOUR, CHARLES. *American Diplomacy during the World War.* Baltimore, 1934.

AMERICA AND THE STRIFE OF EUROPE

SEYMOUR, CHARLES. *American Neutrality, 1914–1917.* New Haven, 1935.

Two volumes marshaling the evidence to show that the United States entered the war against Germany because of the submarine issue. Perhaps too little account is taken of economic and sentimental factors.

SMITH, JUSTIN H. *The Annexation of Texas.* 2d ed. New York, 1919.

———. *The War with Mexico.* 2 vols. New York, 1919.

These works by an excellent writer and thorough scholar should be balanced by a careful reading of the small volume on the Texas question written by E. D. Adams.

SMITH, THEODORE CLARKE, "Expansion after the Civil War, 1865–1871," *Political Science Quarterly*, XVI (1901), 412–36.

An important article by a competent historian, this survey, while not complete, throws light upon the attempt to revive the expansion movement and the reasons for its failure.

STOLBERG-WERNIGERODE, OTTO. *Deutschland und die Vereinigten Staaten von Amerika im Zeitalter Bismarcks.* Berlin and Leipzig, 1933.

A scholarly treatment of the subject.

TANSILL, CHARLES C. *The Purchase of the Danish West Indies.* Baltimore, 1932.

This sound study contains information on the alleged German menace in the Caribbean. Interest in the Danish West Indies was aroused in the United States for years mainly because of apprehensions on this score.

———. *America Goes to War.* Boston, 1938.

An able examination of the factors causing the entrance of the United States into the World War. The best work on the subject.

TARDIEU, ANDRÉ. *La Conférence d'Algéçiras.* Paris, 1909.

So far as France is concerned, little that is new, relative to the Conference, has been discovered since this able journalist and diplomat published his book.

TATUM, EDWARD HOWLAND. *The United States and Europe, 1815–1823: A Study in the Background of the Monroe Doctrine.* Berkeley, 1936.

Further examination of a much discussed subject by a keen student and an uncommonly able writer. Tatum discovers from printed contemporary sources that the Monroe Doctrine was directed mainly against England—perhaps he would say *exclusively* against England, but it is doubtful whether so emphatic an affirmation would be justified. His work should be read along with

CRITICAL BIBLIOGRAPHY

those of Dexter Perkins: the one completely neglects the archives; the other perhaps is disposed to undervalue the printed works.

THOMAS, BENJAMIN PRATT. *Russo-American Relations, 1815–1867.* ("Johns Hopkins University Studies in Historical and Political Science," Ser. XLVIII, No. 2.) Baltimore, 1930.

A satisfactory survey fortified by citations to sources and by a valuable Bibliography; Russian friendship for the United States is evident, and the reasons therefor.

VAGTS, ALFRED. *Deutschland und die Vereinigten Staaten in der Weltpolitik, 1890–1906.* New York, 1935.

This large and masterly work deserves to be translated into English; few American students will have the fortitude to examine it as thoroughly as they should. It supplements the volume by Stolberg listed above, and the two have exhibited the best in recent German scholarship.

VAN ALSTYNE, RICHARD W. "Anglo-American Relations, 1853–1857," *American Historical Review*, XLII (1937), 491–500.

―――. "The Central American Policy of Lord Palmerston," *Hispanic American Historical Review*, XVI (1936), 339–59.

Two suggestive items on the rivalry of the United States and England in Central America. The one dealing with the later period, 1853–57, consists mainly of documents hitherto unpublished. The author concludes that Britain did not recede before the United States between the summer of 1856 and the end of 1859—perhaps an erroneous conclusion reached through failure to take into consideration the terms of the Dallas-Clarendon Treaty of October, 1856.

―――. "Great Britain, the United States, and Hawaiian Independence, 1853–1855," *Pacific Historical Review*, IV (1935), 15–24.

English opposition to the annexation of the islands by the United States; a discussion based on British sources. It would have been improved by an investigation of the French archives, for France was also participating in the effort to prevent the annexation. The Historical Commission of the Territory of Hawaii has published documents on the affair (see its *Report*, Vol. I).

WEINBERG, ALBERT K. *Manifest Destiny: A Study of Nationalist Expansionism in American History.* Baltimore, 1935.

This thorough and intelligent analysis of a subject in which the writer of this Bibliography has been deeply interested for twenty years contains nearly all the quotations employed to illustrate the ideology of expansion in chapters iv and v of the work now being completed. The present author is greatly indebted to Dr. Weinberg.

WHITAKER, ARTHUR P. *The Mississippi Question, 1795–1803*. New York and London, 1934.

———. *The Spanish-American Frontier, 1783–1795*. Boston and New York, 1929.

Definitive works on the topics treated, these volumes reveal the pressure of American frontiersmen on the Spanish borderlands. This pressure and the strife of Europe were the main factors in their acquisition by the United States.

WILKERSON, MARCUS W. *Public Opinion and the Spanish-American War*. Baton Rouge, 1932.

An examination of the war propaganda of 1895–98 in the United States based upon a wide selection of sources.

WILLIAMS, MARY W. *Anglo-American Isthmian Diplomacy*. New York, 1915.

The standard narrative on the subject, rather unattractively presented, but sound. Van Alstyne and Rippy have brought to light new information on the period prior to 1860.

WISAN, JOSEPH E. *The Cuban Crisis as Reflected in the New York Press (1895–1898)*. New York, 1934.

Deals ably with "Yellow Journalism" at its worst: Pulitzer and Hearst in full swing—rival journalists trying to increase their subscriptions and the value of their advertising columns! The public still likes exciting news, but it may be that the day has passed when the American people can lightly be swept into international conflict by the newspapers. War is not the romantic thing it used to be. Yet the power of the radio may prove to be greater than that of the press.

INDEX

INDEX

Abbott, Lyman, and the new imperialism, 89

Aberdeen, Lord, British diplomat, quoted, 116

Adams, Brooks, quoted by expansionists, 86

Adams, Charles Francis, and Filipino independence, 89

Adams, John: favors commercial treaty with France, 3 f.; laments commercial impulses of Americans, 7; quoted on isolationism, 10–14; wages informal war with France, 21; inaugural message as president quoted, 27; opposes early American peace movement, 44–45; predicts transfer of political seat of power to America, 58

Adams, John Quincy: presidential inaugural message quoted, 30–31; criticizes pacifists, 45; declines alliance with Russia, 45–46; envisages continental destiny of the United States, 107–8; views of, on Monroe's message of 1823, 125

Adams, Samuel, favors isolation, 18

Addams, Jane, 195

Addington, H. W., British diplomat, quoted, 116

Aguinaldo, Emilio, Filipino chief, 88, 161

Alaska, 56, 77, 108

Alexander, Tsar of Russia, 43–44, 50, 125

Algeçiras Conference, 178, 180–82

Alliance: entangling, 15, 160; the French of 1778, 5–7, 9, 11–12, 20; offers of to the United States, 19–21, 45–46, 157–58. *See also* Holy Alliance, Triple Alliance, Triple Entente

America, 4, 6, 7, 11, 12, 24, 30, 41, 45, 53, 60, 71, 99, 139; arbiter of European destiny in New World, 17; Little Corsican and, 23; destiny of European possessions in, 24, 72, 130; Europe's strife enables United States to have its way in, 54; a young giant; 75; United States a friend of constitutional government in, 78; regulation of European conduct in, 122–37. *See also* United States

American Peace Society, founded, 42–43

Appalachians, the, 59, 103

Area of freedom, extension of, as expansionist argument, 65, 70–73, 92–93

Asia, 93, 156, 173, 174, 177. *See also* Far East, China, Japan

Asiatic Monroe Doctrine, 177

Austria, 12, 43, 47, 132. *See also* Hungarian Republic

Austria-Hungary, and Spanish American War, 140, 147, 149–152; assassination of prince of, followed by World War, 193

Balfour, Arthur, 152

Bartholdt, Representative Richard, explains expansionist urge, 86

Bay Islands, 112
Baylies, Francis, congressman, quoted on expansion, 66–67
Beckwith, George C., pacifist, 43
Belize (British Honduras), 112, 118
Belknap, Admiral Jeremy, quoted on Hawaii, 78
Bell, John, desires annexation of Canada, 74
Belser, Representative James E., considers United States an asylum for the oppressed, 73
Bemis, Samuel F., 86
Benton, Thomas Hart, quoted on Texas, 74
Berlin-Congo Conference, 49, 51
Beveridge, Senator Albert, expansionist, quoted, 79, 84, 86, 91–92
Bishop, Joseph Bucklin, quoted on Roosevelt, 178
Blaine, James G., 24
Boston Herald, quoted, 79
Brazil, liberal uprising in, 24, 39, 139
Briand, Aristide, 53
Briand-Kellogg Pact, 53, 215–16, 230
British: possessions in the West Indies, 5 f.; resistance to United States expansion, 75, 107–17; resistance relaxed, 118; statesmen and journalists denounce United States aggression, 113–16; friendly during Spanish-American War, 152–53. *See also* England, Great Britain
Bryan, William Jennings, 25, 146; and peace of Europe, 186 f.; and League of Nations, 186, 198; and Spanish-American War, 188–89; visits Tolstoy, 190; visits conference in London, 191–92; secretary of state, 193–97; resigns, 195, 197; declines to join Ford's peace expedition, 195–96; views and policy on neutrality, 197, 221–22, 225–26, 228; enters contest for Bok prize, 198; death, 199; contrasted with Theodore Roosevelt, 199–200
Bryant, William Cullen, quoted, 73
Buchanan, James, 117
Bülow, Bernard von, German acting secretary of foreign affairs, and Spanish-American War, 149, 153, 155
Buenos Aires Peace Conference, 36, 223, 230
Bulwer, Sir Henry, quoted, 115
Burgess, Professor John W., 80, 87
Burritt, Elihu, pacifist, 41, 42, 43
Butler, Benjamin F., quoted, 70

Cambon, Jules, French ambassador, 170
Canada: desire in United States for annexation of, 5, 63, 66, 71, 74, 81; British check United States advance upon, 71, 110
Canaries, the, 159
Cannon, Senator Joseph ("Uncle Joe"), quoted on Philippines, 92
Caribbean, the, policy of United States in reference to. *See* Gulf-Caribbean area
Carnegie, Andrew: Mckinley writes to, 90; writes Roosevelt, 171; Bryan and, 195
Carolines. *See* South Sea Islands
Cass, Lewis, quoted on expansion, 64, 68
Central America: recent control of United States in, 93, 163–66;

INDEX

rivalry of the United States and Great Britain in, 111–17

Chandler, Senator Joseph R., quoted on Hawaii, 79

Channing, William Ellery, favors early peace movement, 44

China, 21, 79, 92, 140, 162, 174, 175. *See also* Far East

Civil War, the American, 24, 49, 64, 118, 128, 133

Clarendon, Lord, British diplomat, 113, 115, 116, 117

Clark, Champ, 87; describes nature of expansionist urge, 84–85

Clark, J. Reuben, *Memorandum* on Monroe Doctrine, 129

Clayton-Bulwer Treaty, the, 75, 112, 114

Cleveland, President Grover, Cuban policy of, 141, 142, 143, 145

Cochran, Representative Charles F., 93

Colombia, republic of, deprived of Panama, 96, 164

Commerce, international: of United States, and Europe's strife, 16–17, 20, 21, 29, 40, 54, 208 f., 228; and investments as cause of new imperialism, 77–78, 83, 84, 95; and World War, 208, 210, 211, 217, 226

Commercial: and investment opportunities in China, 78, 175; and maritime rivalry of the United States and Great Britain, 112, 119; aspect of the Monroe Doctrine, 123–25, 129; motives of Great Britain in supporting independence of Latin-American nations, 133; competition of the United States and Germany, 157, 161

Commoner, The, Bryan's newspaper, 193

Conant, Charles A., quoted, 93

Conferences. *See* Berlin-Congo, The Hague, Versailles

Constant, Baron de, 170–71

Costa Rica, 64, 166

Cox, Representative Samuel E., quoted on expansion, 68, 72

Crampton, John H., British minister to United States, quoted, 113–15

Crimean War, the, 47, 51, 109–10, 111, 113, 117

Cuba: United States' desire for annexation, 20, 64, 67, 72, 74, 141; revolts in, 40, 93, 138, 140, 143 f.; and Platt Amendment, 95, 163; protectorate of the United States, 96, 163, 166; protectorate abandoned, 99, 166; not seized during Crimean War, 110; England and France keep watch over, 110–11; and Spanish-American War, 138 f.; Spain fears loss of, 141 f

Curti, Merle, 186, 198

Cushing, Caleb, quoted on expansion, 68, 76

Dallas, George M., diplomat, 117

Dallas-Clarendon Treaty, 117

Danish West Indies (Virgin Islands), 96, 128, 163

Darwin, Charles, and United States expansion, 80

Davis, Reuben, quoted on expansion, 72

Declaration of Independence, quoted, 22–23

Delcassé, Théophile, French foreign minister, 181

De Leon, Edward, portrays America as young giant, 75

Democracy of New York, urges annexation of Mexico, 68

"Democratic Experiment in Peril," as dynamic concept in United States foreign policy, 22–40, 42, 53, 54, 211, 221, 230–32

Democratic fervor, in United States, 14–15, 22, 23–24, 27, 30–31, 33–34, 36, 38–40, 53, 57, 69–73, 92–93, 98, 211, 221, 230–32

Denby, Charles, quoted on expansion, 83

Depew, Chauncey, describes the new imperialism, 85

Determinism, economic, and United States expansion, 78, 82

Diederichs, German admiral, at Manila Bay, 155

Divinely ordained use of the soil, as expansionist argument, 65, 67–69, 79–80

Dodge, David Low, pacifist, 42

Dominican Republic: desire in the United States for annexation, 67, 72; becomes protectorate of the United States, 96, 164; interference of England and France in, 110, 133

Douglas, Stephen A., quoted on United States' expansion, 75

Duke of Tetuán, Spanish minister of state, interview with Hannis Taylor, 143–47

Duncan, Representative Alexander, quoted on salutary influence of expansion, 7

England: and the American Revolution, 4 f.; politically occupies intermediate position between America and Europe, 15; early peace movement in, 43, 45, 47, 48; and United States Civil War, 118–19, 133–34; and independence of Hispanic America, 132–33; and Venezuela, 134; urges United States to remain in Philippines, 159, 161; and South African War, 162. *See also* British, Great Britain

Enthusiasms, of 1898 and after, in United States, 77–99. *See also* "Democratic Experiment in Peril," Democratic fervor, Pacifism

European concert, effort to effect against the United States, 54, 109, 110–11, 140–52

European powers: and American expansion, 54, 103–21, 138–66; and Monroe Doctrine, 123–37

Everett, Edward, quoted on expansion, 75–76

Expansion: of the United States, 24–25; arguments for, 55–99; curbed by Civil War, 64, 77; first phase of, 103–21; second phase of, 138–66. *See also* Motivation

Falkland Islands, seized by Great Britain, 130

Far East (Orient), 78, 79, 153, 156. *See also* Asia, China, Japan

Fascist and Nazi dictators, 25, 136–37, 230–32

Fernando Po, 159

Filipinos: revolt of, 88, 91; question of government for, 89–92. *See also* Philippine Islands

Floridas, the: attempts to acquire, 38, 63; designed by Nature as a part of the United States, 66; annexed, 107

Foraker, Senator Joseph, quoted on Philippine question, 91

Ford, Henry, peace expedition, 195–96

INDEX

France: and the American Revolution, 4 f.; liberal uprisings in, 24; and United States expansion, 109, 110–11, 113; and the Monroe Doctrine, 132, 133–34; attitude during Spanish-American War, 139 f. *See also* French Alliance, French Revolution, Moroccan Crisis, Napoleon, Russo-Japanese War, World War

Francis Joseph, emperor of Austria-Hungary, 149

Franklin, Benjamin, 11, 12; predicts grand future for Anglo-Americans, 58–59; interested in Western lands, 58

French Alliance (1778), 5–7, 9, 11–12, 20

French Revolution, and the United States, 8, 23, 38

Freneau, Philip, poet, vision of greater America, 59

Friend of Peace, pacifist journal, 44, 46

Gadsden Purchase, the, 110

Geographical predestination, as expansionist argument, 65–67, 78–79

Gerard, James W., Ambassador to Germany, 208

German menace, the, 25, 37, 161–63

Germany: and the Philippines, 89, 153 f.; ambitions in America exaggerated, 135, 163; and Venezuela, 135; and the Spanish-American War, 149 f.; proposes alliance with the United States, 157–58. *See also* Kaiser Wilhelm II, Moroccan Crisis, Russo-Japanese War, World War

Gibson, Representative Henry R., quoted on expansion, 80, 85, 90

Graham, first lord of the British Admiralty, quoted, 115

Grant, Ulysses S., 24

Great Britain: considered antagonist of United States democracy, 71; and Venezuela, 96, 134, 135, 139; ceases to be viewed as antagonist, 119; seeks *rapprochement* with United States, 134; and Spanish-American War, 142 f.; aloofness during Russo-Japanese War, 176. *See also* British, England, Moroccan Crisis, World War

Greek Revolt, and sympathies in the United States, 39–40

Grey, Sir Edward, British foreign secretary, 204, 205, 207, 209, 210

Guam. *See* South Sea Islands

Guizot, French prime minister, 120

Gulf-Caribbean area: control of the United States in, 93, 95–97, 163–66; strategic importance, 126–29

Hague, The, peace conferences at, 50–52, 171–72

Hague Court (Permanent Court of Arbitration), 52, 170–71, 172, 184, 191, 193

Haiti, 133, 135, 163; Napoleon I, and, 106; Woodrow Wilson and, 164

Hamilton, Alexander: quoted on isolation, 17–18; forecasts Monroe Doctrine, 18, 123

Hanotaux, Gabriel, French diplomat, 148, 150

Harper, John A., congressman, quoted, 67

Harrison, William Henry, 39

257

Hatzfeldt, Paul, German, ambassador in London, 156, 159, 161

Hawaiian Islands: sentiment for annexation of, 67, 78–79; Americans seize government of, 84; annexation resolution signed, 157

Hay, John: favors expansion, 83–84; minister to London, 152, 156, 158, 159; hostile to Germany, 161–62; secretary of state, 161, 171, 175, 179

Hay-Pauncefote Treaty, 128

Hayes, Rutherford B., 24

Hearst, William Randolph, and Spanish-American War, 78, 87, 188

Henry, Representative Charles L., quoted on Hawaii, 79

Hoar, Senator George F., rebukes Beveridge, 95

Hobson, J. A., quoted on motivation in history, 84

Holcombe, Rev. Henry, pacifist, 42

Holleben, Ambassador T. von, 155–56, 162

Holy Alliance, the, 23, 47, 43–44, 123, 142

Honduras, British, *See* Belize

Hoover, Herbert, 166

House, Colonel Edward M., 25, 222, 229; peace negotiations, 202 f.

Hugo, Victor, quoted, 82–83

Hull, Cordell: warns against disregard of treaties, 136; quoted, 231–32

Hungarian Republic, 40, 41

Imlay, Gilbert, geographer, predicts vast expansion of the United States, 60

"Inevitable Destiny," as argument for expansion, 81–87

Interparliamentary Union, 171, 191

Investments, influence of United States abroad, 77–78, 83, 84, 95

Ireland, Archbishop, 151

Isolation: sentiment of, in United States, 3–21; maxim, 15, 22, 30, 50, 232; clashes with democratic enthusiasm, 35–40; conflicts with militant pacifism, 50–54; smothered by expansionism, 54, 77

Isolationism: motives for summarized, 15–18; temptations to depart from maxim summarized, 20–21; as justification for expansion, 63–65; as argument against expansion, 77

Isolationists, plight of, 20–21, 54, 217–32

Italy: and Venezuela, 135; and Spanish-American War, 151; and Morocco, 181; Woodrow Wilson visits, 213

Jackson, President Andrew: and nullification movement; 31–32; victory at New Orleans, 107

Japan: autocratic and militant, 25; and Philippines, 89; Monroe Doctrine applies to, 126. *See also* Russo-Japanese War

Jay, John, peace commissioner, 12

Jefferson, Thomas: laments commercial impulses of Americans, 7; views of state of Europe, 14–15; isolationist, 14–15, 16, 17; and the no-transfer principle, 17, 127; presidential inaugural quoted, 27–28; early interest in West, 59; predicts expansion,

INDEX

59; foresees absorption of Spanish borderlands, 61; and Monroe Doctrine, 123

Jusserand, Jules, French ambassador, 179, 182

Kaiser, *See* Wilhelm II
Kansas, struggle over, and expansion, 110
Kellogg, Frank B., 53, 199, 215
Keneko, Viscount Kentaro, 177
Kidd, Benjamin, works mentioned, 80
King, Rufus, 13, 62
Kipling, Rudyard, and American expansion, 88 f.
Kitchin, Claude, opposes United States entrance into World War, 217–19, 226, 232
Knox, Philander C., his Caribbean policy, 97
Kossuth, Louis, Hungarian patriot, 40, 41

Ladd, William, 42
Lafayette, Marquis de, 16, 32
LaFolette, Robert M., opposes United States' entrance into World War, 219
Lansing, Robert, Secretary of State, 222, 229
Latham, Representative Milton S., quoted, 70, 74
Latin America (Hispanic America), 20, 92, 98, 136, 227; Wilson's policy toward, 98–99, 164–65; Franklin Roosevelt's policy toward, 99, 166; Theodore Roosevelt's, 163–64. *See also* Spanish America
Latin-American states (Latin Americans), 97, 131, 135, 223, 227

Law of natural growth, justification for expansion, 65, 75–76, 80–81

League to Enforce Peace, the, 185, 197

League of Nations: United States and its potential activities in the New World, 135–36; Theodore Roosevelt and, 184–85; Bryan and, 186, 198; Wilson and, 193, 214

Lee, Richard Henry: view of Europe, 15; quoted, 60–61
Leibach, reactionary communication from, 45
Lincoln, Abraham: quoted, 24, 34–35; a symbol of democratic ideal, 35
Livingston, Edward, quoted on Louisiana, 63
Lloyd George, David, 196
Lodge, Senator Henry Cabot: quoted on expansion, 79–80, 95; and Filipino incapacity for self-government, 92; hostile to German Kaiser, 162
London Standard, 142
Louisiana: acquired by the United States, 63, 106; England and, 106–7
Love, Alfred, pacifist, 52
"Lusitania," British vessel, 197, 206, 208

McKinley, President William, 50; quoted on expansion, 83; 86–87; and Philippines, 84, 88, 89, 91; Cuban policy of, 148 f., 188
Madison, James: isolationist, 19; involved in war with England, 29; quoted, 74
Mahan, Captain Alfred T., expansionist, 80, 81, 89

Manifest Destiny, 57, 221; O'Sullivan and, 69
Manila Bay: seized, 153; Admiral Diederichs at, 155
Mann, A. Dudley, mission to Hungary, 41–42
María Cristina, Spanish Queen Regent, 139, 149, 150, 151
Mariannes. *See* South Sea Islands
Mason, George, isolationist, 18–19
Metternich, Austrian reactionary, 45
Mexico: war with the United States, 47; treaty with United States, 48; desire for annexation in United States, 64, 66, 68, 69, 71, 74, 218; appeals to Europe for aid, 109; Gadsden Purchase from, 110; Louis Napoleon intervenes in, 119–20, 134
Midway Islands, 77
Mission of Regeneration, as justification for expansion, 65, 69–70
Mississippi River: boundary of United States fixed at (1783), 30, 59, 103, natural right to navigate, 62; United States citizens granted use of, 106
Mississippi Territory, official of, quoted, 63
Monroe, James: isolationist, 19; presidential inaugural quoted, 29; on acquisition of Louisiana, 63
Monroe Doctrine, 29–30, 63; Theodore Roosevelt Corollary of, 96, 128, 129; defined, 122; doctrine of national security, 122, 126; not original, 123; original draft more vigorous, 124; J. Q. Adams and, 124–25; expanded, 126; applied most aggressively in the Caribbean, 126–29; violations and alleged violations, 129–30; reasons for infrequent violations, 131 f.
Morning Post (London), foresees, aggressiveness of United States, 61
Moroccan Crisis, 177–83, 202
Morgan, J. T., 146
Morse, Jedidiah, geographer, predicts grand destiny for United States, 59–60
Mosquitia, 112
Mosquito Indians, 112
Motivation: in history, 55–56; for territorial expansion in United States, 56 f.; for new imperialism, 77 f.

Napoleon I, 23; cedes Louisiana, 106
Napoleon, Louis: opposes United States' expansion, 119; Mexican venture of, 119–20, 134; overthrow of, 139
Natural boundaries, as apology for expansion, 66 f.
Natural rights, 22; as justification for expansion, 62; of inhabitants of Louisiana ignored, 62–63
Nelson, Senator Knute, and Filipino independence, 90–91
Neutral rights, 21, 29, 172, 220, 224
Neutrality legislation, recent, analyzed, 223–25
Newton, Sir Isaac, 75, 81
New World, 5, 58, 81. *See also* America
New York Herald, quoted, 64, 74–75
New York Journal of Commerce, quoted, 69
New York Peace Society, founded, 42
Nicaragua, 111, 112, 117, 164

INDEX

Nicaraguan canal route, 111, 112, 128, 164, 166

Nicholas II, Tsar of Russia, 50, 152

Nootka Sound Controversy, 8

North America, 3, 25, 34

Norton, Representative James A., 93

Olney, Richard: and Venezuela, 139; and Cuba, 140–41; secretary of state, 143, 148

Oregon, 31, 33, 71, 107

"Oscar II," Ford's peace ship, 196

O'Sullivan, John L., 69

Pacific Coast, 67, 108, 127

Pacific Ocean: as natural boundary, 60, 61, 67, 72, 79, 103; Theodore Roosevelt scans, 173

Pacifism, in the United States, 25, 41–53, 169, 171, 186, 221

Pacifists: early, in United States, 42–43; correspondence with Tsar Alexander, 44–45; disappointments, 47; achievements, 48–49; post-Civil War efforts, 49–53

Page, Walter Hines, ambassador, 222, 229

Paine, Thomas, quoted on isolation, 18

Palmerson, Lord, British statesman, 116, 117

Panama: secession of, 96, 164; protectorate of United States, 164–66

Panama Canal, 97, 166

Papal nuncio, at Madrid, peace efforts of, 151

Pauncefote, Sir Julian, ambassador, 128, 152

Peace, of Europe, the United States and, 169–232. *See also* Pacifism, Pacifists

Peace Conference, the Paris, 159–60. *See also* Hague

Peace movement, in the United States. *See* Pacifism.

Pedro II, Dom, emperor of Brazil, 39, 139

Pelew Islands. *See* South Sea Islands

Penn, William, quoted, 3–4

Pennsylvania Germans, isolationists, 3

Philadelphia Convention (1787), isolation sentiment in, 7–8

Philippine Islands: desire for in United States, 78 f.; and the Spanish-American War, 153 f. *See also* Filipinos

Pierce, President Franklin: quoted, 33–34; and Central American problem, 117

Pious Fund, the, 171

Platt, Senator Orville H., and Cuba, 95–96

Platt Amendment, curtails liberty of Cuba, 95, 163. *See also* Cuba

Poinsett, Joel Roberts, politician and diplomat, 32, 39

Political affinity, as justification for expansion, 65, 73–74, 81

Political gravitation, expansionist argument, 65, 74–75, 81

Polk, President James K., quoted, 33

Pope, the, efforts to prevent the Spanish-American War, 151

Powers, H. H., ardent expansionist, 80, 85–86

Prussia, 4, 49, 51, 132

Pulitzer, Joseph, and Spanish-American War, 78, 87, 188

Quakers, and the early peace movement in the United States, 42

Queen Regent, Spanish. *See* María Cristina

Queen Victoria. *See* Victoria

Reid, Whitelaw: quoted, 79, 80; Theodore Roosevelt's letter to, 178 f.

Revolts: in Spanish America, 39; in Europe, 40

Richthofen, Baron von, German diplomat, 158, 159

Río Grande: republics from to Cape Horn, 23; as natural boundary of United States, 66

"Roaring Forties," the, in United States, 23, 33

Rocky Mountains, 66

Roosevelt, Franklin D.: quoted, 36, 98–99, 230–31; and consultation with Europe, 53; his Latin-American policy, 99, 166, 227–28

Roosevelt, Theodore, 25; quoted on expansion, 84, 93–94; and the Kaiser, 162–63, 173 f.; his Latin-American policy vigorous, 163–164 and peace of Europe, 169 f.; and Hague Court, 170–71; and second Hague Peace Conference, 171–72; and Russo-Japanese War, 173–77; and Moroccan Crisis, 173, 177–83; and notion of American balance of power, 173–75, 183; and war with Germany, 183–84; and League of Nations, 184–85; receives Nobel Peace Prize, 185

Roosevelt Corollary of the Monroe Doctrine, 96, 128–29

Root, Elihu, 163 n.

Rouvier, Maurice, French foreign minister, 181

Russell, Lord John, British diplomat and statesman, 116

Russia: friendship for United States, 107, 108, 132, 133, 177; recedes from Far Northwest, 108; war with Japan, 173, 174–77; and Spanish-American War, 148–58; an ally of France and England, 181, 204

Russo-Japanese War, 173, 174–77

St. Bartholomew, island, transferred to France, 130

St. Louis Globe-Democrat, and political gravitation, 81

Salisbury, Lord, head of British foreign office, 151, 159

Samoan Islands, 78, 157; partitioned, 160

Samoans, 92

Sanctions, battle of the, in United States Congress, 53, 220, 223, 228, 230

Scudder, Representative Townsend, quoted on Cuba, 96

Self-defense, as justification for expansion, 62, 63–65, 81

Seward, William H., 24; quoted on expansion, 67, 72

Slavery issue, and expansion in United States, 56, 76, 111

Smith, Gerrit, quoted on Mexico, 70

South America, 72, 125, 137, 162. *See also* Spanish America, Latin America

South Sea Islands, negotiations regarding, 159 f.

Spain: and the Anglo-American revolution, 4 f.; invaded by French, 46; cedes borderlands to United States, 61, 106; fails to secure aid against colonies,

INDEX

132; seeks coalition against the United States, 141 f.

Spanish America, 38, 70, 107, 132. *See also* Latin America

Speck von Sternberg, German ambassador, 178, 179, 181, 182

Spring Rice, Cecil, British diplomat, 174; quoted, 193–94

Stimson, Henry L., secretary of state: his non-recognition doctrine, 53; quoted on Briand-Kellogg Pact, 215–16

Straus, Oscar, 194

Strife of Europe, 96; influence of on the American policy of the United States, 3 f., 103–66; and expansion of United States, 103–30, 138 f.; and enforcement of the Monroe Doctrine, 131–37

Taft, William Howard, 97, 179; continues Roosevelt's Caribbean policy, 164; at Tokio, 177; and League to Enforce Peace, 197

Taylor, Hannis, minister to Spain, diplomacy of, 142–48

Texas: desire for annexation in United States, 33, 71, 74, 107; Great Britain and, 109

Thoburn, Bishop James M., quoted, 83

Tillman, Senator Ben, opposes expansion, 94

Tirpitz, Grand Admiral von, 203

Tolstoy, Count Leo, Bryan and, 187, 190

Treaties of Versailles, 212–14

Treaty of 1783, 7, 12, 103

Treaty of 1848, arbitration clause in, 47–48

Trimble, Congressman William, quoted on two spheres, 123–24

Triple Alliance, 139, 209

Triple Entente, 139, 197, 207, 209

Trueblood, Benjamin, pacifist, 52

Tsar Alexander. *See* Alexander

Tsar Nicholas II. *See* Nicholas II

Union, Interparliamentary, 171, 191

United States: isolation sentiment in, 3 f.; considered an experiment in democracy for the benefit of all the world, 22 f.; peace movement in, 41 f.; fundamental motives influencing foreign policy of, 55–56; motives for expansion, 56 f.; expansion of, 103–21, 158–66; regulates European conduct in America, 122–57; concern with peace of Europe, 169 f. *See also* Civil War, War of 1812, World War, various presidents by name, etc.

United States Democratic Review, quoted, 68–69, 75

Vanderbilt, Cornelius, in Central America, 111

Vanderlip, Frank A., quoted on expansion, 80

Venezuela: punitive expedition against, 96; boundary dispute with England, 139

Victoria, Queen, and Spanish-American War, 151, 152

Wake Island. *See* South Sea Islands

Walker, William, filibuster, 111, 117

War: of 1812, 29, 42, 107; Mexican, 47, 109; Franco-Prussian, 49, 51; Spanish-American, 138 f. *See also* Crimean War, Russo-Japanese War, World War

Washington, George: farewell advice, 3, 8–10, 21; reasons for his policy of isolation, 9, 16–17; first inaugural quoted, 26

Washington Post, quoted, 89, 95

Wayne, James M., expansionist, quoted, 68

Weinberg, Albert K., 66, 94

West Florida, boundaries reduced, 106

Western Hemisphere, United States suzerainty in, 81

West Indies, 5, 72, 117, 162. *See also* Cuba, Danish West Indies, Dominican Republic, Haiti, Puerto Rico

White, Andrew D., ambassador to Germany: quoted, 153; his diplomacy, 157–58

"White Man's Burden, The," as expansionist argument, 81, 87 f.

Wilde, Richard H., quoted on Indian land titles, 68

Wilhelm II, German Kaiser: and Spanish-American War, 96 f.; designs on New World magnified, 134–35, 163, 220; criticism of by American leaders, 161–63; Roosevelt and, 162–63, 178 f.; House and, 202–5

Williams, Professor Talcott, quoted, 193

Wilson, Woodrow, 25; and peace of Europe, 25, 35–36, 42, 201 f.; quoted on Lincoln, 35; summons people to "new freedom," 97; quoted on Philippines, 97; on Latin America, 97–98; his Latin-American policy, 164–65; his "Fourteen Points," 201, 212; in Europe, 213–14; death, 215

Wolcott, Senator Edward O., quoted, 93

Wolff, Sir Henry Drummond, British ambassador to Spain, 142, 143

Woodford, General S. L., minister to Spain, 148

Worcester, Noah, pacifist, 42, 44

World War, the, 25, 52, 174, 183–84, 193–98; 201–14; 217–22; causes of United States involvement in, 211, 220, 221, 228–29

"Young America," 75

Zimmerman, Alfred, German diplomat, 203, 206

[PRINTED IN U·S·A·]

327.73
R486a